THE
UNLIKELY
SETTLER

Lipika Pelham

Other Press / New York

Poems on pages 167 and 247 from *Anthology of Modern Palestinian Literature*, edited by Salma Khadra Jayyusi, translated by Lena Jayyusi and W. S. Merwin. Copyright © 1992, Columbia University Press. Reprinted with permission of the publisher.

Production Editor: Yvonne E. Cárdenas
Book design: Jennifer Daddio / Bookmark Design & Media, Inc.
This book was set in 13.4 Fournier by Alpha Design & Composition of Pittsfield, NH.

1 3 5 7 9 10 8 6 4 2

Library of Congress Cataloging-in-Publication Data

Pelham, Lipika.
The unlikely settler / Lipika Pelham.
pages cm
ISBN 978-1-59051-683-6 (hardback) — ISBN 978-1-59051-684-3 (e-book)   1. Pelham, Lipika.   2. Women motion picture producers and directors—Israel—Biography.
3. Women, East Indian—Biography.   4. Interfaith marriage—Personal narratives.
5. Interracial marriage—Personal narratives.   6. Arab-Israeli conflict, 1993—Personal narratives.   7. Jerusalem—Ethnic relations—Personal narratives.   I. Title.
PN1998.3.P446.A3 2014
828'.9203—dc23
[B]
2013026641

For my father

Many things have happened in Jerusalem. The city has been destroyed, rebuilt, destroyed, and rebuilt again. Conqueror after conqueror has come, ruled for a while, left behind a few walls and towers, some cracks in the stone, a handful of potsherds and documents, and disappeared. Vanished like the morning mist down the hilly slopes. Jerusalem is an old nymphomaniac who squeezes lover after lover to death before shrugging him off with a yawn, a black widow who devours her mates while they are still penetrating her.

AMOS OZ, *A TALE OF LOVE AND DARKNESS*

PREFACE

I could have written an autobiographical novel. In fact that
was how it had started many years ago. But I found it hard
to stay plugged into the voice of the third-person singular,
increasingly breaking into the protagonist's mind, and before I realized, her voice started to echo mine. At one point
the third person merged into the first and *she* became *I*.

While this is a memoir, and a memoir is expected to be
one's personal account of the life that one has left behind,
and one is supposed to chronicle the events as they happened and not brush over them with too many imaginary
shades, I must confess that I have taken a few liberties and
have not let my confusion about the exact timeline obstruct
the flow of writing. I have tried to weave these stories of
love and destruction, passion and apathy, anguish and pleasure, as I had experienced them with shock and wonder, and
not always with clarity. But then life, when it has been run

through extreme emotions, may appear like fiction. On occasion my imagination may have colored it for extra poignancy. I have also at times resigned to the sensible god that exists in even the wildest of souls amongst us, to take control of my untamed pen to tone down, to bowdlerize my recollections of certain circumstances.

My deep apologies to my family if they are not comfortable with some aspects of this book. I would not say that I was not aware of this while writing it over the years. But this was my way of making sense of the events that more than often left us estranged from one another, with irreconcilable conflict of interests, as we found ourselves caught in the conflict on the ground itself. I recounted these stories as they enwrapped us as a family, but also as they blasted us apart with so much force that coming together never seemed complete enough; coming together always carried the traces of a trauma that had been corrosive and residual. We emerged with healed scars where the flesh of the original innocence had been clawed away.

But these are also memories of intense joy. There was never an ordinary moment. During the times of extreme happiness we floated high and beautiful, as a family or simply as a couple. We traveled off the beaten track to the end of the Middle East and the rest of the world, feeling uplifted and so passionately in love with each other that we were grateful to be alive in each other's arms.

THE UNLIKELY SETTLER

PROLOGUE

During our fifth year in Jerusalem, I was faced with a dilemma: where to give birth to our third child. In London, where our two older children were born and where my husband wanted me to go? In Bethlehem, because our friends recommended the Holy Family Hospital there? Or in Jerusalem, where I had met a Jewish Orthodox obstetrician I really liked?

I tried not to rule out Bethlehem. Many of our expatriate friends—journalists and diplomats—went to Palestinian cities to deliver their babies to avoid probable future difficulties for their work life in the Middle East. I went to see the hospital in Bethlehem. It had a beautiful setting amid lovely gardens, and a state-of-the-art neonatal unit. The delivery rooms were spacious and airy with a view of the primordial hills. But it sounded so clichéd. Born in Bethlehem. Implicated in too much compassion and sacrifice. A

[1]

birth loaded with expectations. Given that Bethlehem had one of the highest birthrates in Palestine, the land should have been inundated by now with hundreds of thousands of compassionate apostles. If only forgiveness had been the core value of this place, peace would have flourished in the hills around Jesus's birthplace, rather than outposts of hate. I could not help my eye being drawn to the ugly architecture of the Israeli settlements that dotted the landscape around Bethlehem. It was too ominous a place to give birth.

I carried on seeing my doctor, who traveled from his home in a Jewish settlement in the West Bank to his practice in Jerusalem's ultra-Orthodox neighborhood of Mea Shearim.

"How can you compromise your politics by seeing a settler doctor? Don't you think you are implicitly supporting the Israeli occupation?" said Leo, my husband, an expert on Middle Eastern affairs.

"It's up to the mother of the baby to decide where she feels comfortable to give birth," I replied.

He would stare at me speechless in disbelief. Leo worked for a think tank involved in conflict resolution in the Middle East and spent sleepless nights going through possible difficult scenarios at Syrian passport control. He feared that a passport with the place of birth listed as Jerusalem would have an impact on traveling with our baby to the Arab world.

My own origins were of no help. I was born in Bengal with a mélange of religions that would only complicate our case with the Syrian Mukhabarat, the secret police. I grew up with my grandmother's strong cultural Hinduism, challenged by my father's Islam. My preference for my ancestral "pagan" faith above my father's monotheism would definitely not go down well with an Islamic nation.

I got to know my Orthodox doctor not long after I first came to Jerusalem. I was doing some journalism for the BBC and was asked by *Woman's Hour* to make a feature on his research into the so-called halakhic infertility. Ultra-Orthodox Jewish women often failed to conceive naturally due to the strict regime of "ritual purity," or *niddah*, decreed by a rabbinical commandment. For two weeks of every month, from the first day of menstruation, sex is forbidden between couples. (Although I had come across alternative mitzvah whereby a particular rabbi had shown some degrees of leniency toward young men visiting prostitutes while their wives were in niddah.) This resulted in many women missing the small window of ovulation. My doctor denounced this practice, endorsed by halakha, or Talmudic law, which deprived healthy women from getting pregnant. Many were put on ovulation drugs that sometimes led to serious heart problems and hypertension. He demanded that the law on the purity of the female body be revised, which was hugely controversial in a country where its rabbinical courts defined the laws of marriage and divorce. His views held much deeper implications than those of the secular doctors, as he himself was religious. He was popular and well regarded in his profession, which showed in the number of ultra-Orthodox women in his waiting room. It was courageous of these women to attend his practice in a culture where a handshake or even innocent eye contact was not permitted between the opposite sexes (with some ultra-Orthodox men campaigning for separate pavements for men and women). It was unusual for Orthodox women to visit male doctors.

When I found out that I was pregnant, the obstetrician whose name came to my mind was this doctor who, since my *Woman's Hour* feature, had written a book that was being serialized in one of the main national papers. I felt comfortable having a doctor I already knew. And, although I would never admit it to Leo, the thought of upsetting the Syrian and other closed Arab regimes with a child born in Jerusalem filled me with a perverse pleasure, due to my own complicated relationship with and rejection of Islam in my childhood. I felt that since it was my prerogative to criticize Israel's "colonial" policy along with the majority of the world, it was also my right not to comply with the infantile demand of certain despotic Arab countries to determine what I should wear, whom I could talk to, or where I should give birth to my baby.

I was fascinated by my "settler" doctor who wore a *kippah*, a skullcap, under his motorbike helmet when he commuted into work from his home in the Judean desert. I was intrigued by the women, and some men, in the waiting room of the doctor's clinic during my routine visits: women in wigs and long black skirts, black-hatted religious men with *payots*, curly sidelocks ("curly-wurlies," as nicknamed by our children), swaying their heads as they read from the daily scriptures. To me, the atmosphere was deliciously sexually charged. I would be sitting with these demure, pasty-looking women whose bodies as I understood were regarded solely as their husbands' property, and yet there they were, lying exposed (with their legs in stirrups) before a male gynecologist behind closed doors while their husbands prayed outside. In my fantasy, this was these women's silent revenge—their little adventure.

My own external differences included not only my dark Bengali complexion amid the Haredi's milky-white never-exposed-to-the-sun bodies, but also what I wore, how I spoke, and what I read. I tried my best to dress modestly—in full-sleeve shirts and long skirts. One day a woman kept pointing at the front of my dress, and at first I had thought she was enchanted by the smocked pattern of my frock. But she started nodding vigorously, and I thought she was probably going through a particular prayer that needed wild swaying of one's head. She was sitting opposite me, but when I remained seated with a baffled look and a polite smile on my face, she came to sit beside me and without hesitation pulled up the front of my dress. I realized that the cut of the neckline showed a faint line of cleavage—harmless in my eyes but offensive to the men sitting in the room. I also felt I was offending them by flicking through the pages of the *Economist* while I should have been holding one of the black gilded Hebrew prayer books that were on the table at the entrance to the waiting room.

Strangely, I felt that my child was blessed amid all the scriptures and praying heads around me. My baby was safe every time the doctor said, clicking through the ultrasound pictures on the monitor beside me, *"Baruch Hashem,"* God be praised. The baby looked great and healthy, and he passed all the genetic tests successfully. Despite being an older mother, I did not have to go through any of the invasive tests that women were routinely put through beyond a certain age, because my doctor said, *"Baruch Hashem,"* everything looked good. I would not deny that I was secretly terrified, having skipped the diagnostic amniocentesis test for chromosomal abnormalities because of my doctor's faith. He believed in my "healthy" baby, and so did I. From the start of the pregnancy, I had been following such emotionally driven, naïve, ambiguous directions. Perhaps it was the pregnancy hormones, Leo claimed, that made me so blasé about the possible risks.

"How can you say you have faith in your doctor's faith? You don't even have a religion."

"I can't explain. This is how I feel and I should just follow my instinct."

Follow my instinct I certainly did, and in this case my instinct was directed by fear. I was afraid of the invasive test. I spent my pregnancy under a hidden blanket of terror that was lifted only the moment my boy was born and the doctor announced, after his initial checkups, "Well, I don't see any signs of Down syndrome or any other abnormality in your baby! He is a good baby."

How did he know that I had been worried?

"I know you were being brave, but I told you all along that I had a good feeling about your baby."

Now that my child was born healthy and I was devoid of pregnancy hormones, I wondered how I would have reacted if luck hadn't been on my side, how my religious doctor's "good feeling" would have helped if the baby had been born with abnormalities.

———

My baby was lying in the glass-walled neonatal unit of Hadassah Hospital in Mount Scopus in northeast Jerusalem—the scene of fierce fighting during the Six-Day War in 1967 over the ownership of this strategically situated hill. Although the view would matter very little once I was in labor and would decide to have a natural birth without the intervention of an epidural. At one point, as I was groaning in bed, I heard Leo ask the attendant midwife if she would move the curtains so that I could have the view of the valley from my window.

"Maybe that would relieve her pain a bit?" he suggested.

He was sternly stared down by the midwife. "Do you really think giving birth is like being on holiday in a seaside room with a view? Do you think she really cares?"

Despite the maddening contractions, I felt sorry for him. He was only trying to help ease the pain that would not be alleviated until the early hours of the morning in late August 2010. As the sun peeped through the curtains, my eyes filled with tears of wonder as our baby was handed over to my arms and Leo said, "It's a boy. Born in Jerusalem. You've won."

He held the baby still covered in blood and mucus and inspected his face.

"He definitely has my eyebrows!" Leo said, kissing our son's forehead still covered in laguno. His dark hair came down to his eyebrows. I looked at his mouth and replied to Leo, "He has your mouth too." Leo nodded in agreement as he put our baby son on my chest. I stroked his face, his wide mouth like his father's, his bushy eyebrows.

"Our third child, who would have known!" Leo said as we watched the little miracle in our arms. The baby was wide awake, only a few minutes old but he did not cry. He watched us cross-eyed, probably skeptical at the two conflict-ridden strangers in charge of bringing him up.

—

The babies are lying in a neat row in clear plastic cots in a brightly lit room, with student doctors tending to the needs of the newborns. New mothers queue outside the glass wall, trying to spot their babies in Russian doll wraps.

I cannot recognize my baby and I start panicking. Have they put the right name tag on him? My boy has a head full of dark hair. But through the glass, many other babies seem to have similar features, and my heart begins to pound when after searching over all the faces I still can't identify my child.

In my panic-stricken postnatal state, I am distracted by a woman just behind me, in an Islamic long djellaba, her head covered in a tight scarf. She looks tired, but she gives me a smile of reassurance, as if to say, "Don't worry, you'll find your son." But there's something else that I feel is strange about her standing there with other mothers. The other mothers—I start going over their faces: the woman immediately behind the head-scarved Muslim woman is a head-scarved Jewish mother. The woman behind the Jewish mother is a very young head-uncovered Palestinian who is deeply engaged in a whispered conversation in Arabic with the woman behind her. Surprisingly, at this early hour, the young mother's face is made up with mascara, smoky eyeliner, and bright magenta lipstick. I wonder why these mothers lining up outside the baby nursery in this hospital seem so strange; why, despite extreme fatigue, I am being filled with generous optimism, and why I am glad I've given birth here in this ward with all these women.

The Jewish and Palestinian mothers are waiting to be handed over their sons and daughters—the future generation of this land, while their fathers might be fighting petty battles at checkpoints and borders, at separation walls, in nightly incursions into the refugee camps of Gaza and Jenin; some might be preparing for retaliation of the most destructive kind, self-immolation.

But the bringers of the future generation to this land are standing here, side by side, chatting or smiling to each other, all with the same goal—to nurture and nourish their offspring.

As I walk through the rows of cribs in the neonatal ward with the tiny babies in white wraparound muslin, they all look the same and a vision hovers over me. Some of these babies would one day hold guns to shoot down the "enemy," some would vow to become suicide bombers, some stone-throwing insurgents. But for now they are all lying there together in unity and peace. There, lying among them, I finally find my son. He is asleep and I identify him by the most distinguishing feature on his face, his father's eyebrows. I am overwhelmed by an immense sense of responsibility. The burden of the past is weighing on me and I feel vulnerable. Exactly at that moment he opens his eyes and observes the world above him, which is my anxious face.

PART
ONE

.1.

PREQUEL TO A TALE OF
LOVE AND DARKNESS

I first met Leo on April Fool's Day, three months after I had arrived in London in the early 1990s. I had just had a successful interview at a London University college to study Hinduism and Buddhism and had been doing some freelance journalism for the BBC. It was through a colleague at the BBC's Bengali section that I had started working for a Marxist student newspaper, which held its meetings in one of the conference rooms of the London University Union. Early for one such meeting, I slipped into the crowded student bar to kill time. I walked toward the only available chair in the room. Leo was sitting beside it, his face buried in a newspaper. When I asked him if I could take the chair, he looked at me with impatient eyes and started fidgeting with the paper and the empty beer glass on the low table.

I said, "Hello!" He was startled and pointed at the available seat next to him, "unable to utter a word," as he would tell me later.

I smiled at him. Thick clouds of cigarette smoke were hanging over people's heads. I looked at my watch. I would have to spend another fifteen minutes before the meeting began.

"Do you come here often?" he asked. "I've never seen you before."

He reminded me of an early Woody Allen in his round, rimmed glasses.

"No, no, I don't come here often. I am waiting to go to a meeting, but I'm not sure if I really want to go. It's nice just sitting here watching people."

"What's this meeting about?" He looked up and we made eye contact for the first time. I immediately developed a liking for this inexplicably nervous-looking man in front of me, whose name I did not yet know.

"If I told you about it, you would laugh, because in this country young people don't tend to spend their evenings with Marxists! It sounds so archaic!"

"How intriguing! Are you some sort of an ex–Soviet agent or something?"

"You could say so." I laughed. "I probably inadvertently contributed to the KGB cause by working for the Novosti Press for a year before coming here."

"You worked for Novosti? How incredible! Where? I can't imagine it was in London!"

"You ask too many questions!" I said. "What's so shocking, anyway?" I wasn't ready to say more on my work as a young subeditor for the Soviet Press agency.

"It's interesting because for us," he said, "I mean, for the people in the West, it is very difficult to understand that there are young people around the world who still believe in a Soviet-style revolution. Student politics is almost nonexistent in the West, whereas my counterparts in Asia can bring down a government! I am amazed by the immense popular support those students enjoy. Can you imagine a Tiananmen Square uprising in Trafalgar Square?"

I burst into laughter.

"Would you like a crisp?" he said, holding out the packet he was munching from. And I took one.

"Well, after your meeting, if you are free, I could perhaps make some suggestions?" he said as I silently shared more than one of his salt-and-vinegar crisps. I felt secretly excited by this chance encounter. I felt a strange thrill, the thrill of a new challenge, to get to know this stranger. But I tried not to show it.

"If I had time, I would have wanted to know your suggestion, but I am afraid I have to go in three minutes." I didn't know why I said this, because I was totally uninterested in the meeting and wanted instead to sit there, drink beer, and feel light-headed with my Woody Allen.

"Three minutes is a long time. Enough at least to tell you my name. I am Leo."

"Leo? Are you a student here?"

"I was here too for a meeting, with some British Islamists . . ."

"Islamists? You mean British Muslims?"

"You must be from the subcontinent?" He asked me, "Are you Muslim?"

No, not that question, I thought. Why can't I ever escape the tedium of explaining myself. "Yes to the first question," I said. "Not sure of the next one, though. How would you feel if I asked you what your religion was?"

"Which part?"

"What do you mean?"

"Which part of the subcontinent do you come from?"

"From Bengal."

"Which part of Bengal?"

"Just from Bengal. Why aren't you happy with that? Which part of Europe do your ancestors come from? With your curly black locks, you don't look that English to me. Are you Gypsy? Jewish?"

I knew I was being unfair to him and evasive about myself, but there was no simple way of describing my personal history and confused national identity. How could I explain to a stranger my strong connection to Hindu culture despite having a Muslim father? Or that, despite being born in Bangladesh—in a village barely meters from the political border—I considered myself Indian? That even as a child I could not accept the arbitrariness of the division of Bengal, the eastern part of which eventually, after much political turmoil, became Bangladesh and the western part remained in India? My father, who was born in undivided India, was destined to belong to the Muslim majority East Bengal because of his faith. My past was so convoluted that any casual question regarding my origins threatened to unleash unwanted emotion. In a situation like this, I always felt an urge to leave or to divert the conversation. Luckily, I had to go and see the editors of the Marxist newspaper. I stood up.

Leo looked puzzled at my change of mood. I collected my bag. He stood with me and said, "Look, it was really great to have met you, though only for a very short time. We could perhaps see each other again this evening? I am meeting some friends from college at the blues place in Covent Garden at eight o'clock. It would be nice if you came along. If you want, we could meet back here at half past six."

To my surprise and great relief, I instinctively agreed.

"By the way, I'm Jewish, since you asked!"

I remembered feeling tremendously exalted but at the same time restless in the face of the fast-unfolding, unpredictable course of that evening. I could barely wait to leave my meeting and come out to see Leo again. When I walked back to the student bar, he was sitting at the same table, exactly as I had left him, with his newspaper.

"Have you been waiting here all this time?" I asked him. Leo smiled enigmatically and said, "I couldn't risk losing you!"

He collected his things and we walked out of the smoke-filled den.

We strolled through the vibrant London streets to the blues bar. When introducing me to his friends, he stammered as he tried to pronounce my name correctly. Earlier in the student café, I had written it down for him on a napkin and had explained which syllable to put the emphasis on. The laughter of his friends attracted every pair of eyes in the bar. He apologized as he checked my name again on the napkin. He ordered a bottle of wine and a pizza to share. The blues singers arrived. Although we were sitting close together, we had to shout in each other's ears to make ourselves heard. Leo drew meaningless lines on a paper napkin. I was fascinated to see that not once during the whole time we were together did he put his ballpoint pen away, even when he was pouring wine. He was constantly drawing and writing down things I said, including the word *kaak*, meaning "crow" in Bengali, although I'm not sure why that word came up in our very first conversation. Perhaps because he demanded in his persistent way that I say something in Bengali, and *kaak* is one of the first words that Bengali children learn in school, as it conjoins the first consonant, barely separated by the second vowel.

Throughout the course of the evening we talked about our lives, our interests in books, and our travels. I was surprised but also slightly put off by what increasingly appeared to be his single-minded pursuit of his interest in Judaism, the Arab world, and Islam. During his gap year he had gone to Syria to study Arabic while I was backpacking in Nepal and meeting misfits from around the world, including a Swiss bank robber turned heroin dealer and a Danish mountaineer who had been living in the recesses of the Himalayas for as long as he remembered. I pictured Leo as a curious Jewish boy sitting in the souq of Damascus, studiously memorizing verses from the Quran and learning to speak what's considered the most sophisticated dialect of Syrian Arabic. He struck me as someone who did not believe in aimless wandering. Everything he did, he did with a specific target in mind, with the principal objective to collect information that catered to his quest for coexistence among followers of different faiths. He did not ask me what I did in Nepal in my late teens, but what my Muslim father thought of me when I chose to grow up with my ancestral religion of Hinduism. I told him that ultimately I hated all religions. I had no faith. My Hinduism was only cultural, a façade behind which I hid when the external pestering about my origins became too much to bear.

By the end of the evening, my initial irritation toward his over-inquisitiveness was mixed with awe. I saw a man before me full of unfamiliar paradoxes: a young expert on Arab affairs, an intellectual with in-depth analytical knowledge of the Middle East's past and present, and yet he was captivated by its religions. He believed that somehow the two warring creeds, Judaism and Islam, are interconnected and a common ground is within reach. He was not a carefree young man but rather someone who had a crystal-clear idea about his future. He wanted to be closely involved in shaping the modern Middle East.

I was unnerved by this. The Middle East was, to me, a place rife with extreme ideas and the subjugation of women.

"How can you nurture such prejudices?" Leo said, when I expressed a much edited version of my neurosis. "Take Iran. You have no idea what the women of Iran are like. They are filmmakers and parliamentarians."

"Yes, but nevertheless many of them look to me like walking black tents!" I retorted.

"It's their minds that one should be concerned with, not what they wear. Often, as in this case, they don't have a choice."

"But they do have a choice, first and foremost, to strive to throw away the burka! As they strove to secure their places in parliament. What's more important, to struggle for the right to walk freely without having to carry a black tent around or to sit in men's parliament all shrouded?" I said.

"How can you talk like this, as a woman, about these amazingly accomplished women!" I heard a hint of exasperation in his voice.

I sat there fuming. For me the burka was a pure violation of a woman's control over her own body and had to be eradicated before there could be any talk of emancipation. I was annoyed by Leo's vindication of the veil, how presumptuously he expressed his view on things relating to women, and how he made me seem like an unempathetic, a-religious bigot—an amateur feminist.

Nevertheless, I felt exhilarated by his constant probing into what I did, what I believed in. I was fascinated by his upbringing in the middle-class north London community where his parents still lived. I was also intrigued by his faith, how important his Jewish identity was for him, and how he balanced it with his unfaltering fascination for all things Islamic. I was attracted by the paradox of our respective personal histories: there I was, an Eastern woman devoid of religion, sitting opposite and falling in love with a Western European man with a strong faith.

I wished I could talk to Leo about my past and my beliefs with the frankness that he talked about his. But his immense curiosity about me made me fearful for other reasons. I knew that if I started talking about my childhood, I would be censoring myself. He would get only the idyllic part of growing up in rural Bengal—swimming in rivers filled with *shushuk*, the Ganges River dolphin, or searching in tree holes for the vengeful female cobra in case it came to bite us in the night because my father had killed the male that was hiding under my bed. I could not deceive my love with stories of the beauty and adventures of a wild childhood and hide the horror that lurked beneath. Because what defined my disposition was not only the river swimming, tilapia fishing, and dolphin spotting, but also repeated sexual abuse at the hands of one of my father's subordinates in the food distribution center that he managed. Both my parents had turned a blind eye to my plight in the name of honor. Despite my pleas to my father who fearlessly killed cobras, he had failed to protect his nine-year-old daughter in this instance.

We came out of the blues bar in the early hours of the morning. Leo called a taxi and gave the driver his address south of the river Thames. I said I would prefer to go to my place in Hackney, in northeast London, a rambling Victorian house that I shared with two sisters and their brother, Sarah, Emma, and Robert Wiseman.

"Wiseman. You didn't tell me you lived with a Jewish family!"

"Because I didn't think it was necessary to define the religion of the people I live with! They could very well be Huguenots! Copts! Zoroastrians!"

As we heard the dawn break with the passing of the milk van and the sound of the glass milk bottles being delivered with a soothing clink to my front doorstep, Leo asked me whether I wanted to go on holiday with him to Scotland in two weeks' time. He had just passed his driving test and his parents were lending him their four-wheel drive for a fortnight. He said that he and three other friends from college had booked a holiday cottage in Lochgilphead. I told him that I was in charge of looking after the twin boys of a single mother air stewardess whose house I slept in two nights a week while she was on night duty, and I could not join him because it would be difficult for her to find my replacement. He argued that we were embarking on an important phase in our life together, and we must spend more time in each other's company. I replied that we had met barely twelve hours ago, and I had a bit more exploring to do before settling with someone I had just stumbled into. He said that he really wanted me to come with him on this trip. His voice was calm but persuasive all the same. I was too tired to argue, and before I fell asleep in his arms, I might have said to him, "I'll think about it," because it was strangely comforting to lie there cocooned in his embrace. Only yesterday he was a stranger; today he was talking about going on holiday together. In fact I had already decided that I wanted to go to the Scottish Highlands with him. I was arguing for the sake of it. I wanted to see more of him. I was intrigued to find out more about his world.

Two weeks later we were back in my basement room after a magical evening. We'd been to the Duke of York's Theatre, where we had watched a fabulous performance of Ariel Dorfman's *Death and the Maiden*. Deeply moved by the dark and tormented character of the play's protagonist, former political prisoner Paulina Salas, I'd said to Leo that I wanted to hear the sound of the sea, which featured as a dramatic backdrop in the play, so he'd driven me to Brighton. We drove back in silence in the early hours of the morning with Schubert's String Quartet no. 14 in D minor, a haunting piece called *Death and the Maiden*, a cassette of which we had bought earlier at the theater, playing on the car's stereo.

After only two hours' sleep, Leo woke me and said that he had to go to his new job.

"What's that?" I asked sleepily.

"I work as a paralegal to a Pakistani lawyer," he said. "He has a private practice where he advises his South Asian clients on Islamic law."

"Where's that, the private practice of your Pakistani?"

"Islamic Law Chambers, in Whitechapel, not far from here. I think I'll walk. Stay in bed, you don't have to get up. I'll let myself out."

"No, no, stay for breakfast," I said. There was a pull in my heart at the thought of him leaving so soon. "I'll make you some tea and Marmite on toast."

Marmite, the infamous yeast extract that the British loved on their morning toast, which I had discovered soon after my arrival in England and grown much attached to since.

"Thank you, but I won't eat bread, it's Passover."

"Why should that stop you from eating bread?"

"You are meant to eat only unleavened bread during Passover."

"What's unleavened bread?"

"Bread made without yeast. Unrisen bread. Eating your Marmite on toast would be having yeast on yeast! A double whammy!" he said, leaving me dumbfounded by this early-morning discourse on yeast.

I felt distracted and started pondering the impracticability of our probable future together. Holidaying in Scotland and no bread! The following weekend in Scotland, as we climbed Britain's highest mountain, he would refuse to eat my sandwiches made with leavened bread and would instead beg for energy-replenishing Kendal Mint Cake from fellow climbers during the five-hour ascent to the summit and back. We would have our first real big argument on top of Ben Nevis in the middle of a howling blizzard, over his observance of Jewish dietary laws.

It was the first of many arguments, yet over the next two years we fell deeply in love. Leo's ideas challenged me, kept me excited about our relationship. He made me feel at ease with my immigrant background. I knew that he never exoticized my "otherness." I was no *la femme Indienne* for him, as an old French boyfriend used to call me. I felt exhilarated by his thirst for travel and was amazed at his perfect sense of navigation in totally new places. We started traveling from the beginning, mostly in the Arab Middle East. Even when we weren't in the Middle East, he searched for the legacy of the Arab-Muslim civilization in places such as Andalusia, Turkey, North Africa, and of course the Indian subcontinent. "I cannot imagine my life without you," we had said to each other as we stood on the steps of the Acropolis in Athens and he smeared vermillion powder in the center parting of my hair, in a symbolic Hindu matrimony. We had a child together, a son. We got married—although of course we could not agree on a type of wedding, Jewish or Bengali, so we married in a registry office, with Leo's promise that one day we would find a rabbi and a Hindu priest who would agree to do a joint service. Interfaith dialogue would continue to be his primary aspiration as a Middle East analyst.

In those early days, we (or rather I, a majority of the time) struggled to cope with the pressures of being young working parents, but we never lost the thrill that we first felt being in each other's company in that London University bar.

How, then, did we manage to cause each other so much pain in the ensuing years?

.2.

WHEN THE MOTHER
IS NOT JEWISH

It is a dark Yom Kippur evening in London, Leo comes home from the synagogue to break the twenty-four-hour fast. It is the end of a cold, late autumn day and I have just come back from a twelve-hour newsroom shift at the BBC World Service in Bush House. My fingertips tingle, my back hurts, and my eyes, having been open under the fluorescent glare for so long, are trying to accustom themselves to the softer yellow glow of my kitchen, where I have dumped my bag and coat and sat with a mug of tea. Our six-year-old son, Kiran, is drawing stick people with round faces and his trademark googly eyes. I say hello to Leo, who is standing behind our son looking over his drawings.

"How was your day?"

"Good."

"You look pale."

"Do I?"

"How is Rabbi Glick?"

"He's fine."

"Would you like some tea?"

He does not answer. With the same sullen face as when I walked in, he starts rearranging things on the kitchen table without making eye contact with me. I realize what I have just done and start wondering whether I should say sorry. Before I can articulate a phrase to convey my apology for being insensitive to his fasting for Yom Kippur, he says in his characteristic quiet but firm voice, "This is the holiest day in the Jewish calendar. I know you are not interested in religion, but you could at least respect."

"Of course I respect. What do you mean? I even take our son to the Saturday kiddush service in the synagogue when you are not around. I like Rabbi Glick and his family very much."

"Then how can you drink tea in front of me when I am fasting? You could have waited another half hour or so before the end of the fast."

"Please, don't start! I was at work the whole day. It was very stressful. Israel has been shelling southern Lebanon indiscriminately, you might be interested to know . . ."

"How could you go to work on Yom Kippur? You know how important it is for me."

"I beg your pardon? I can't believe you are saying this. I am not Jewish. I have no problem with you observing your religion, but why do I have to fast and why should I not have gone to work? How can you be so despotic?"

"You don't seem to understand. Throughout the year I suppress my feelings; on this day I wake up with a shudder knowing that my children will never be Jewish," he says. His voice is trembling and I fear the oncoming familiar row that we have at least once a year, on Yom Kippur in particular, over whether our children should be Jewish or not. For them to be Jewish, I must convert.

"Because I am not Jewish? So what do you expect me to do? Put a wig on, eat kosher, not be able to eat seafood, and go through the three-year conversion process? Are you out of your mind? I thought we were a great couple; we wanted to prove that we could live together and bring up the children with sound liberal values despite coming from different continents and customs. Ours, I want to believe, is a great cross-cultural love story."

"But on Yom Kippur, I feel differently," he says, with dismay at the non-possibility of my ever converting. But he is now preoccupied with our son, and I decide to leave the subject and head toward the bedroom to change, to go to his parents' house in Hampstead to break the fast.

"I'd never ask you to convert, but if you loved me, you'd know what mattered to me."

I stop at the bottom of the stairs as I hear him say the most impossible thing that anyone can ever expect of me.

"Because I love you, I let you have our son circumcised, when he was a tiny baby, soon after we came back from the hospital. It was the hardest thing that I'd ever had to come to terms with," I say as I climb the narrow staircase to the bedroom.

"*I can't convert, Leo.* You know that. I don't have a religion to convert from! Had I been a believing Hindu or a Muslim, it would be easier. But I am neither. You know that," I reiterated to him a few weeks after that Yom Kippur evening.

Now, looking back, I often thought where that rabid atheism came from. It must have resulted from my rejection of my father's faith. And the rejection of my father's faith must have followed his failure to protect me when I was a child.

Perhaps conflicted between his faith-bound inner despair at his Talmudically non-Jewish son and his Very English Public School background of rational thinking, Leo hugged me with reassurance and said, although in a trembling voice, "I like you the way you are. I would not expect you to convert."

"I had to agree with you on Kiran's circumcision, but I did it for you, not for our son," I said to him.

"Yes, I understand. Thank you for that."

His thanking me melted my heart and I went on giving him more concessions, although I didn't mean to, but this was how I would find myself act out my schoolgirlish love for Leo. This would become a recurrent theme in our relationship. I had a desperate need to be appreciated by him. I would struggle against my better judgment in order to accommodate Leo's vision for our family. My continued acceptance of what I saw as his infuriatingly self-serving rules in our lives pushed me to the brink of insanity, but I would be unable to break free. Because breaking free was to embrace once again a mountainous challenge of being alone in a great big world; I had already been there when I not only left my parents' home but also severed my connection to the past. It was not pleasant. Besides, every time I accepted one more piece of the precepts of Leo's Middle Eastern mission, I would be rewarded by some unexpected, charming demonstration of love, which would erase any doubt that I had about his persuasive ways.

"I won't mind if you want to bring them up, Kiran and our future children, with Judaism," I heard myself say.

He looked into my eyes with deep emotion. And I immediately regretted what I had just promised him. I wanted to take it back, but it was too late. I wanted to cry out that my Hinduism, although devoid of belief in God, was important to me, and I wanted to pass that on to our children too.

Those were the years when the repetitive tapestry of passion and desolation in our marriage began to weave its first yarn. While the unpredictability of our emotional peaks kept us perpetually infatuated with each other, it also tore us apart as we became its unwitting victims when the inevitable lows befell us. I jokingly referred to Leo as "the Peacemaker" because of what appeared to me his single-minded determination to put world affairs before our family. In the beginning, I made sacrifices easily. Filled with an abundance of the adrenaline of youth, I enjoyed the role of superwoman: managing a career at the BBC and young motherhood while he concentrated on his work as a roving reporter for a number of British and American news agencies in the Middle East. When my peacemaker lover suggested that we leave England, I jumped. Leo said that he could never envisage his life in London, that he didn't study Arabic to rot in the English capital, that he was meant to do better things than living and paying off a mortgage in the grimy metropolis. I saw reason in what he had said then, and I thought that I had nothing to lose in leaving London, where I had comfortably made my second home after having left my Bengali years behind. It would not be so hard to make a "third home" elsewhere if that kept the family together. So I left London for Morocco, only to find out that Leo had better things to do elsewhere in the region, and our little boy and I were frequently left for long stretches of time in a lonely beach house that felt as if it had a thousand windows through which the cold squall of the Atlantic blew day and night. We were burning newspapers, driftwood that we collected from the beach, at one point even old novels in the fireplace; we were boiling eggs in a kettle because we had yet to settle in and had no utensils or furniture or coal for fire. The capital, Rabat, was thirty-five minutes away by bus, and we had yet to rent a car. But Leo, the reporter, had gone away with a UN mission touring around North Africa with Kofi Annan while Kiran and I shivered in our seaside house, laughed at by the demons of the Atlantic.

I left Rabat a year later and came back to London without Leo. At least half the time during that year I fantasized that I was Hideous Kinky. I would try to lose myself in the maze of the medieval city of Fez and haggle with carpet makers in the colorful bazaars of Marrakesh, or just walk in the blue and white alleyways of the casbah, in the Udayas neighborhood of Rabat, where the Atlantic crashed down below against the Mamluk ramparts with destructive possibilities. But I did so with a talkative, uninhibited child trailing behind me and always asking questions like, "Mummy, when are we going to the snail man? I want to eat twenty-six snails this time." His previous record was eighteen, and the man behind the stall of this Moroccan delicacy would say to me, "Your boy will make many women very happy"—referring to the aphrodisiac powers of the fourteen herbs that the snail broth was said to have been infused with. That was his chat-up line and my cutoff point when Kiran and I would saunter back into the ancient maze of the city to do some more haggling just to kill time. However, I would never be brave enough to leave everything behind and lose myself in the mystery of the inner maze of Morocco's medieval cities. Instead, at the end of a long day, our legs would ache and I would find myself on the bus on the beach highway going back home with my son, now filled with two dozen snails, asleep on my lap, and his child's trust placed upon my quivering heart burdened with guilt and self-doubt.

Following my return from Morocco, I reestablished myself very quickly in London, with a full-time position in the newsroom and a German au pair. There was suddenly this new reality in my life: my boy, the nanny, and I; the bimonthly visits by my Middle East–trotting husband; my bustling life in London with my fabulous friends and my great job. It all seemed perfect, for a while.

After all the socializing and Ecstasy parties, and after all the cooking and feasting in London's best restaurants with my closest friend, a super chef and Chinese cookbook writer, after a lot of fantasizing about having recriminating flings during Leo's travels, which never really materialized, and after all attempts at having a good time despite my lover's absence failed, by the time our baby girl, Maya, was born almost eight years after our son, I felt that I could not deal with that life in London anymore. As a mother of two young children, I clung to Leo and started imagining myself as a fuller, happier woman, an undemanding mother like my own mother, a trusted wife like my mother-in-law, blindly loyal to the work and mission of the father of my children. "What's the big deal about a BBC career? I can leave everything for love and unhazardous happiness," became the recurrent theme on my mind. All I needed was to drown myself in the intense blissfulness that I felt being with Leo. I had not given it a second thought as I took a year's unpaid leave while I was at my prime in the newsroom as a regional editor. My bosses looked at me in disbelief, and I must have been seen as a traitor, a protégée whom they promoted and who then betrayed them.

One fine day when I was feeling high—higher than I ever felt during those hallucinogenic trips in my bold and superwomanly midtwenties—I told Leo that I would go to Syria with him. That was where he wanted to go when the talk of another Middle Eastern sojourn came up. To continue on the path to learn from some of the best teachers from the days when he was a student of Arabic in Damascus, Leo said. But the closed Syrian regime would not let him settle in Damascus as a reporter. The reason, we suspected, was that they had him listed as a Jew during his one-year stay in the Syrian capital while he was learning Arabic. During that time he was going through a period of religious awakening, visiting the country's few remaining synagogues. He was sure that his movements had been recorded by the Mukhabarat. Our suspicion had been confirmed by the "not-so-secret" police during a holiday trip to Damascus while I was pregnant with our daughter. Leo was interrogated for hours at the airport, during which they must have embellished their previous dossier on him, as they asked the names of his parents, grandparents, and great-grandparents, and even the names of my parents and grandparents, in order to double check and reestablish his Jewish genealogy. Following that visit, his repeated applications for a visa to reenter the country were either ignored or rejected. Leo concluded that his Damascene dream was to be left, for now, unfulfilled. He therefore approached two serious British papers and asked them to send him to Amman. It was on the eve of the talks of a possible American attack on Saddam Hussein's rogue regime. The editors of those papers were delighted to find this young enthusiast of Middle Eastern affairs who spoke perfect Arabic and volunteered to report from what would become the most dangerous place in the region. A few months later we were traveling to Amman, where we would live for a year. During that year, Leo frequently went to Baghdad to cover the war in Iraq for several mainstream British newspapers.

I did not know then that those thirteen months in Amman, during the second Gulf War and its prequel, would be the first taste of what it was going to be like to live with Leo in the Middle East. Most of those months I spent in Jordan, deeply perturbed not only by being alone with two children in an unfriendly place while Leo traveled to Baghdad, but also by the terrible stuff in the news of insurgents kidnapping and beheading Westerners.

When British citizens were evacuated from Amman, I left the city and traveled with Maya and Kiran to the Gulf on the first leg of my journey to India.

In Abu Dhabi as the temperature rose to 50°C, I became restless and wandered around the capital of the UAE, burying my bare feet in soft green grass. I was less than a kilometer away from the vast uninterrupted tracts of sand that stretched all the way east to the shores of the Gulf of Oman, to the west across Saudi Arabia, up to the eastern bank of the Gulf of Aqaba on the Red Sea. In Abu Dhabi's manicured parks, in the shade of a flame tree, I enjoyed speaking Hindi to South Asian workers who—from sweeping the streets to running department stores—were involved in maintaining each square of the country except government offices and immigration kiosks at the airport. These positions were exclusively held by the men dressed in all white, the Gulf Arabs in their trademark white keffiyehs and long white dishdashas.

From Abu Dhabi I flew to Dubai, running away from a war that would create a heinous, continuing legacy in the history of the Middle East and the rest of the world for many years to come. In Dubai, I boarded a plane to my next destination, the Indian subcontinent, the first stop being Delhi. During the next three months, my little daughter would make her first steps in a Bengali village as she tried to reach for a bucket of water, and she would speak her first coherent words in Arabic at a Dubai mall: *"mish mushkil,"* no problem, mimicking a shop assistant.

As the American war on Iraq was still raging, I came back to London with our son and our daughter. When Maya turned two, I returned to the BBC, where once again I found my old, comfortable place in the newsroom. I considered myself lucky that the news organization had a policy of offering its female employees extended maternity leave. It saved me time and time again from being licked by the lolling tongue of depression, as I frequently found myself alone in London, this time with two children.

Leo worked in Baghdad one more year while I wrote news stories every day on the war in Iraq and woke up many nights shivering with terrible visions. Every time the news agencies reported on another foreign journalist going missing, I would shut my ears and my eyes to push away the shattering terror.

He came back eventually and spent a year writing a book on Iraq's new religious order as instilled by the United States. During this year we talked about going away again.

I was more into North Africa: Morocco again, or Tunisia, even Algeria, but Leo, first sheepishly, then more decidedly, announced that the only place where he saw himself being useful was in Jerusalem.

"I'd never go to Jerusalem. You must be joking! Why on earth would we subject ourselves to living among a divided society?" I would scream at him in frustration as he hammered his Jerusalem travel scheme into my brain several times a day like a persistent drone. I locked myself in the bathroom so that I didn't have to hear about Jerusalem. I saw friends in the evening in order to stay away from his interrogation of whether or not I was ready to go to Jerusalem with him. I started going to sleep early so that he didn't have a chance to talk about Jerusalem in bed. At one point his drone attacks seemed fewer than before, and I was about to relax, thinking that he got the point, when one evening he came home and announced that he had got a job with an international crisis resolution think tank. He was to be based in Jerusalem as its Middle East analyst.

"You always said how much you wanted me to have a job that won't involve too much traveling. Well, this job would enable me to stay in Jerusalem, with my family, and only occasional trips to the West Bank and Gaza. I won't be going away to war zones. I won't be covering the regional politics. Just the Israeli-Palestinian conflict."

"Are you sure?"

"Yes," he said without a tremble of doubt in his voice. "I am sure. Will you come with me?"

"You are going to go there anyway, whether I join you or not," I thought, as I tried to weigh up the costs and benefits of the two choices available to me: to be left alone with two children in London—déjà vu all over again—or to follow him and live together as a family, albeit in a divided city of security walls, checkpoints, and bus bombs.

In the end, I agreed to go with him to Jerusalem. In the months preceding our departure, I tried to imagine what it would be like to live in Israel, whose prelude into my life had been an interesting one. When I was eighteen and back-packing in Kathmandu, I had marveled at the raucous Israeli youths, who were on their "normalization holiday"—government subsidized "time off" for the ex-conscript—in hashish-flooded Nepalese towns and villages. I would have laughed at Destiny if it had told me then that I would one day be living among the young boys and the girls who were enjoying themselves in a strange language in Kathmandu's dingy cafés and food joints. That I would be speaking Hebrew in my everyday life, raising my children with a Jewish kind of identity.

However, the Jewish desire to go to Jerusalem was not unfamiliar in my experience. Before I met Leo, I became well acquainted with the Zionist dream to return to Jerusalem when I was living with the Wiseman brother and sisters during my early days in London. Jerusalem was so deeply ingrained in the Jewish psyche that, even for extreme left-wing followers of this oldest Semitic faith, the city offered a certain message, a message of hope. Leo always said that peace would start from here, from this contested city, once the warring sides had agreed on a cease-fire and nonviolence. He believed this because this was the city wherein the two peoples had placed their hopes that one day their dream to live there simultaneously would blossom into reality. And it was in this city that they both shared the same trepidation that this dream might be tarnished according to their respective political point scoring. Somehow, what was trepidation for many in Jerusalem was hope to Leo, because he thought that at least it involved both sides, unlike in cities like Tel Aviv where, with a self-imposed oblivion of the conflict that was on their doorstep, the residents were living in denial.

Despite my reluctance to uproot our family and re-settle in the conflict zone of Jerusalem, I felt a familial bond with the Jews. I felt that way because I had two half-Jewish children—although according to the Jewish law they were not part of the Great Jewish Family, as Judaism passed on through the mother. Biology prevailed over the Talmud, however, and to my soul devoid of faith, they were half Jewish through their father. I also came to accept the concept because it made Leo so happy. Agreeing to bring them up with Jewish traditions had at first seemed like a compromise, although soon I began to enjoy lighting candles on Shabbat and eating the evening meal together as a family. I was in many ways also intrigued by one of the world's strongest tribal faiths to which ironically there were so many adherents from Europe, the continent that had long ago shed the mildewed mystery of religion.

The link that I felt to the Palestinian people was political, and much more than that. I felt an affinity with the fellow citizens of the third world, of the East. I understood their passion, emotional flare-ups, family values, and also, to some extent, their Islam, even though it was very different in shade and expression from the subcontinental version that I was familiar with. In a way, I felt closer to Islam in terms of religious street culture—the mosques, the prayer calls, the alleyways of the Old City of Jerusalem with shop fronts spilling over with multicolored spices and China-made toys, with Palestinian vendors shouting out prices. I grew up in rural Bengal with the same hustle and bustle of its markets: with prayer calls and temple bells and expressive faces with glittering eyes that exuded similar raw emotions.

But then I would wander around the empty streets in West Jerusalem on a Saturday morning and the chorus of the Shabbat prayer coming out from the synagogues would fill my heart with strange emotions. The person I loved most in the world belonged to this tradition. The children I had with him half belonged to the tradition, to the hymns, and to some extent to the city that I now lived in—the city that for three millennia, Jews from all over the world remembered routinely every year in the Passover prayer: "Next Year in Jerusalem." Having been by now part of a Jewish family for almost a decade and a half and having spent almost every Passover with the extended family around the table reading from the Haggadah, the story of the Exodus of the Jews from Egypt, I must have said the prayer at least fifteen times.

On the day we finally arrived in Jerusalem, I accepted it as my destiny. "So, what shall we say this year, then?" I asked Leo in the taxi from Ben Gurion airport. "*This* year in Jerusalem!"

Leo nudged me with a huge beam on his face, his eyes luminous, imbued with the kind of emotion he exuded when he could not express how much he loved me, saying, "We'll make it work."

THIS YEAR IN

JERUSALEM

Our first house stood just off the popular West Jerusalem street called Emek Rafaim, which means "the valley of ghosts." When we were first visiting it, house hunting, we asked many people, but they didn't know the origins of the street's name. Later, I did my own research, and out of at least four different interpretations that I found, I would settle for this: "some biblical sources suggest that prior to the conquest of the land in Deuteronomy, the enemies were seen as 'ghosts' or 'giants,' *rafaims*." Here in the new, barely half-a-century-old Jewish state, the new "enemy" must be the Palestinians. What could be a more fitting description than that, of the bygone residents who had left behind palatial houses along the leafy street where no one heard an Arab voice anymore? Even the few Palestinians who worked behind the kitchen counter in various cafés and restaurants kept a low profile and spoke immaculate

Hebrew to their Jewish employers and customers. They and the absentees, the exiled Palestinians, were the ghosts of Emek Rafaim in the twenty-first century—a view that would be endorsed later by one of the relics of the past whom I would befriend.

Of course, to the new traveler's eye, the street, lined with buzzing cafés, restaurants, theaters, and designer lingerie and dress shops, was anything but ghostly. All these and more were only a five-minute walk from our house. Kiran started taking guitar and drum lessons at a well-known music conservatory, which was also on Emek Rafaim.

The cavernous, rambling, and elegant ground floor of our house, with its high arched windows, used to be part of a grand Arab mansion. The post-1948 owners had added two more floors, dividing up the former mansion into two independent houses. The architects who had refurbished and redesigned the building had played around with the structure to suppress its Arab character. The pioneers of the new school of architecture in the new country called these homes "Arab style," as opposed to just "Arab." In line with these architectural concepts, "Arab style" could be anything. It could be that the house was built after the old Arab style post-1948, or it could just be an authentic Arab dwelling from before that time. I would feel soon after we moved here that the theme was kept deliberately vague to confuse the new generation of Israelis about the historical continuity, about a certain phase in their country's past. Later on, as we traveled around the country, we would be faced with many other such blurred examples of Israel's Palestinian history. We were told every day by the mainstream media and television documentaries of an archaic past: of the great King David who unified the Jewish nation, or even of the Ottomans and the Byzantines because they were no longer a threat to the Jewish state, but there was not a word mentioned about the most contemporary history of the land, the history of an absentee generation and their offspring, the history of the Palestinian people.

The top floors of our Emek Rafaim house, added in the 1950s, had a touch of what came to be known as the New Temple architecture about them, with very tall windows through which light and air flooded our huge master bedroom. The pioneers of this style introduced another megalomaniac scheme to the Jewish state, possibly to topple the predominant beauty of the old Arab architecture, which was to build hotels, shopping malls, and swanky homes after the mythical description of the Second Temple, destroyed by the Romans in AD 70. My landlady, a-religious but fanatically Zionist, a very tall and big woman who worked in the Israel Museum, often joked that the members of her German Jewish family were so large that she'd had to rebuild the top of the house high and spacious enough to accommodate them. She was reluctant to reveal who the original owners were, but she very enthusiastically told us that there had been two murders in the house—but only after we had exchanged contract and transferred three months' rent in advance into her bank account. The first was by a jealous wife who killed her husband, or the other way round, and the second murder was committed apparently by a Palestinian gardener who killed his Jewish employer because she had not paid him for his work.

I did not want to probe too much into these stories, as I was slightly unnerved by them so soon after moving in. I would find myself spending the evenings on my own quite a lot of the time with the two children, and Kiran, who was obsessed with murder mysteries, blood, and gore, would ask endless questions about what might have prompted the killings, to unsettle me more.

I found the house difficult to be in on my own. It was too noisy for Leo with the children playing downstairs; the center of the house was hollow like a church, and the noise reached his upstairs study after echoing and strengthening to five times its original *dong*, so he went to work in a café. Our simple narrow three-story Victorian home in London had been cozy, warm, and carpeted. The Emek Rafaim house was echoey. It had hidden noises and dancing shadows that leapt out whenever I found myself alone, and enticed me into taking a virtual tour at their invitation. On these tours I became a shadow myself, a hollow, bodiless receptacle of an alternative narrative of the bygone era.

The domed high-ceilinged kitchen must have once been the middle courtyard under an open sky, with potted rosemary and *za'atar* lining the edges against the outer wall. The courtyard might also have once boasted a solitary almond tree with its fragrant yearly blossoms around which the children of the house and the neighborhood played. It was all closed up now, with huge transparent plastic domes through which light fell. I often felt as if I were in a church,

Entrance to our first "Arab" house

especially on evenings when Leo was out, the children were in bed, and I had dimmed the lights to sit at the built-in kitchen bar listening to music through headphones.

We chose the house because of the effervescent café culture of Emek Rafaim, but we soon realized how deceptive the whole thing was. Its inhabitants were predominantly American Jews (with the exception of a few English and French scattered in between), who visited their palatial Arab houses only during the Jewish holidays. The rest of the year the houses remained vacant and locked up. In the street's numerous cafés and restaurants there was an overwhelming Anglo presence. Within the first month we, Leo more than the children or myself, realized that we had landed in an area full of English-speaking Jewish expatriates. In cafés the waiters refused to speak Hebrew to him, which made Leo furious. Before we could settle in properly, he started regretting moving into such a bubble of an Anglophone world. He would not join us for the famous Israeli breakfast, which was so big that the whole family could share just one order. We were eating out almost every day for the first two months, as the shipping company that we used to transfer our possessions from London to Jerusalem had lost track of our things and we were in our cavernous house without any furniture, even without beds to sleep on. We lived with echoes, alive and animated, pervaded by the ghosts of the valley.

Café Hillel—our house was right behind it—was a notable landmark venue on the street: a twenty-two-year-old suicide bomber had blown himself up at the entrance to the café in 2003, two years before we arrived, killing some twenty people, among them important Israeli intellectuals who were apparently opposed to the occupation. The café, which occupied the ground floor of an elegant old Arab house, had been rebuilt in the past year with a modern glass-fronted façade and had since reclaimed its reputation as a popular meeting place. "In fact it is busier than ever before," the owner said to me, "because the old customers never stopped coming here after it was rebuilt, and many more new customers started to join us just to see the place in the aftermath of the bombing." I could not help thinking that human beings have a natural fascination with death, destruction, and unknown fear. Or is it our innate challenge to the possibility of terror, to overcome fear by visiting dangerous places?

We would roll into Café Hillel every morning and order its breakfast: a huge herb omelet, coffee, fresh orange juice, five different dips, hummus, green salad, raw vegetables to go with the dips, a piece of sweet something, and fresh crusty bread. The children would devour the food. They were always hungry. There was no cooked food in the house as our pots and pans were still in transit somewhere. Our kind neighbors lent us three mattresses on which we slept on the stone floor—fortunately it was late August and so it was the hottest month of the year. During our second week I bought a pot and a pan to do emergency fried eggs and simple pasta, but stupidly, I forgot to buy plates. I realized this one morning after I broke some eggs into the frying pan as we felt too lazy to get dressed and go out for breakfast. I went to our neighbors who had given us the mattresses and asked whether they could lend us some plates. We had enough plastic cutlery that Kiran and Maya had collected from our many take-out dinners.

"I am afraid we don't have any spare plates," the neighbors, Alan and Carol Rosenthal, said, with clear awkwardness in their voices.

"We only need a couple for the children, just for a short while. Our stuff should arrive very soon," I said to them, unable to understand why they were turning down such a simple request.

"So sorry, my brother has borrowed the spare ones for a wedding and we don't really have any to give you." Carol sounded genuinely apologetic.

I was taken aback. They were a big family with three children, they lived in a big house—the other half of the duplex—surely they could lend us two plates. I was standing in our spacious terrace, which we shared with a low bamboo partition in the middle, looking lost and confused. So the kind-faced Rosenthals said, "Anything else you need, just ask. Do you need sheets, towels?"

"No, thanks," I said absentmindedly, still not sure why they did not have a couple of plates to spare. I thought of the eggs in the frying pan. I could hear Maya and Kiran squabbling over who was going to have the softer egg. Kiran was particular about his fried eggs; they had to be perfect sunny-side up. Sometimes I would turn them over, especially when they had just come out of the fridge, and after cooking for two minutes the "sunny side" would still be cold. But Kiran would refuse to eat the turned-over yolks in their soft white parcels.

My neighbors were in a hurry to get back inside. So was I, because of the eggs, but I stood there dumbfounded for another minute or so among the flowering cactus and the pink and white geraniums.

The children ate their eggs directly from the pan using plastic forks.

It did not sink in until later in the evening when I told Leo about it.

"You are mad. You can't ask religious Jews for plates and cutlery. They eat kosher."

It all fell into place. Why did it take me so long to work that out? I had known about kosher rules for years. When Leo's religious relatives from Jerusalem had come to stay with us in London, they had asked whether we ate meat. We were vegetarian then and so I said no, which was why they had stayed with us. But I did not tell them that although Leo and I did not eat meat, I occasionally cooked hot dogs for our son. I could not bring myself to tell them, because that would have meant buying a new kitchen set or disposable ones and cooking separately for them. One was not even supposed to use the same oven where nonkosher meat had been cooked. Leo had said then that his cousin, Yakov, knew that Kiran ate meat, but he pretended not to in order to stay with us. Otherwise he would have had to find alternative accommodation in one of the Jewish neighborhoods in north London. This way he could save several hundred dollars during his two-week stay in one of the world's most expensive cities. However Amos, Yakov's thirteen-year-old son, who wore a kippah and attended a religious school in Jerusalem, was not so gullible—he went through our freezer and kept asking then three-year-old Kiran whether he liked chicken fingers. He replied, to my great relief, that he liked the dinosaur shapes most that were served at his school lunch.

After my extensive education on kosher food from Yakov and Amos, I could not help thinking that this was one important area in the Jewish religious tradition that I felt uncomfortable with. I did not have patience for such an exclusive custom, which alienated not only the non-Jews but also the non-religious Jews. It hardened the hearts of the most kind-hearted men and women. My neighbors were happy to share their linen and towels with me, but not a plate. If my meat and my shrimp touched their plates, they would have been washed in the dishwasher at 70°C—but then the dishwasher itself, where plates and cutlery touched by nonkosher food were washed, was considered to be nonkosher.

"Religion is not about logic, it's about rituals," said Leo. "Ancient rituals passed on to you by your ancestors. It's tribal, but it's important all the same for many people."

Despite our languid mornings on the sunny terrace of Café Hillel with plates full of the delicious dips and breads, Kiran didn't feel entirely at ease there.

"It is hard to tell where we live," he said one day. "All the people sitting at these tables are speaking English. It feels like we're in some American town!"

"So it seems, doesn't it?" I said. "That's why Daddy never joins us here."

"Does Dad not like America?"

"He doesn't like the American Jews here who flaunt Judaism in your face."

"Then why does Dad insist on taking me to the synagogue and having my bar mitzvah?"

"I suppose he feels that he wants to pass on his tradition—or tribalism as he often calls it—as it had been passed on to him by his ancestors."

"What about your ancestors?"

In answer to that question, I asked him to eat up. It was important, for some, to belong to a tribe, I would later tell my son, because it was comforting to know that you were not alone in this vast, unkind world. For me, I had to cut the cord with the ghosts of my personal history, or histories, which I believed led to the next stage from the world of ancestors. It led to a new generation of reckless, lonely souls. Wraithlike beings who nevertheless strove to belong but didn't.

So where were the real rafaims—ghosts of the *Emek*, of this valley, then? The ghosts that should be roaming these houses and the streets? This café where we were spending our mornings? The ghosts of the original residents who had left behind these huge ornate palaces?

I would soon meet them. At least one of them, albeit a reincarnated one, Elyan.

He had renamed himself Elan—a popular Jewish name, dropping the Arabic "y" after he was given an Israeli passport, which attested to his very special "Israeli Arab" status. He was the retired headwaiter of the café-restaurant at the Jerusalem YMCA where Maya would start nursery school. The YMCA ran the one and only Hebrew-Arabic bilingual peace kindergarten in the city. One morning when Maya was crying for a *pain au chocolat*, Elyan descended as a prophet and fulfilled her wishes three times over. It would then become our morning ritual. We would arrive at eight every morning, and before we could reach the bottom of the steps of the majestic building from the British mandate era, my daughter would start running up, hurrying across the ornate hall, and arriving at the sumptuous café terrace with Armenian stone tables. She would find Elyan, who still habitually came to the café every morning, having his coffee under a sun canopy. He would take her to the buffet counter and offer her a tray full of sweet breads to choose from. To keep me happy, she would very diplomatically pick one piece of cheesy boreka for me, which I would accept with a forced smile, secretly disapproving of her hands full of mini chocolate rolls. "*Hilue, hilue,*" sweet, sweet, Elyan would mutter and softly pinch her cheeks full of chocolate while I would be thinking of her rotten teeth and cursing the affectionate Arab.

But then we would become friends, as I would eventually learn to get used to this "sweet" Arab tradition of feeding little children with an unlimited amount of sweets until they became sick. You could not live in Palestine and reject the Arab hospitality. After my reluctant acceptance of my daughter stuffing herself every morning with sweet bread rolls ("only milk teeth, Mummy," she would defend herself!), Elyan and I started having our morning coffee together. That was how I came to know that he grew up roaming the streets of Emek Rafaim as a little boy in pre-1948 Jerusalem. His family owned a large swathe of land that reached the outskirts of Emek Rafaim, which used to be called Baqaa and was part of the now shrunken district of Beit Safafa, an Israeli-Arab neighborhood. Elyan was born and still lived in Beit Safafa.

"My father knew the owners of each one of these houses," said Elyan, when one day he took me out for a drive through our street.

"Emek Rafaim was the Arab millionaires' road, so to speak. The post-48 Jews have renamed it appropriately the valley of ghosts. I can feel when I drive through this street that my father's friends are breathing down my neck."

Elyan spent his childhood playing around the old railway line—now disused and gentrified into a bicycle and pedestrian path with fancy restaurants on both sides—while his father drank Arabic coffee with his friends sitting on low divans in some of the splendid houses on Emek Rafaim. Although the houses and the street as a whole had gone through a considerable face-lift and modernization, or the so-called de-Arabization process, since 1948, one could still find on concrete façades of some houses verses from the Quran written in the finest Arabic calligraphy. The balconies retained exquisite ironwork and the windows still had their grand Ottoman arches. They were somehow gothic shaped, but the colored tiles and ironwork of the Arab school of architecture added an air of lightness to the otherwise dense Jerusalem stone façades. Some of the houses still preserved old stained-glass windows on the top half, with blue or green shutters. It was usually the renovated houses, like ours, that hung between modern and Arab style, that looked fussy and heavy from outside. However, many of the houses immediately on both sides of Emek Rafaim were still intact, feminine, and very distinguishably Arab in character.

"Wealthy Palestinians lived here. Just look at them, more than enough space for a modern family. They were clutter-free so that children could run around. The main house merged into the surrounding vast gardens. In a way the huge space that each house enclosed within its walls was justified, as it was open to all," Elyan explained.

The big mansions were now cut up and partitioned to accommodate several small families. But at least the houses here were finally listed and so the exteriors could not be dismantled or drastically modified, which was not the case with the smaller Arab houses in many other areas. There were streets that had been cleared of their former ornate Palestinian houses in the 1950s to make room for the *shikunim*, the ugly high-rise, concrete-paneled estates erected to solve housing problems for the hundreds of thousands of new arrivals. Jewish immigrants from all over the world were enticed by the new state to boost its demographic ratio.

"We used to have a lot of birds here. West Jerusalem was villagelike and leafy, with tall eucalyptus and Aleppo pine trees that the British had planted. Even the birds have fled after my people left the city," said Elyan.

We drove toward the south to Talpiot and then Beit Safafa, where his family, the ones who had not left, now lived.

"They'll take everything. The Jewish state has a biblical mission. They'll take the entire land from the Nile to the Euphrates. Then they'll be happy. Or maybe they won't."

That was not the first time I had heard this popular hypothesis among the Palestinians about the expanse of the Jewish dream for land.

With Elyan, my journey through the valley of ghosts was emotional, without precise political or historical footnotes; it was based purely on his personal memories. It was literally a journey through the ghost road of the past.

A few weeks later I found myself doing the same journey with a Palestinian tour group organized by Al-Quds

University in East Jerusalem. This time there were no ghosts. This time it was real, with political and historical footnotes and related analyses. It was a specially designed tour where a number of former residents of Emek Rafaim, who were now living in Jordan or the United States, were taken back to their former homes to give them a chance to talk about their feelings.

I took along Joy, my mother-in-law, on this tour. She was visiting us, or rather, she was on a rescue mission for her daughter-in-law and her only grandchildren at the time, who had found themselves once again in a strange country, in an empty house devoid of furniture. It was reminiscent of our early Moroccan days where there too she had come to our rescue while we were shivering from the cold winds and isolation that the Atlantic blew over our little family and her Middle East–trotting son was away. Joy was excited about the trip. She had been born in Egypt to a wealthy and respectable Jewish family just years before the 1956 Suez crisis, which caused her family to be forced out of their homeland, never to return to their elegant, rambling house in Alexandria.

Huda, who was the main organizer of this tour, was also the daughter of one of the "former residents" of a palatial house on Emek Rafaim. As we stood before her father's childhood home, which was next to a big house that belonged to her uncle and was adjacent to a spacious building that belonged to another uncle, she did not look particularly perturbed by emotion, unlike some of the others, who had moist eyes. But the others were older and had personal memories of growing up in these homes. They talked about

pomegranate trees in their back gardens, about juicy kum-
quats and carobs; of patterns of Hebron tiles on the pathway
or on the floors of their living rooms. Each one of them created a picture book sketched out by his or her memories.

In Huda's case it was different. She was the daughter
of a wealthy father, had wealthy uncles and other family
members who had remained influential even after they were
dispossessed of their Emek Rafaim palaces. Huda was the
only one I met in Jerusalem who had taken the new owners to court, to claim back the family property. The case
had been adjourned many times, but she fought on until it
reopened. Outside her father's house there was a pathway
with beautiful tiles, like the ones we had in the living room
of our "Arab" house, but these were more striking. They
were black and white, and they stood out against the green
lawn. It was Saturday, and through the window we could
see people eating lunch. Several families had gathered for
the Shabbat meal.

I could see that Huda, who had a fiery disposition, was
getting more and more agitated as she watched the families
eating and enjoying themselves.

Two of the men, wearing kippah, came out.

"They called the police the last time I was here," said
Huda proudly.

I was hoping that on Shabbat, the observant Jews would
not call the police. After all, we were not causing any trouble. We were just standing outside the front gate admiring
the tiles on the pathway, which Huda said had been taken
from elsewhere in the house.

The men stood outside the front door. There was a lush garden between us and them that stretched about fifty meters with a huge, blossoming askadinya tree in the middle.

"My father still talks about the elaborate dinner parties they used to have, when the entire neighborhood would sit there around a big table—where those people are now having their Shabbat lunch—eating maqluba, drinking mint tea, and smoking nargila.

"And today," continued Huda angrily, "they threaten to call the police when I stand in front of my father's house, which was taken by force; my father had to leave on short notice, with his brothers and uncles and nieces and aunts, and there has been no compensation whatsoever."

"Compensation? You must be joking," said one of the older women whose house we had just visited. She now lived in America. She too was not allowed to go inside her house. "I just wanted to see the olive tree that we had in our back garden, which we loved to climb as children. My father never pruned it—something you would normally do every year to olive trees—because he said that it was a climbing tree and he just let it grow naturally. I still remember, it was wild, with a huge bushy head with strong branches."

The two men marched toward us and I felt a desperate urge to leave the premises, but Huda wanted to wait and see what happened if we stood there, if she asked for permission to visit the interior of the house.

"*Sabah el khair,*" Good morning, she greeted the men in Arabic. It seemed from the expressionless faces that they knew her, that they remembered her.

She then said to them that the house belonged to her father, and that it would be so kind of them if they would let her group at least see the house through the front door and the windows.

"For fifteen minutes only," Huda pleaded, but her voice hardly hid the tone of defiance. What she really meant to say was, "Who the hell are you sitting in my house eating lunch?"

The men just stood there. They did not say anything for a while, then one of them said to the other, in English, "This woman came before and stole tiles from the builders. Maybe she bribed them. I sacked the builders, brought in a new lot. She came again to get more, but this time the new builders won't give her any. That's why you can see we couldn't finish the chessboard pattern in some places on the pathway. Look here, some tiles are missing here and some over there."

Then, without looking at us or saying anything directly to Huda, they turned around and marched back inside the house. Huda could hardly hide her fury. It seemed as though she was expecting some reaction from the current owners; she had probably been gearing up the whole morning to taunt them, to get them involved at least in a verbal fight. She suddenly went all quiet, and the whole entourage too stopped talking. We did not know what to say. Did Huda really want to put up a fight? Did she want them to call the police again, because that would have at least proved that she could still stir up a fuss before her father's house even though she did not, could not win in court? That she could still sow seeds of discontent in the quiet complacency of the Shabbat observers? By refusing to have any dialogue or confrontations with her, those men in skullcaps in a way struck a raw nerve in her.

Finally, when she could pull herself together, she said to us in a trembling voice, "Most of you probably can't imagine how it feels to stand before your father's home that you can no longer enter. You didn't sell it. You didn't hand it over as charity. You were just told to leave, with your lunch on the cooker. You left and you can never return."

"I know how it feels," said Joy, inspecting a flowering lemon tree whose fragrant branches outstretched across the periphery of the walled house that once belonged to Huda's family.

"My family also had to leave their house in Alexandria. All the Jews were forced to leave Egypt after 1956. They had very little time to pack their things. I was born there and spent my childhood there. There was no compensation. I was not even allowed to visit Alexandria for many years, where in the family mausoleum my little brother is buried. They didn't ask us before they turned the house into an orphanage—but that's the only consolation I have now, that my house is being used for a good cause, at least."

"When you *could* go back to Alexandria, did you visit the house . . . the orphanage?" asked a kind-voiced Palestinian-American woman from our tour group. Her voice was emotional.

"Yes I did, and it did help," said Joy. "Of course, since it is an orphanage now, they had to make a lot of changes to the structure of the building, but it still helped to reconcile, at least psychologically, with my own personal sense of loss. I don't ever dream of being compensated." Then she turned to Huda, who was speechless, and said, "I totally understand how you feel."

So the party of memory keepers, the living ghosts of the recent history of the Arab-Jewish conflict in the Middle East, started walking away from Huda's father's house. The bus was waiting to take us to our next destination: another "abandoned house" by Palestinian refugees now owned and occupied by Jewish immigrants from Europe.

"The Jews didn't forget, for two thousand years, that this was their homeland, and they finally came and claimed the land from its current rightful inhabitants. How can anyone expect the Palestinians to forget what they have lost after just sixty years?" Leo always said this to his family and close friends.

.4.

NO CLAUSE FOR "NOTHING" AS RELIGION

In terms of schools, there were not many great choices, especially not for Kiran. We went for the most obvious option available for him at this stage, the Anglican International School, where we felt that with his London primary school background he would find it easier to integrate. He resisted learning Hebrew. He didn't understand why his father insisted that he learn the language of Israel when he himself vehemently fought against its policy. He would argue with me for hours whenever I suggested, "Do you not want to learn the language of the land where you live?"

"None of my friends speaks Hebrew."

"You live here. You must learn to speak to the people in the street!"

"Why should I? Everyone in the street speaks English."

"Well, it's an objectionable excuse, one that always stopped the English from learning a second language properly."

"I'll learn French."

"But that won't be useful here."

"It'll be useful later."

"But you are living here now."

"I'll do Arabic, then."

"What's wrong with Hebrew?"

"It's not useful. At least Arabic would be useful later if I wanted to travel in the Arab world, since you said I must learn a useful language."

"But your father would be so happy if you learnt Hebrew, because then you would be able to read from the Torah at your bar mitzvah."

"I don't want a bar mitzvah. I am not Jewish."

"You are half Jewish."

"No, I am not. It goes through the mother. There's no such thing as half Jewish."

"Biologically you are half Jewish."

"Mum! Religion doesn't go through biology! So far as I know, I am not Jewish."

"Come off it! You are being unnecessarily difficult and arguing like a teenager. Judaism is also a cultural identity. And so you are half Jewish."

"Still, I don't need to learn to speak Hebrew."

He would always outwit me when it came to establishing what we considered as his identity. From very early on he asserted that he could not be Jewish under Jewish law. Where did he get such definitive language to argue with? Some of it came from his father, except the bit concerning his attitude to Hebrew. He had seen his father tirelessly testing the Israeli xenophobia, on buses, in taxis, at airport security counters. Kiran had often seen his father opening Arabic newspapers on Israeli buses just to annoy the passengers who wanted to be annoyed. He had seen him turn on loud Arabic music on Saturday evenings as the expatriate Jewish worshippers gathered in the synagogue next to our house for the *motzei*, after-Shabbat service. Every time we were on the road, Kiran heard his father rant about how the highway signs often did not include Arabic, and when they did, it was sprayed over with racist graffiti.

I could not really argue with the observation of an eleven-year-old concerning the attitude of most Israelis to the Arabic language, spoken by almost two-thirds of the population: it was the language spoken not only by the Palestinians but also by most of the Jews who originated from the Arab world, which constituted roughly half of the Israeli Jewish population. It was not just in the everyday life where Arabic was absent. Even on popular music channels such as Galgalatz it was rare to hear Arabic music.

It was sad, Leo would say, this insular attitude toward Arabic, because in the homes of Iraqi Jews, the voice of Umm Kulthum, the Egyptian queen of Arabic music, was more likely to be heard than popular Hebrew songs. When the zealots erased the Arabic from road signs, they also wiped out a large chunk of their own history— the Middle Eastern history of the Jewish people. Maimonides, one of the greatest Jewish philosophers, from twelfth-century Andalusia, published most of his work in Arabic. The minds of the obliterators of Arabic verged on paranoia on a national level, with the same zealousness of the converted people. When the textbooks in Pakistan left out the Indian epics such as the Mahabharata and the Ramayana, they were reinventing history and deculturalizing the population. It was clear from the exclusion of Arabic music from the Israeli radio stations and the overwhelming presence of English pop songs in their airwaves that Israel was still living a myth sixty years after the victory of the European Zionism that led to the creation of the modern Jewish state. Despite its Middle Eastern geographical reality, it had a European heart, albeit beating rather erratically.

However, despite his reluctance, Leo and I decided that Kiran should continue with Hebrew as a second language. The offhand manner in which he accepted the language never ceased to bother me. After a year of three hours of Hebrew a week, he still could not string together a simple sentence such as, "I am hungry." Maya somehow made up for her brother's lack of enthusiasm in Hebrew by being the perfect "Israeli" child with an immaculate Ashkenazi accent.

Despite his insistence on teaching the children Hebrew, it had not been Leo's intention to bring up his daughter as an Israeli. We had chosen to send her to the only mixed Arab-Israeli kindergarten in Jerusalem. The Peace Pre-school was situated on the first floor of the elegant YMCA complex in West Jerusalem. With its tall phallic bell tower, the building on the exclusive King David Street was a Jerusalem landmark, and it conducted many other inter-communal and bridge-building operations between the Israelis and the Palestinians. But it had its limitations. After all, the management was Israeli, and I should have seen the warning signs when I found myself grappling with the kindergarten's admission form, which had a clear section for the applicant's religion. I had left blank, as I always did on application forms, the space requiring religion.

"You have to write your family's religion."

"We don't follow any particular religion."

"You have to write something. We have a quota system, half and half, half Jewish, half Arab."

"What about the ones who don't fall into these categories?"

"You still have to write something. What is her father's religion?"

I hesitated for a moment. I really didn't want to jeopardize my daughter's chances of getting into this very special kindergarten. Moreover, Leo did believe in his religion, so it would be a lie to say he had no faith.

"Judaism."

"And yours?"

"None."

"What were you born with?"

"None. No one is born with a religion."

"I mean your parents."

"It's too complicated."

The admissions secretary looked visibly irritated at my cryptic answers. But before long she came up with, "Okay, I'll put your daughter in the Jewish section, then. As you said, you didn't have a religion, and we don't have a section for 'Nothing' as religion. So she shall be Jewish."

"I suppose you are right."

I was itching to say that Maya's grandfather believed in Islam, although her maternal ancestors were Hindu. But it would not have been prudent to register my daughter with what might have been regarded by the school authorities as a messed-up family history. So for her sake and for the sake of the preschool quota system, I had been coerced to having a fully Jewish daughter as opposed to her being half "nothing." I wondered whether that could be passed on through the mother.

The kindergarten, which was supposedly a "peace" school, awakened in Maya quite early on a keen interest in the Arab-Israeli conflict. One day, as we were having breakfast, she said, "Mummy, did you talk about Lebanon on the radio when you worked for the BBC in London?"

"Yes, I did. There was a war then, about which we talked on the radio almost every day. What do you know about Lebanon?"

"I know Lebanon and Israel had a war."

I was taken aback. "How do you know that?" I asked.

"I just know, someone told me . . ."

"Who told you?"

"I think Daddy might have told me."

"What did Daddy say?"

"He said there was a war, when we went up to the Golan and you didn't want to come with us. Daddy drove to a place called Lebanese border, and the soldiers won't let us stay there very long. Daddy had an argument with them."

"What else did Daddy tell you?"

"Are there Arabs in Lebanon?"

"What did he exactly say to you?" I repeated, feeling intrigued and at the same time perturbed by her war talk. But she ignored me and continued instead, "Mummy, you didn't tell me if the Lebanese people were Arabs."

"Yes they are," I said absentmindedly.

"Like the Palesti-ninians?"

"Yes." I noticed again, with fondness, the extra "ni" that my daughter always used as she pronounced "Palestinians." The Ninians, the Ninjas . . . I began playing with words until she brought me back to reality with this: "Israelis are stronger than the Arabs."

"How on earth . . ." I barked at her. "Now, who's been saying this to you?"

"Gili, my best friend in school." She looked at me, baffled by my sudden, angry reaction.

"I thought Layal was your best friend."

"Gili is my best Yehudi friend and Layal is my best Arab friend." She said in Hebrew, "Do you know, Layal didn't come to school on Yom Ha'atzmayut? My teacher Ariela said, '*Hayom ʒe Hayom bishvil ha Yehudim, lo bishvil ha*

Muslemim.'" "Independence Day," according to my daughter's kindergarten teacher, "was a day for the Jewish people, not for the Muslims."

I often wondered how the bilingual, mixed Palestinian-Israeli "peace" school dealt with days like Yom Ha'atzmayut: the day that marked the creation in 1948 of the Jewish state and was viewed by the Palestinians as al-Naqba, the Catastrophe, when more than seven hundred thousand Palestinians left or, arguably, fled their homes and became refugees. Obviously the kindergarten at the YMCA, the much reputed, politically correct educational institution, which catered to liberal-minded Jews and open-minded Palestinians (open to mingling with Jews within the institution), had failed to deal with the question of Independence Day. So the broad-minded Arabs were reduced to shutting themselves up in their homes until the festivities were over. Somehow my daughter's understanding of religious differences, as she saw her friends in the light of their perceived religions, was beginning to worry me.

I tried to think what it had been like in my Bengali school. I still remembered the names of some of my classmates, Bani, Tushar, Laila, Bithi, Aisha, Camellia . . . none of these had ever appeared to me as being tied to any religious identity. But now, looking back, and as the names fluttered before my eyes on the translucent wings of a multicolored butterfly, they detonated a multitude of explosions of religious identities: Hindu, Muslim, Buddhist, Christian. As children, we without question believed that the festivals of Durga Puja, Eid, Buddha Purnima, Ramzan (Ramadan), and Christmas were all part of our life, our culture, and our understanding of the myriad traditions that enriched our daily experience.

Nevertheless, I felt intrigued by Maya's perception of Israeli-Palestinian politics, and I wanted to probe further. I asked her, "What do you think of yourself, then? Are you with the Israelis or the Arabs?"

"You tell me."

"No, you tell me!"

"My daddy is Jewish, so should I be with the Israelis? I think Israel is stronger."

"But your daddy also speaks fluent Arabic, and I don't think he'd agree with you on this."

"But in school I speak Hebrew. Even Layal, my Palestininian friend, speaks Hebrew better than Arabic."

Hebrew would soon dominate as the language of the ruler-occupier of the land, and Maya would be coming home waving the Israeli flag and singing jingoistic ghetto songs that went like:

Eretz Yisrael Sheli My land of Israel

Yafa ve gam porakhat Beautiful and also blossoming.

Mi bana ou mi nata? Who built it? Who planted it?

Kulanu b'yakhad. We are all together.

Ani baniti bait b'Eretz Israel I built my home in the land of Israel.

Az Yesh lanu eretz, So we have a land

Ve yesh lanu bait, And we have a house

Ve yesh lanu etz, ve yesh lanu kvish, yesh lanu gesher, We
   have a tree and we have a road and we have a bridge
B'Eretz Yisrael. In the land of Israel.

The simplicity of the nationalistic pride felt by most
Israeli children amused me at first to the extent that I did
not stop Maya from decorating our house with blue-and-
white Israeli flags or singing, before our horrified UN
guests, patriotic songs about the glory of the land of Israel.
Leo, who advocated that Jews should at least issue an apology to the Palestinians for taking their land and that the
Israeli-Palestinian conflict could be resolved by promoting
a one-state solution, was mortified in front of the representatives of the international community that considered Israel an occupying power, and therefore his daughter was an
embarrassment.

Most of our expatriate friends—from the UN, other aid
agencies, and the Western media—did not learn Hebrew,
because they saw it as the language of the occupation, and
also because some found it useless. But there was always a
flurry of enthusiasm among the newcomers from the peace
camp to enroll in various language schools in East Jerusalem
for courses in colloquial Arabic. Except for just a handful of
journalists, no one had ever set foot in an ulpan, the institution for intensive Hebrew lessons designed for new Jewish
immigrants. After six months in the Hebrew ulpan, one was
meant to be fairly fluent in the language for everyday use.

Learning Hebrew was not politically correct. Many of
our friends, after having spent four years in West Jerusalem,

could not ask for a glass of water or buy a newspaper, and they found this disinclination to learn Hebrew somehow a source of pride, a political statement. The international community had limited interactions with ordinary Israelis. Most lived in Arab East Jerusalem and some of them even were reluctant to or would not visit restaurants in Jewish West Jerusalem. Some younger types, however, sometimes rebelled against this unwritten rule. One would know which bars were the UN or the EU favorites by spotting the white number plates on their cars outside. The international community could park their cars anywhere and everywhere, even on pavements. This special privilege was assigned to the members of the peace-negotiating, food-distributing, and refugee-repatriating teams in recognition of the critical nature of their work. But it was disconcerting to see the WFP (World Food Programme) or ICRC (Red Cross) cars parked outside bars, restaurants, and nightclubs in West Jerusalem, blocking the footpath. The owners of these cars could be seen sipping margaritas, discussing the latest internal organizational politics and, of course, the hot topic of the Israeli occupation. The comfort and the European ambiance in Israeli bars and restaurants provided a perfect home away from home; many found respite from the conflict talk and from the pressure of the overtly politicized "Arab" areas where most of them lived. Only a few hundred meters from the bars and the clubs at the city center stretched Arab East Jerusalem linking the West Bank, where the aid and conflict-resolution agencies did their fieldwork. I could understand the sense of despair that I often detected among these "Western" crowds sitting on barstools, philosophically downing the Maccabee Beer or hard liquor late into the evening. What they did was in a way a thankless task, the results of which were not going to be seen or felt in a clear-cut way. Over the years, the peace process had been deadlocked in the discourse of peace with or without justice. A conflict that involved two peoples fighting for the same piece of land could not be resolved with real justice being done to either of them. In the past sixty years, there had been many outsiders who came here on two- or four-year contracts, and finished their terms without realizing the completion of what they were doing, because there was no permanence in the work that the international agencies—the peace industry, as described by cynics—did in the Palestinian territories. No sooner did one project come to an end than another intifada or unrest broke out. Or just before a promising dialogue—for which there would be a lot of preparations over many months or years—was scheduled to start, a bus would be blown up in West Jerusalem and the international mediation would be pushed aside to make room for Israel's retaliation.

It was primarily this retaliation by Israel, which showed in many forms against the occupied people in the Palestinian territories, that made the Hebrew language unattractive and synonymous with oppression to the members of the international community. I could see a point there. I had never been in a place before where the visitors showed deliberate "politically correct" reluctance to learn the local language.

I had made several attempts in the past at taking Arabic lessons. And while learning modern classical *Fus-ha*, I was amazed to see how much Indian languages had borrowed from Arabic. But while it was easy to recognize numerous Arabic words and expressions, and Arab culinary traditions in the northern Indian languages and culture, I found it extremely difficult to learn Arabic. The "h" and "gh" were impossible to master, and the different dialects of the language in each of the Arab countries that we visited varied so much and it was so confusing that I would be reluctant to practice in Palestine the Arabic that I had learnt in Morocco. Even the numbers and simple words such as "straight on" changed from country to country. After more than six months of learning the Palestinian dialect, I could barely speak it, although I understood a fair amount. That I believed was largely due to my habit of searching and finding links to Hindi and Urdu.

I had no reservations in giving preference to Hebrew over Arabic when we moved to Jerusalem. The sound of Hebrew was familiar to me from the Shabbat prayers that I had heard on Friday nights before the meal, since I met Leo. We decided to live in West Jerusalem, in a Hebrew-speaking area, as opposed to the Arabic-speaking eastern half of the city. When we came to the Middle East's only country where a Semitic language other than Arabic was spoken, we wanted to give it a try. As well as the connection that I felt to Israel because of my Jewish husband and our half-Jewish children, I was captivated by the workings of the Jewish state founded on European values and how that functioned in the Middle East. Simple things intrigued me, such as how the Eastern European ultra-Orthodox in black coats and hats dealt with the desert heat or how hummus— the mashed chickpea dip, a classic Arab starter—had been taken into the homes of the Ashkenazi Jews as "Israeli food." It was also interesting to see a language that had been dead for almost two millennia come alive and be carried forth as the main mode of literature, science, poetry, and astronomy of the new state. I often wondered what it would be like if Sanskrit were spoken again. How would one describe a computer, a thermometer, and a plug point? In my Hebrew ulpan, I was amazed to learn that all three words could be said in biblical Hebrew (in which "computer" is translated as "thought machine," *makhshev*). The ingenuity and the constant evolution of the language fascinated me. A language whose current spoken form was less than a hundred years old, great novels were being written in it, so were political treaties, songs, poetry, and pornography.

But my enthusiasm for Hebrew suffered a significant blow when one day my son came home from school and announced, "Mummy, I heard that Daddy's been looking for an intensive Hebrew ulpan for me. Is that right?"

"Yes, because you don't have very long before your bar mitzvah. I think you should have your bar mitzvah. You may not like it now, but as Daddy says, when you are older, you'll look back and you may appreciate the cultural experience."

"No, I won't. Don't embarrass me in front of my friends. Dad doesn't want any of his friends or colleagues to know that he is Jewish, so why should it be different for me? My close friends in school are all Palestinians and they would think that I am on the Israeli side. It's bad enough already that they've found out I have a Jewish family."

"How have they found out?" I asked him, concerned by my son's denial of his roots. Leo always avoided his Jewish identity being revealed in public, because he felt that as a former Middle East reporter and now as a peace negotiator between Israel and the Palestinians in the occupied territories, he would lose his credibility.

Nevertheless, it upset me because it left me and the children in a difficult situation. Because I was excited by Leo's and the children's Jewish lineage, I liked telling my acquaintances in Jerusalem that I was here because of my connection to the city through my family.

I felt sad that Kiran felt embarrassed by the Jewish part of his identity, more or less for the same reasons as his dad. He was afraid of what his Arab friends would make out of his sense of justice for the Palestinians if they realized his connection to Judaism.

"You know, in the computer room, we were just messing about . . ." Kiran went on as I still pondered the absurdity of the situation. While I empathized with why Leo felt he had to hide his Judaism and why Kiran too had to copy his father, part of me felt that this attitude toward the Arabs in general somehow verged on paranoia. In my experience, most Arabs may be anti-Zionist, but they are rarely anti-Semitic.

"So . . ." I asked Kiran, "how did your friends find out about your Jewish family?"

"They Googled me. And imagine how embarrassing it was that my middle name, Akiva, came up in a family tree."

"What family tree?"

"You are also there. It's a Jewish family tree; my ancestors apparently came here from Lithuania in the 1880s as Zionist settlers."

I didn't say anything. I tried to imagine how the poor boy must have felt sharing this information with his Palestinian friends.

"And now that they know my middle name, they started teasing me in school, calling me Akiva."

"Yezan, too? Your best friend?"

"No, not Yezan. I don't know what he's thinking. He might not come now and spend the summer holiday with me as we've arranged, with my grandparents in England."

"I'm sure he will. The Barghoutis are broad-minded. They might be fighting Zionism but not the Jews."

The extended Barghouti family included the charismatic Palestinian leader and political activist Marwan Barghouti, now serving five life sentences after being convicted by an Israeli court of the murder of civilians. He was a distant uncle of Yezan's. Traditionally the Barghoutis were part of the upper echelon of Palestinian intelligentsia. Yezan's parents had been educated in England and France, and they were now sending their children to the Anglican school where the fees were as high as in any English public school. They lived in a vast house in East Jerusalem. Foreign dignitaries and Palestinian ministers made regular appearances at their social gatherings, where fine wine and delicious canapés were served by the hosts themselves. Leo was very excited that their son was coming to spend his summer holiday with us in England.

"But my ancestors were among the first Zionist settlers in this country, Mummy, so says the family tree on the Internet. They have taken Palestine away from Yezan!" said my distraught boy.

.5.

"TOO MUCH HAPPINESS"

The first months went by dizzyingly fast. I jumped from one ecstatic mood to another as I attempted to redefine my identity in the divided city. I tried to avoid the numerous expatriate parties and gatherings to which we were routinely invited as part of the international community. I'd had many depressing experiences of the expatriate life from our year in Jordan. Having failed to form friendships with Jordanians, who frequently spoke to me disrespectfully, seeing me as one of the hundreds of South Asian maids who served the wealthy locals as well as the foreigners, I had sought shelter in the European circle. But they made me equally sad with their own exclusivity in the "safe" havens of enclosed clubs with pools and playgrounds—for their children only.

Leo's work involved a fair amount of dealings with international NGOs and diplomats in Jerusalem. We were invited to parties thrown by the UN, the World Food

Programme, the Norwegian Refugee Council, the International Crisis Group, the British council, and many of the other hundreds of agencies that worked on peacekeeping, crisis resolution, refugee care missions. But I preferred to spend time with Leo's cousins, Michal and Yakov, who lived in West Jerusalem and were religious.

I felt that I was not like most of my expat acquaintances, that I had a real connection to this place because Leo's great-great grandparents had been among the first Zionist settlers in what would become Israel. I was fascinated by Jewish rituals, intrigued by the recitations of the Shabbat prayer with our religious cousins, who had a picture of the Wailing Wall in their living room painted by a well-known Jerusalem artist, but there was a very important omission—the Dome of the Rock was missing from the painting!

Leo's cousins were very private people; they kept to themselves with their old-fashioned, often reactionary, religious Zionist values. Michal and Leo shared the same maternal great-grandfather, who was of European Jewish or Ashkenazi background. Michal came from a secular Zionist family but married a religious "Arab Jew" from Yemen, defying her parents and the whole Ashkenazi establishment of the time. Yakov's worldview was mesmerizing to me, the most refreshingly honest and politically incorrect opinion that I would ever come across. He called himself an Arab Jew, to the great displeasure of the predominantly Ashkenazi Israeli "high society" and even to his own wife (but I think, now that Michal was no longer among us—she died of cancer—that she actually loved the quirky views of her

Yemenite husband and that she changed into a religious woman to annoy her a-religious Ashkenazi parents), spoke Arabic to his mother, who immigrated to Israel from Yemen as a young woman with two small children in the 1950s, and went to a synagogue where the service was conducted to this day in strong Arabic-accented Hebrew, exactly how it had been done back in Yemen for a thousand years.

For me, spending my weekends with Yakov and Michal was so much more inviting than listening to foreign diplomats discuss Middle East politics. The talk of peace in the Middle East somehow went round and round and satisfied the egos of the European misfits who attributed certain prophecy to themselves and deluded themselves, some unknowingly, some believingly, that they were participating in making a difference to this region. As a journalist, I should have dived into this frenzy. But instead I was put off by it all.

I was not overtly critical of Israel as was expected of me by the foreigners around me. I found myself tremendously interested in the way that the new country asserted its command and "sophomoric" aspiration. I was intrigued by the many shades of Zionism that I came across in my everyday life.

Perhaps I was trying to fit in among the West Jerusalem locals, which explained why I didn't, at least in the beginning, join the league of expatriates and radical Israelis to voice openly the immense unease that I felt toward Israel's policy in the West Bank.

The first person I befriended in Jerusalem was Orli, a Spanish-American Jewish immigrant who was virulently a-religious, a Zionist with matching vigor. The term "left-wing Zionist" was used to describe people like her, who believed in a two-state solution as opposed to the right-wing Zionists for whom the land of Israel spread from the Mediterranean to the Jordan River and was for the Jews and Jews only. She and Leo did not like each other from day one. But I was happy to have met Orli, who befriended our children too and snatched me away from the first attacks of loneliness as we started our life as a family in the big, hollow house on Emek Rafaim.

I was completely charmed by Orli, who wrote poems in French, dreamt in Spanish, and conducted daily conversations in English and Hebrew. She was voluptuously beautiful with endless legs, flawlessly golden and firm under her tiny skirts. She was forty years old. And single.

She somehow portrayed what I thought I too was meant to be. I wanted to feel "young" like her, although I was younger than Orli, with overflowing strands of creative juices, boast long legs in a miniskirt that I would never have the guts to wear in Jerusalem, and be single. Single? Perhaps not. I was not so sure of the last attribute, as I loved those "manly" embraces too much, embraces that, Alice Munro said in her story "Too Much Happiness," offered a marvelous assurance, which was "more delightful of course if they love you, but comforting even if it is only a kind of ancient noble pact that they have made, a bond that has been signed, necessarily even if not enthusiastically, for your protection."

I was not sure if Leo ever felt that he was protecting me with his embraces, but I loved them all the same. He had strong arms, strong milk- and meat-fed arms of the middle classes, unlike my puny, muscleless, stringlike limbs, meat-deprived in my Bengali childhood. He often said he was worried that he might snap my wrists by pulling me too hard into his arms.

His embraces were always comforting to me, even if they were part of a bond that he may have signed not enthusiastically but as a noble pact out of his Very English education.

So on that front I did not envy Orli.

Leo said that I was in love with her, that I was finally living my hidden lesbian fantasy. He did not understand how I could look forward to seeing Orli every day and that I had not spent a single moment fantasizing about being in love with her the way he meant.

But I loved her all the same. The children longed to see her. She was this aunt who fell from the sky in Jerusalem and whose company they adored. Kiran, in particular, who, deprived of meat at home at the time due to my own mostly vegetarian (with fish) background and Leo's political vegetarianism, gorged on her burgers with anchovies, her mussels with bacon, and her ageless Peter Pan lifestyle.

Orli lived in a Templer house in the same neighborhood as ours in West Jerusalem, with wild, rambling gardens surrounding it. "The German Templers were adequately compensated by the state of Israel," she said one day, before I even fathomed the intricacies of the debate on the return of the refugees. Why did she say that? I had wondered, because I at that point refused to judge her by any of her political views or nonviews. It was totally politically sound even to people like Leo, she said, to live in a house formerly owned and inhabited by the German Protestants who had fled persecution back in Germany and settled in Palestine but who too were made refugees along with the Palestinians after the creation of the state of Israel. Israel had subsequently compensated the Templers in return for hefty German reparations for the Holocaust victims and survivors. Somehow that made it all right to live in an abandoned Templer house confiscated by Israel just because the state had recompensed the losers. Or did it? What about the *act* of forced abandonment? But for now, I would not ask this question.

I was lucky that Orli had happened into my life and to the lives of my children so soon after we arrived in Jerusalem. What would I have done otherwise? How would I have coped with so much loss and so many expectations? How would the process of uprooting that was to last for the next several years have set in without knocking us all off our feet?

Michal, Leo's cousin who would die a few years later, provided another aspect of the integrating factor that we needed so much to belong here. I did not want to float indefinitely or indecisively, bobbing up and down and around, to be propped up by the representatives of the foreign NGOs, the NGOs that were the parallel government here and that in a way ruled the hearts of the international community in this city. In short, I wanted to avoid feeling indebted to those who already had enough on their plate: administering all those refugee schools educating Palestinian children and the aid carts that delivered food to Gaza, refugee camps, and other occupied and stranded Palestinians.

"That should be the responsibility of the occupying force, i.e., Israel," Orli would say, giving me food for thought. "If those organizations stopped meddling in the affairs of this place, Israel would have been forced by international law to look after the refugees and the occupied Palestinians. Well, as they say in Arabic, '*Ahlan wa sahlan*,' Welcome to my family. That's what we say to the UN and the other aid organizations; they are subsidizing what must be the responsibility of Israel! By taking over refugee repatriation and the welfare of the occupied territories, the international agencies have prevented Israel from doing its job."

I would soon acknowledge the futility of the international presence in Israel and Palestine. Orli was right. But I felt then, and I would continue to feel in later years, that her comments were not directed to me. I was not one of them. I belonged here. My children belonged here.

Kiran, however, continued to refuse to belong. "They have taken Palestine away from Yezan."

I would lie awake thinking about what my son had said. When I told Leo about Kiran's desire for his friends not to know that he was half Jewish, he found it very funny. He teased him for a bit, saying, "So I hear they call you Akiva, it's a nice Jewish name, after a famous rabbi," before becoming serious when Kiran ran back to his room and banged the door shut to another mention of his Jewish name that he loathed so much.

That evening I spread a China-made lambskin that we bought from the Old City on the beautiful tiled floor in our spacious sitting room and sat with Leo with two glasses of wine. I was feeling emotional by the rare delight in recent weeks when the two of us could spend the evening without having our peacemaking friends among us. I was feeling nervous.

In a trembling and cautious voice I asked him, "So, tell me about your ancestors, then. Funny that I never asked you this. Kiran for the first time made me think."

"My little foray into peacemaking has not been a happy event," said Leo, looking out through the arched windows of our Arab house. "In the 1880s a great-great-grandfather lit the flame of the first Arab-Israeli conflict when, as the founder of the first Jewish colony, he stole some cows from the nearby Palestinian village. I vainly hoped that I might have a small part resolving it."

I was astonished. I had known him for a decade and a half and there were still things that I knew nothing about. How come I was only now told this important piece of information concerning his mission as a peacemaker in Israel-Palestine, information that shaped my present and probably would dominate my future too to a great length? As we sat on the floor in the empty, furnitureless room with my eyes fixed on the abstract patterns of leaves and flowers on the Hebron tiles, I would hear more astounding revelations of Leo's family. The great-great-grandfather was not only charged with the theft of an unknown number of Palestinian cows but was also accused of throwing a Palestinian villager into a well—"probably the owner of the cows," Leo added, with warped humor in his voice.

It was this perpetual enigma around him, his left-wing politics and yet strong Jewish faith and the uninhibited demand that we keep a semi-Jewish home, that kept me interested in him still like a new lover. I felt that I hardly knew him after all these years. As the sudden Middle Eastern dusk descended out in the gardens and in the house, darkening the tiles into holograms of frozen testimonies of a bygone people, I began to realize why he did not want to live in an "Arab house." Underneath all his joking and fooling around this particular legend concerning his Zionist ancestor, there was a great deal of guilt. He took personal responsibility for the exile of the Palestinian refugees. From the far corner of a just world, Leo said, "that great-great-grandfather then ran away to England dodging a subpoena. One hundred and twenty years later I came here to atone for his alleged sin."

He laughed again. I wish he had not. I could not take his self-deprecating humor at times like this, when I would have liked to have been able to hold a normal, sensible, grown-up conversation. When I wanted to show him my support, when I was ready to say that if it troubled him too much to live in an Arab house whose former residents were refugees, I would very happily move. I knew he had agreed to my choice of the family home where we started the new chapter of our life in Jerusalem because he wanted to make me happy and show his gratitude toward me for chucking my life and job in London and following him to the Middle East again, so soon after our botched Jordanian trial.

But it was not possible to hold empathy for Leo for very long. It was as if part of him just naturally rejected or pretended not to notice when his loved ones genuinely wanted to do things for him. The moment I thought, sitting close to him in the darkened room, that I would propose to move out of this house and go somewhere free of guilt of desecrating the Palestinian past, he answered a phone call from someone who sounded like a diplomat wanting to pick his brain on the impending Israeli disengagement from Gaza. He left the room as if he were in a great hurry, leaving me in the gloom of the dusk with my desire to reach out to him callously snubbed. A few minutes later I would hear the front door shut as he went out to see the diplomat at a nearby café. The streetlights came on and long shadows of the ornate iron grilles of the open windows fell upon the tiles. There could easily have been ghosts laughing at my powerless frustration at yet another missed opportunity, the parallel paths that my love and I strode and how they hardly ever crossed.

"Nonsense," Orli said later in the evening when I invited her to keep me company in the lonely house after the children had gone to bed. "No need for you to feel spooked in this fabulous house! You know your husband, he is a self-hating Jew! Refugees cannot return in practical terms, although the desire to return is perfectly valid. For many hundreds of years this will remain a literary dream. Poems will be written on it, a whole area of literature and art on the Palestinian displacement and exile will probably flourish.

That's a good thing. But advocating their physical return may unleash another war. There isn't enough room for all of us to live together in this tiny dot on the world map."

Orli's argument was, in short, that after the displaced people had moved on, the memory of displacement could be used as poetic inspiration. As it had been for the Jews for many hundreds of years while they yearned for an eventual return to Jerusalem in their prayers, their dreams, and their art.

After we drank a bottle of wine on the terrace under the clear Jerusalem night sky, I could not help admitting to myself that I was not convinced by Orli. Even after the rough edges of my previously agitated mind were beautifully blunted by the merlot, which by the way did not come from any Jewish settlement in the occupied territory, I felt that Orli was just playing with ideas. She did not believe in what she was saying. Suddenly, I had a flash of insight—she was voicing such an absurd argument because she wanted me to pass it on to Leo. She wanted to taunt him, his self-hating Jewishness.

It appeared that I was right in my conjecture. "What a load of colonial nonsense!" Leo snapped the following morning at the breakfast table, spreading Marmite on toast for Maya. "What does she know about the pain of the refugees? She is an invader, an outsider from the Americas, and she is not even religious, and yet she thinks she has a more valid reason to be here than the rightful inhabitants of this land who were kicked out by the most absurd colonial enterprise of the twentieth century!

"What does she want?" asked Leo. "Why does she want to turn you against me?"

"Now, now, where do you get this from? Orli's been wonderful to us, to me, to the kids. She fills the void left by your erratic work engagements."

"Here we go, the cracked record playing again. You'll never be happy whatever I do, do you not see that by now? I have tried for fifteen years."

"Have you?"

"Yes, I have, in my way as best as I could. I never planned to make you *un*happy."

"You never consciously thought of making me happy either. You remained preoccupied with your own self-absorbed mission or whatever you want to call it."

"You've hardly been Mother Teresa."

"Actually, I have been. I left everything that once mattered to me so that you can pursue your dream in this bloody region. You still want more. You want to control my friends, whom I should or should not see."

"You like seeing people who dislike me, that's how you get God knows what. Your kicks? Revenge? I don't ever deliberately try to hurt you, but you still get hurt. It has become your obsession to get hurt, to play victim. You are like the Israelis, you thrive on the celebration of victimhood. I can't think how I can make you happy when you're set on being unhappy!"

"Of course you can't think, you are insensitive to the needs of your immediate family, you are too busy saving the world. You don't get a credit for being with the family, so why should you care?"

"Pure paranoia. And I can't help but run away from all this. Couldn't you just go one week without shouting hysterically at me? All I'm saying is that I don't feel comfortable with your newfound friend in our house. A *friend*, who's doing everything in her power to separate us, to cause friction between us. She gives out this air as if she owns you all, you and the kids. You play on that—you use other people to show me that you don't need me. Well, I can't be there for you whenever you press the buzzer. I have a job to do, and it's a very critical time in this country."

In this country. He would never say "in Israel," or even "in Palestine." Over the years we would be living in this country. Faceless, nameless, like an abstract god that ruled over our lives. We had assigned ourselves to living "in this country" for as long as it took to create peaceful borders or abolish all borders under Leo's scheme, until we all became part of the mythical "one state." What name would that state have? We did not have to discuss it right now, he would say. "I would be very happy to live in Palestine, so long as it will have equal rights and justice for all the religions."

I would always give in and we would just continue to live in this country. When I was called back by the BBC at the end of my sabbatical, I told my boss that I was not coming back. I was asked if I would be interested in extending my leave for another year, to give me time to make up my mind. But I had already made up my mind. I chose to offer myself on the altar of destiny, our joint destiny, the destiny that had been designed by Leo and by his faith in the myth of a binational state in this country.

I would not of course stop seeing Orli, despite the evident conflict between her and my husband. I would see her at least three times a week, sometimes with the children but often without. We would go to Jerusalem's famous Mahane Yehuda market to buy produce for her elaborate feasts; she would introduce me to the best fishmonger with the freshest catch of the day. She would pick up "free" tilapia fish heads for the broth of her mussel soup. We would slip behind the counter for our clandestine supplies of shellfish—live mussels and prawns in three layers of plastic bags to conceal their existence and smell in a kosher market. We would open the parcel in the kitchen of her Templer house and laugh in childish enthrallment at having done something prohibited in the religious city.

Orli would introduce me to the owner of the Iraqi Jewish café in the market, who would open the whole world of the Arab Jewish community: Jews, many of whom still dreamed of returning to their "homeland" in Iraq, Kurdistan, Morocco, Tunisia, Algeria, Yemen. A world where I would feel at home, and snippets of an idyllic Bengali childhood would come back as a source of immense joy and self-discovery. I became forever indebted to Orli, who inadvertently took me on a journey to the chapter of my life that I thought had been buried under more dominant memories of trauma, the memories that I had been running away from for as long as I remembered. For the first time since I left my village town stuck between two Bengals, I came face-to-face in Jerusalem with the bright, untainted side of my childhood, which I did not know that I also carried within me, hidden underneath the many layers of shattered innocence.

.6.

FROM YEMEN
WITH HILBE

"*This is hilbe*," said the man behind the counter, spooning out some of the yellow gelatinous substance from a big plastic tub and displaying it right under my nose.

It smelt sour, with a pungent whiff of coriander.

"In the Yemen, this used to be our hummus, the national dipping sauce for everything, from bread to meat. Well, it still is, here in Israel, and not only among the Yemenite communities. Hilbe has been successfully adopted by the 'Israeli cuisine.'"

Which included, among other oddities, I thought: Polish gefilte fish, jellied herring, Japanese sushi, and of course the entire Arabic kitchen with mutabbal, maqluba, falafel, hummus, and so on. The traditional Arabic breakfast was widely known as "Israeli" breakfast in cafés and restaurants in West Jerusalem. Leo often said, "They took their cities, their villages, their beautiful houses with arches, their olive

The Iraqi souq in the Mahane Yehuda market.

and almond groves, their music, and their food, but there's something missing. Where's the human factor? Where are all the people?"

The man behind the counter of exotic condiments said, "We have been making this for generations, grinding fresh fenugreek seeds with a stone mortar and pestle. This particular spoonful is ground by my mother in our house, after her village recipe from the south of Yemen."

I took the spoon from him, inhaled the aroma of the sour-smelling jelly with chunky bits of green fruit in it. Locked in some long-lost bouquet of childhood, I absent-mindedly asked, "What else is in here?"

"Mango, crushed fenugreek seeds, mustard, water, salt, pepper, and lemon juice," the man from Yemen said with dramatic hand and eye movements. The hustle and bustle of the

Mahane Yehuda market flew past me, lingered around me, with shoppers and hawkers noisily making their demands. I was wrapped from all around in the aroma of freshly ground spices, pickled olives, fresh fish from the Mediterranean, smoked mackerel, and ripe pink pomegranates. Mounds of nuts and dried fruit lined a particular stretch of the market known as the Iraqi souq. The apricot seller opened a dozen of the bright orange fruit and offered the juicy halves on a tray to the passersby to entice them to buy.

I hesitated with the spoonful of hilbe held under my nose. I was trying to unearth some familiar but long-forgotten mystery that was emerging fast, taking shape from under the jumbled pile of memories.

"Ah, the mango achar!" I cried out loud, having found the connection. It really smelt like the sour mango concoction of my childhood, the green unripe fruit sliced with a sharpened mussel shell and mixed with lime juice, crushed fenugreek, salt, toasted chili flakes, and fresh coriander.

The hilbe man gave me a surprised look as I, still holding the spoonful of fenugreek jelly, squealed with excitement at the sudden discovery.

"I remember something similar from where I grew up, with an extra dose of green chili and fresh lime juice," I explained to him. "So it originated in the Yemen then . . ." I dropped the spoonful of spicy-sour mix into my mouth. The mango slipped into the food channel effortlessly, leaving a velvety, strong, bitter, sweet, and coriander-infused taste.

"But the Jews didn't take it to India, I can tell you that," he said. "It must have been the wandering Muslim men, the holy ones, who went to your country to spread the words of Muhammad. We Jews, we never left our country, we were in high positions; until about sixty years ago, Jews worked as advisers to the kings of Yemen."

My thoughts traveled back to history textbooks. In the village primary school I remembered memorizing something like this: "In the fourteenth century, wandering Muslim holy men from the Yemen arrived in northern India to spread the message of Prophet Muhammad." These roving messengers of the new religion from Arabia came to be known as pir and dervish. There is a mausoleum in the city of Sylhet in Bangladesh, where one of the Yemeni pirs, Shah Jalal, had settled, married, preached his Prophet's message, and died. Did Shah Jalal bring the gelatinous hilbe to the east of the Indus River?

"You seem lost, my Indian friend. So, which is better, this or the Indian version?"

"I can't really tell. Ours is less sticky and more spicy, it's hotter with loads of fresh green chilies."

"Everything is hot in India, like your film stars. What beauties you've got there! I used to watch Egyptian films after I came to Israel to keep in touch with Arabic, but the girls there look like rusty pipes compared to your stainless-steel dazzlers! I am learning Hindu from the films. '*Namaste! Ap keise hain?*' Hello! How are you?"

"*Hindi*, not Hindu!" I said as I received his Indian greeting.

"Oh! In my next life—you believe in rebirth, man having many lives, don't you?—in my next life I want to be born as a Hindi."

Instinctively I was about to say "Hindu" but could not be bothered, as I was by now used to hearing at least once a day the general confusion among the Israelis and the Palestinians over the difference between Hindu and Hindi. I wanted to concentrate instead on the origins of hilbe, which most probably the Yemenis had introduced to India.

"So you are the creators of this delicious hilbe, and back home you were kings' advisers. Why did you come here, then?"

"Oh, you know, the old story. After the Jewish state was created, none of the Arab states wanted us anymore; they saw us as traitors. Before 1948, we lived with real privileges. Jew, Muslim, no problem. We ate in one another's homes."

"Did you? So you didn't eat kosher food then? Your family wasn't religious?"

I could not help sounding doubtful about Jews and Muslims eating meals together. But the spirit of the proud deliverer of hilbe from Yemen was buoyant as he said, "Of course we ate together. The kind of religious exclusivity you see here is a very Ashkenazi, European Jewish thing. Our Arab friends ate halal, we ate kosher, both comply the same terms of draining the blood of the animals when you kill them."

He was more comfortable with a nostalgic past that excluded the discriminatory treatment of the Jews, which existed in many of the Arab countries. The hilbe seller was not interested in digging up bad memories of being the Jewish minority and being confined to Jewish ghettos, *mellah*, for centuries despite holding "high positions." In Yemen, Jews were apparently not allowed to wear shoes in public. As I observed the spice seller, the self-proclaimed descendant of a former adviser to the king of Yemen and now known as the King of the Market, I thought of other nostalgists and former "landowners."

"Back in East Bengal we had so much land, we lived like zamindars, aristocrats." I heard this so many times from the West Bengalis who had lived through and been displaced by the division of India. The partitions of India and of Palestine left similar legacies for the people of the both nations: some had to leave, others had arrived from unknown shores as refugees, some were granted asylum, others were kicked out. Hundreds of thousands were denied citizenship in the countries of their ancestors. The partition reduced landowners to refugee status and endowed refugees with new homes that had been stolen, confiscated from the very landowners who had to leave. The former zamindars from East Bengal arrived in Calcutta to sleep in refugee camps, out of which grew the present-day slum city in the place of what was once the majestic capital of British India. Five million Palestinians still lived in refugee camps sixty years after the partition (to many, the death of old Palestine, al-Naqba, the Catastrophe). The partition created a great chasm between the religious groups that once enjoyed coexistence in the same village, town, or city, from Hebron to the Galilee. The hatred that it spread had grown out of control over the past six decades. Jews had once again ended up in ghettos that they created for themselves to live with their own kind in order to hold on to the land that the state of Israel declared "abandoned," creating physical walls around them to keep the Arabs out. From Poland to Palestine, the ghetto had traveled and expanded far and fast.

"We look like each other," said the Yemeni man, leaning forward and holding his arm against mine, to compare our skin tones. "We could be from the same family." His dark eyes sparkled as he smiled. "Well, if the situation here doesn't get better, I might actually move to India."

"And sell hilbe in the market in north Calcutta!"

"I could, couldn't I?"

"You have to make it less gooey with fewer fenugreek seeds, though."

"And more chilies."

"And more chilies. Don't forget the fresh lime."

With this last note, I was about to walk away when he leant forward again and tapped my shoulder. "So, what brought you here? You don't talk like a foreign worker. You haven't left your beautiful country to look after some old Ashkenazi Jew with Parkinson's, have you?"

He whispered as he shook his body in a mock show of the symptom of the disease. I said to him, "It's not just the European Jews who get Parkinson's disease . . . Yasser Arafat also suffered from it. Besides, there's nothing wrong in looking after old people, Ashkenazi or non-Ashkenazi."

"My mother is eighty-four years old, she can barely walk. I applied three times already for full-time help, but each time, my application was thrown into the waiting list. If I were a blue-eyed, white Ashkenazi and had a blond mother, a girl from India, Sri Lanka, or the Philippines would have arrived at my door in no time at all."

"Is that so? I had no idea." I lied, of course. I knew from Yakov and Michal's family of Israel's discriminatory treatment of nonwhite, non-European Jews.

"Our country has become what South Africa used to be like, white, black, colored, Indian. Here we have hierarchy not just between the Jews and the Palestinians. We also have very white Jews, olive-skinned Jews, nearly white Jews, brownish Jews, brown Jews, nearly black Jews, completely black Jews, and a whole new species, the Russian Jews, most of them are not even Jews, some are in fact Nazis and some Muslims! Your entitlement depends on the thickness of the melanin under your skin, except in the case of Russian Jews, as I told you, they are a different lot, some are very privileged, some not so much. Some enjoy political power and opportunities as white Ashkenazis and some are dumped together with the Ethiopians—probably the least privileged." The spice seller looked pleased with himself after his long, elaborate rant on what he thought was his country's South Africa syndrome.

Orli, who took me to this especially crowded Friday morning market, was restless. She was pulling me by my arm; she must have heard it so many times as a regular customer of this man from Yemen. I was dithering whether to encourage him to continue with his animated disgruntlement or move on to see the rest of the market when he said, "When you see those frail old Ashkenazi Jews with their nice little Indian or Filipino helpers, what does it remind you of? Have you ever seen a black Jew with domestic help? An Ethiopian Jew supported by a Filipino? Here we have the typical apartheid scene: whites with black or brown servants."

"You seem very bitter," I said, then added, to lighten up what was beginning to turn into a long, winding racial discourse on the Israeli society, "as bitter as crushed fenugreek!"

"So you are not a domestic helper, you are too beautiful for that, *habibti*," he said, ending with the popular Arabic word of endearment, "my love." "Why are you here?"

I smiled without answering.

"You, married?"

"Ah, here we go!" I thought. "Once you've started along this line, you could never leave." I smiled again, guardedly this time, and said, "May I have a pot of hilbe, please?"

I placed a five-shekel coin on the sticky counter and let myself be swept away by Orli's arm through the crowd along the narrow alleys of the old Jewish market. I elbowed through a sea of people, taking in the smell of sweat, smoked fish, dried fruit, goat cheese, brown truffle, salted cod.

Why did I feel so good in this market? The Iraqi Jewish fishmonger, Nissim, greeted us wielding a cleaver, chopping off heads of the dark and scaly ancient Tiberian tilapia, known as St. Peter's fish. Legend has it that Jesus fed five thousand people on the shores of the Sea of Galilee with two St. Peter's fish and five barley loaves. The heads were being thrown into a pile—from which Orli picked a couple. Nissim filleted with the motion of a swordsman the silvery sea bass, the fat bream, the delicate red snapper. His Palestinian helpers picked up the fillets, the steaks, or the whole cleaned fish according to each order, weighed them, and handed them over to the anxious buyers who had been standing there since the early hours of the morning. It was soothing for the eyes to see the Jews and the Palestinians working together. Even though the roles were those of masters and their sidekicks, it was still nice to see the apparent harmony, the mélange of the two that one did not see that often in this place. There were perhaps only two places where this kind of direct contact between the two warring communities existed in Jerusalem—the city's hospitals and the Mahane Yehuda market. The market was a slice of old Jerusalem unchanged despite conflict and suicide bombs, in the days of superstores and cellophane-wrapped merchandise.

Increasingly, as months passed by and the primary reason behind our move to Jerusalem—to help fulfill Leo's mission to contribute to the peace mediation—seemed farther and farther away, I clung to other modes of justification as to why I was here. Why did I continue to live here? So that I could walk through this crowded market any time of the day, see life so vibrant such as this, when many of my former colleagues would be "copy-testing" in a frantic newsroom with robotic precision. So that, I concluded with sudden impulse, I could buy the fish I want, the way I want it, so that I could see my fish gutted right before my eyes because I hated buying skinned, deboned fish wrapped in many layers of packaging off the freezing shelf of a sterile supermarket. I literally and symbolically enjoyed the experience, which was raw and visceral, which struck a hidden chord in my heart and helped me, with its simplicity and transcendence, to rediscover and relive a lost childhood. And somewhere out there within my reach immeasurable energy was being unleashed.

———

"*You have to start thinking about working here*, perhaps for the BBC. Why not? . . . Did you ever go to the bureau here and check it out?" suggested Orli one day. "You have been here long enough. Also it would help you to put behind Leo's frantic life, which you seem to be so fixated on at the moment. If I may say, you harp on what he does and doesn't a bit too much, and it's starting to get a bit repetitive."

"I think so too, and I am sorry if I have bored you with my personal woes."

"I am happy to listen. I think you should find your own footing."

My own footing I definitely wanted to find—I too was tired of constantly bickering over the same issues. Little did Orli know that we had been bickering exactly in the same way for almost as long as we had known each other. I must

find my own world, not just a world of substitute friendship and company and empathy that I found in Orli, but a
world that would enhance my social status, instill pride in
me. I must get back to work. I needed to make use of the energy that I felt inside me. The storyteller that bubbled in my
heart was striving to get out, to tell the world my side of the
Middle Eastern tale that had been told in so many ways already. But Orli filled me with such reassurance that I would
tell this story differently, as I, she said, did not come here
as a "white prophet" from the West to change her country.
From that point of view she was a valuable friend. Between
us, there was not a speck of professional jealousy.

During the first year I had been immersed in some kind
of a daze, feeling constantly baffled at the schizophrenic
place that I found myself living in, which did not adhere to
any stereotype or a particular model of the world's other nations. "This country," Israel-Palestine, straddled the East
and the West. I could, if I wanted to, lie on the golden sand
of a Tel Aviv beach in a skimpy bathing suit, feeling the
warm waves of the Mediterranean tingle my bare toes while
watching beautiful dark bodies pass by in a heavy, hedo-
nistic stupor as if there had never been any conflict, as if it
really were the biblical land of milk and honey. While only
a few kilometers away Bedouin goatherds would be scour-
ing away in the scrubby desert searching for dry cactus for
their scrawny animals, and Bedouin women in long black
robes and head coverings would be walking to the edge of
the desert to fetch drinking water. In Tel Aviv, it was easy
to forget that there was a war just around the corner. That a

short distance away at checkpoints, teenage Israeli soldiers in camouflage garb watched with expressionless eyes as old and frail Palestinians fainted under the hot sun waiting to get through to go to hospital, work, or homes of estranged relatives separated by Israeli barriers. Israel was caught between democratic illusions and the rule of the jungle where the mighty with nukes impounded the already barricaded indigenous inhabitants accused of throwing rotten fruit at their tanks. The store windows in the high streets in Tel Aviv spilled over with the latest range of designer clothing; it would be hard for a new visitor not to imagine that he or she might be in Rome or Paris. But just an hour's drive away, there was not a decent road between Jerusalem and Ramallah.

The source of energy that I found was embedded in such contrasts of life on both sides. I found the contrasts invigorating, albeit disheartening, as they constantly threw questions at the observer's vulnerability, at the inadequacy of his or her political sensibility. In the homes of my friends of the Israeli left, I had been made to feel ashamed of my political incorrectness when I arrived with a bottle of Golan Heights red. "How can you support the occupation like this?" they would say. "Each time you buy a product from the occupied territory, you help the regime to continue with its apartheid policy." I would be scolded by my peace activist Israeli Jewish friends for not buying the right products, for not eating the right eggs. The most widely available and the best-known organic variety came from a hilltop settlement in the heart of the West Bank, which I had been told was the most right-wing and militant of all. A few months after my arrival, I was to learn that the eggs laid by "settler" hens traveled in armored vehicles through occupied land to reach the Israeli market, and so I could not bring myself to buy organic eggs.

But when I was being really politically sound and took along a Bordeaux bought at London Heathrow to my Palestinian friend's home in East Jerusalem, Bashar Barghouti greeted me with a fantastic, rich aromatic glass of Gamla red from the occupied Golan.

"When it comes to drinking wine, I don't look at the label. Between a bottle of politically correct and a bottle of good wine, I go for the latter. When it comes to appreciating music, I don't like to face the question 'Do I like Mendelssohn more than Wagner?' From the occupied or the land of freedom, I would welcome the master winemaker into my house. Here, have a glass."

The contrasts continued to thrive, their message hovering over my everyday life. The essence of life was there; within my reach was the vast abundance of resources, a treasure chest full of tales of love, contradictions, hate, and resilience, all intertwined in a human cycle. This was what my English years lacked—the direct human contact, the quarrels, the making up, the flare-ups of unpredictable emotions. During the first year, when I was making up my mind whether I wanted to stay on or to leave, I would notice people talking loudly on the bus, laughing or discussing family matters: children's marriage, bar mitzvah, circumcision—all unashamedly openly. I came to feel embarrassed by my eavesdropping on other people's lives. But then I spotted my obsession, the desire to travel by bus despite the fear of possible suicide attacks. I would feel guilty at times, especially when I took my daughter on the bus to and from school. I was obsessed with the experience of the *real* life and its contrasts. I would notice the veiled travelers—Muslim women from East Jerusalem sitting quietly, usually at the front of the bus. I would be shocked by my innate prejudices as I took a furtive glance at their stomachs, searching for imaginary explosive belts. I would realize that I was not the only one on the lookout for them; the man sitting next to me with the Torah pages before him had also been secretly watching the Arab women in veils, and while doing so he had hastened the pace of his reading from the prayer book and the swaying of his body back and forth. Armed security guards carried out random checks on the passengers on the bus. Once a young, hard-faced Russian came straight up to me and asked me to open my bag. "Do I look sufficiently *Arab* to you?" I said as I obligingly unzipped my rucksack full of smoked fish and goat cheese from the market. I saw a moment of hesitation in his bright blue eyes. I seized the moment and added, "Or are you doing it so that you can show that you are searching not just the Arab passengers but the rest of the bus too?"

Eavesdropping on buses and noting down people's behavior and expressions in my diary would continue to be my obsession in the coming months. I voraciously tucked in the exuberance and dynamism that were presented to me on a golden platter. I was hungry for life's petty talks and ordinariness, which I had been deprived of since I had settled in a stiff-upper-lipped England in my early youth. The bus in Jerusalem was a vehicle to a notion that I called "home," where people talked and shouted and screamed and burst into floods of tears without the restraints of European modesty. And I would risk at least one journey a day even in difficult times when a bomb had gone off elsewhere and we had been warned not to take the bus.

It was in Jerusalem's stiflingly politicized societies that I found invigorating inspiration to search for my footing, as Orli said that I must. The glaring white stones of the Old City wall projected day and night the wrath and fury of ordinary Palestinians at the complexities of the Israeli control over their everyday life. Fury emanated also from the Western Wall sheltering the swaying Jews lamenting over the destruction of the Second Temple some two thousand years ago. While just behind the wall, in the adjacent golden Dome of the Rock, prostrating Muslims vindicated the rightful continuation of the seventh-century Haram-al-Sharif mosque complex reportedly built on the site of the Temple.

The lives of the two peoples were interdependent in every possible way, their places of worship, their land, their vision for Jerusalem. One was entrenched into the other so intrusively that Jerusalem could not cope with the pressure; it was perpetually at a boiling point. Disquiet was reflected day and night onto the city's residents. No one could escape it. Everyone, even the foreign peacemakers, were included. And yet everyone was expendable. Outsiders in Jerusalem believed their presence was needed as mediators, writers, and reporters; the religious Jews believed it was their biblical right to be there; Israeli politicians saw Jerusalem as their eternal, undivided capital; the peace activists needed to be closer to the West Bank and so Jerusalem was their home; and across the checkpoints on the other side of the security wall, hundreds of thousands of Palestinians cherished the belief that one day Jerusalem would become the capital of a Palestinian state.

Somehow these dreams, contradictions, and eventual disappointments fed into one another and regenerated new energy, with the process repeating over and over again, probably as had been happening throughout the history of the city. The cycle reminded me of the work of the Hindu trinity, of the gods Brahma, Vishnu, and Shiva. Brahma the creator represented the people of the land, the dream makers, the believers; Vishnu the preserver continued with the creation, which was the role of the peace negotiators, the discourse makers. Until Shiva destroyed it all. The god of destruction embodied the disenchanted: the settlers, the suicide bombers, the failed politicians of the failed state and the nonstate: Israel and Palestine. Promised land, political recklessness, desecration of dreams and, finally, regeneration—this seemed to be the divine plan of the Israeli-Palestinian conflict, the participants in which were all by now well used to this familiar rotation.

Still and all, away from the gloom of the occupation, there was the Mahane Yehuda market, where fish were chosen, gutted, scaled, and sliced before my eyes. The last time I saw fish covered in blood and slime was long ago in Bengal.

In Mahane Yehuda, I would let myself be carried away by naïve, inexplicable self-indulgence: I would learn to shut out the conflict and to overlook the recurring cycle of frustration, muted hope, negotiations, and all too often unavailing endeavors by Leo and his copeacemakers to alter the course of history. At least once a week I would stop by Nissim's fish counter to buy the fat earth-colored St. Peter's fish from Tiberias, which I would take home reminiscing about a distant childhood that, to my great joy, was fast becoming tangible.

.7.

MY "ISRAELI"
DAUGHTER

I went back to work. As we were victoriously approaching the end of our first year in Jerusalem, one day I called Simon Wilson, at the time the bureau chief of the BBC. He was very warm on the phone. However, when I went to see him, he said that I was welcome to use the bureau, but I must discuss all the stories with him and that the appointed BBC correspondents would have the first choice of a story even if I was the one who had stumbled upon it, which meant that I would not be allowed to follow that story any further. But most important, he said that according to the BBC's employment regulations, I would have to first resign from the London newsroom if I wanted to freelance from Jerusalem.

One other thing he added was that I was not to cover the "main news story." That was the job of the bureau correspondents.

I did not mind much the last part, because I was not interested in the main story anyway, as it was bound to be the political news of the Israeli-Palestinian conflict. I was more into the other aspect, the human factor of the conflict. I discussed with Leo the impending "huge" decision that I was about to take that would involve resigning from the BBC as a permanent member of the staff. I asked him whether it would be a good idea, as it would mean severing myself from the possibility of a fairly comfortable continuation of my career and the retirement benefits. That would mean indirectly depending on Leo's resources in case I failed to make it work as a freelancer. He said, "It's your choice, whatever you want to decide."

"Well, it's not, because if I don't resign very soon, I will be summoned back to the newsroom when my extended leave ends. Would you come back to London with me?"

"I can't, you know that I can't. My work is here. What I always wanted to do is here—if I ever wanted to be useful anywhere, or contribute to making a difference, it's in this country."

"How about my goals, my mission, my life?"

"When you married me, you knew what I wanted. You married knowing who I was. I can't change myself. I am not good at changing myself."

"You are avoiding my question—what happens to *my* dream?"

"You make it work the way it's best suited to you."

"How? By going back to London? What happens to the family?"

"You choose what's best for you and the family. But I won't come back to London."

"I am not talking about going back, I am just asking you to appreciate that I am faced with what most people would consider a very important decision, to leave a permanent job at the world's most sought-after newsroom. Yes, I have already made up my mind to resign, I just wanted to hear some kind words of reassurance from you."

I raised my voice as I said the last sentence. As always, my demons defied me and burst out, showing their lolling red tongues, leaving me baffled at the rage that I felt toward Leo's nonchalant attitude to my future. I said totally sensible things, but the way they came out, they sounded just the opposite.

I stormed out and called the world service news desk in Bush House. Within thirty seconds I was put through to the right person. The soft voice of the editor who had interviewed me and selected me as part of the newsroom team was on the line. I could detect her disappointment in the cold, unfriendly tone with which she said that I must send a formal e-mail to the Human Resources Department, which would then e-mail me back with a confirmation letter of my discharge. And, she added, I must send by post my BBC staff ID. "That and any other BBC properties that you may have in your possession."

I sat in silence and tried to take in what I had just done. I felt calm and numb to some extent. It was so easy? Giving up a job for which most journalists would do anything, just like that, over the telephone, in two sentences?

Later in the evening, as the reality of my action began to sink in, what bothered me was not the fact that I had just resigned but that the newsroom editor had asked for the ID back. I looked at it, a young, happy, smiley face from what seemed like many years ago, after I had just been initiated to the BBC club of reporters. They can't just dispossess me like that of my claim to the institution that I worked for since I was twenty-three.

I decided that I was going to keep my old ID.

That week, I was hoping that Leo would propose to celebrate this occasion. But it was not even mentioned. I thought that it was probably a good thing that my resignation was not being hailed as a big deal. And it was not, considering all the other things that I had already left behind to keep us together. I argued with my demons: I was different, I did not hang on to the past, I had the courage to accept and adapt and to move on. I did not need to be tied to the BBC's pension policy! I definitely did not want to grow old in the newsroom, a graveyard for former correspondents.

On Monday the following week, I dropped Maya off at kindergarten and boldly entered the BBC's Jerusalem bureau on the third floor of a commercial media building near the city center. Simon Wilson greeted me, and I was given an empty desk, where I sat and looked out the window at the busy Jaffa Road below to calm my nerves. During this pause, I resolved that I was not going to leave this place, this city, as a loser. I would reinvent myself and move on as I had to so many times before. Within the course of the day, after a few calls to London, I acquired commissions for several "packages," illustrated reports for two of the BBC's well-known slots.

I was late picking up Maya from kindergarten. There were a few other children still being collected by frantic parents who had to abandon their cars at various places, as King David Street, where the YMCA and its peace school stood, was closed to the public to allow the convoys of some dignitaries to pass. Maya was waiting for me with a handful of drawings in blue and white. Israeli Independence Day was in a few days' time and everything the children drew was along the same theme, depicting the colors of Israel. I even received a note from the school saying all the children should wear white T-shirts and blue jeans on the actual day to greet the celebratory procession along King David Street, waving blue-and-white flags. The city was decorated with these colors and there were flags everywhere, from private homes to checkpoint towers. Almost every other car had the Israeli flag flying from the radio antenna.

Maya went back to her drawer to collect something that she forgot. When she came back, I was surprised to see that it was a miniature Union Jack.

"Who asked you to draw this?"

"My teachers. Each child had to draw the flag of her country. I didn't even know that this was the British flag. My teachers showed me a picture and I drew it. Do you like it? It's for you, Mummy, for when you miss home."

"So they want to make it look normal, drawing these Israeli flags all day long, so long as you also drew the Union Jack? What about the Palestinian flag?" I said to my four-year-old daughter and immediately noticed how stupid that sounded.

"What's a Union Jack?"

"This, what you are holding."

"Oh, I didn't know the British flag is called that."

"What are you going to do with these drawings in your hand? Shall I take them from you?"

"These are Yom Ha'atzmayut decorations. I'll put them up in my room."

Nowhere else in the world had I seen such obsession with the national flag. There were flags in people's balconies and windows. Hikers wore baseball caps with flags, and on men, I even saw the skullcap woven with the blue star and two stripes of the flag. As I walked out of the elegant YMCA building with Maya, she screamed, *"Degel shel Israel!"* Israeli flag! as she pointed to the dozen or so flying from the flagpoles outside King David Hotel.

"Degel shel Israel" would remain one of her favorite phrases during the coming months, no matter how hard I tried to convince her that drawing or waving flags was not a very sound thing to do. But she refused to understand why it was not and why she should not draw the Israeli flag on her bedroom wall or in my work notebooks. To the great annoyance of her pro-Palestinian brother, she even started wearing an Israel Museum badge with a flag on it. Any attempt to take that off created huge scenes of tantrums and tears. In the end I decided to ignore her flag obsession, hoping that she would soon lose interest. But it was not easy for Leo, as he was worried about his Palestinian friends finding

out that he was Jewish and had an "Israeli" daughter! That was another issue I was still struggling to come to terms with: it made Leo furious whenever I mentioned to anyone that we observed Shabbat and lit candles on Friday nights. Some of our huge arguments soon after our arrival in Jerusalem resulted from the fact that I was openly talking about our half-Jewish children and that the reason we were here had a lot to do with his connection to the land and Judaism.

"You wouldn't like me going around telling people that you may be Hindu but close members of your family are Muslim!" Leo said, angrily. To which I said, "Of course you can say that, but it's not the same. You know that my background is not straightforward, I don't practice any religion. I am an atheist, and that's my true identity. Besides, we are not in India, we are here, and so far as I'm concerned we are here because you are Jewish."

"I don't want to be subjected to any stereotyping. Besides, it probably would not be very good for my profile among the Palestinians I work with, if they knew that a Jew is telling them how to have peace with Israel."

"If you have to hide something that is so important to you, why should they trust you? How would they feel if the fact that you are Jewish came out someday?"

"I'm making recommendations in my reports on the basis of my meetings with people; I just don't want to prejudice their views about me. But I fear that I would be risking it if they found out," said Leo.

"I am sorry, I am not getting it," I went on. "If you are worried about the Arabs finding out about your religion and turning therefore against you, then you are wasting your time here. The recommendations for peace have to come from the people who belong here. Otherwise it would seem like a colonial enterprise. Why should they listen to the outsiders? What have they brought to this land after sixty years of negotiations?"

"I don't want you to publicize that I am Jewish, that's all." I heard the familiar sternness in his voice when he was upset with me.

"Of course I don't publicize anything! But I think you must tell them who you *are* and that they would be really wrong to doubt your impartiality."

I felt lost. I did not see any purpose in my being in Jerusalem if he was constantly in denial of his roots. I had agreed to come to Jerusalem *because* of his connection. I did not want to be another foreigner willingly or inadvertently exploiting the Israeli-Palestinian conflict by being here as part of Western liberal colonialism. Orli called Leo a self-hating Jew, which infuriated him. What he wanted to convey was that what Israel was doing in the name of Judaism was appalling and he wanted to dissociate himself from that. But there must be another way to express that without hiding his identity.

"You are giving conflicting messages to the children," I said.

Well, despite her father's reservations about Israel and confessional Judaism, our daughter was not the slightest bit confused about where she belonged. Maya loved Israel.

We had walked to the next bus stop, as the ones on King David street were not functional during these visits of foreign dignitaries who stayed in the hotel of the same name. There were quite a number of people already waiting for the Number 18 bus. Several suicide attacks had been carried out on this service since the second intifada began in 2000. I was still taking the bus despite repeated warnings from the British consulate against doing so. Taking the bus was one step toward belonging to the society that we lived in. Everyone here boarded the bus with the nagging fear of suicide bombs in the back of their mind. That fear was successfully transmitted to me whenever I traveled. But I felt that I was linked to the people around me somehow, through our common fear.

Maya and I took the 18 every day to school. Today we were waiting for the bus to go home to pick up the car, and then we would be driving to East Jerusalem to collect an Israeli human rights activist. I had arranged to do an interview in a refugee camp for my "package" for the BBC. When we saw our bus on the hill at the traffic lights, I said to her, "You have to be really good today because I'm going to have to take you to work."

"I'll be good, Mummy, I promise, when you interview people. I will take my crayons and drawing paper. I like going with you to your work."

"But don't please draw Israeli flags! Take all your crayons except the blues and the whites."

She was familiar with my dragging her along to my work assignments.

"Please please don't draw any *degel shel Israel* there, please," I said to her again.

"Why, because we are going to Palestine?"

"We're going to a refugee camp."

"Where the Palesti-ninians live?"

"Where many Palestinians live."

"Is it in Ramallah?"

"It is on the way to Ramallah, in East Jerusalem."

"Have I ever been there before?"

"No, you have not."

"I've been to Palestine before, Ramallah is in Palestine. And Bethlehem. You can't speak Hebrew in Bethlehem," she said to herself.

I remembered the time when we were driving in Bethlehem and Kiran caught her sitting in the back flicking through Hebrew storybooks. He quickly snatched them away from her and hid them under the seat. Later on, standing in the middle of the market, she had screamed to annoy her brother and me, "Imaa a a a aaa . . ." Within six months in Jerusalem she decided that she wanted to call me *Ima*, "Mummy" in Hebrew, which was not a sensible thing to do, especially while traveling in the West Bank. And I did not dare think what would happen if we traveled to Syria and if the Mukhabarat, the secret police, heard her and turned their attention to a South Asian ima!

I thought that in the Shuafat refugee camp where I was going to do the interview with a Palestinian whose house had been demolished by the Israeli army for the ninth time in as many years, it would be wise to keep my "Israeli" daughter under control, and she must not call me Ima there. How could I explain this to her, that in that overcrowded camp with sewage flooding the streets, anger and hatred spread like poisonous fungus? That in the squalid existence where some ten or more children grew up in each family in two-room shacks, every child developed a soft corner in his or her heart for martyrdom, where mercy toward the occupier would be the hardest thing to show.

But I could not find a babysitter for Maya, and it was my very first assignment for the BBC in my new freelance status; I could not afford to jeopardize my chances of rebuilding my career. Besides, we would be accompanied by Jeff, the Israeli peace activist, director of the Israeli Committee Against House Demolitions. It did not seem like a huge risk to take a little drive through the refugee camp. So this was how I prepared her, "Don't please speak Hebrew there. We might get into trouble."

"But they won't shoot at us, will they?"

"Well, they might do if you, by calling me Ima, give them the idea that we are Israeli."

When the bus came, she ran to the door before anyone else and I regretted saying this. It was irresponsible. How could I have uttered something like that, to confuse my little daughter? What was I doing telling her that the people of the refugee camp roamed around with guns? But it was too late to retract what I had just said. She was already quite obsessed with the idea of who shot whom in the street and who carried guns. Seeing guns every day on her friends' dads, her father's cousins, turned the notion of people carrying guns into such a normal thing to her that she did not understand why Leo and I found it so objectionable. When we walked in the street, she would always admiringly watch soldiers with huge rifles dangling from their sides even when they were off duty. As the bus sped through the café-lined avenue of Emek Rafaim, I looked out the window and saw at least four people with guns on them waiting at the nearest pedestrian crossing. Inside the bus, Maya was smiling at the soldier sitting opposite her with a gun on her lap.

"Do you know, my friend Asaf's dad, Dudu, has a pistol." She had a sharp memory, she hadn't forgotten what we—well, *she*, had been discussing before the bus came.

"Does he?" I said, feeling perturbed that she knew the word "pistol" at the age of four. I wanted to divert the conversation, but it was impossible.

"He puts it in a pistol bag on his belt. Asaf says that his father protects us."

"Protects you from what?"

"From terrorists. So that no one can come to our school and shoot us."

"What are you talking about? Who are these terrorists?"

"I think Palesti-ninian terrorists. The ones who put bombs in buses."

I did not know how much she knew about the bus bombings. It was a bit disquieting to be talking about bus bombs while riding on the Number 18. She never asked me why we still took the bus home instead of a taxi. Emotionally it was strange to me that I never felt that fear quite deeply enough—the fear of being blown up. When my Hebrew-speaking daughter and I traveled together by bus with

Israeli and some Palestinian commuters, I felt we were part
of the local community. Sitting next to me on the bus, Maya
would talk freely about pistols, guns, Israeli security, and
terrorism. Words I did not know until I became a reader of
crime fiction in my early teens.

The first time I had ever touched a gun was in the house
of Yakov and Michal, who had three children in the army.
It was soon after my arrival in Jerusalem. I was still trying
to get over the initial shock of seeing so many armed young
people in the streets. Every café, restaurant, bookshop, bar,
cinema, and all the local schools had armed guards at the
door checking bags before letting anyone in.

The first time I touched a gun, I had had cold shivers
transmitting through me. I felt I had just broken a certain
code of decency, that I had just committed an act of obscen-
ity. Yakov and Michal's son, Amos, who was twenty, was
posted in the West Bank and routinely took part in raid-
ing homes of suspected terrorists. One day we were having
Shabbat dinner in their house when he said, "Come to my
room. I want to show you something."

Earlier I had talked about how irresponsible the Israeli
army was to let eighteen-year-olds go home with guns on
their days off.

"But we have to be alert all the time, in case we are at-
tacked!" Amos passionately defended the army.

His room was in the basement, which also doubled as
a bomb shelter. Each new house in West Jerusalem was required to have a bomb shelter. The small room was cold,

and through the only window I saw that it had one-meter-thick walls. The window reminded me of the porthole on a ship; it opened with a wheel-shaped device that I presumed you drew toward you to shut the window. It was open, but still the room had a stuffy smell. The gun was lying on his very messy bed.

"I've been cleaning it. We are supposed to oil it once in a while," said Amos.

"You just left the gun here with the window wide open? There are no grilles!"

"Nobody is going to steal a gun. They are all numbered, the army computer knows that this particular one has been issued to me! All the neighbors are Jewish and they all have guns. I told you, we are supposed to be alert and ready to strike at short or no notice at all. That's why the whole of Israel is like an active army. We are ready to fight anytime, the enemy can't take us by surprise. The Arabs underestimated us in 1973 during the Yom Kippur War, thinking everyone would be busy fasting or praying, but the army was awake and alert. They learnt the lesson of their life!"

"Is the gun loaded?"

"Of course it is loaded. What's the point otherwise? I just told you, we have to be ready to go, immediately."

"Why should anyone attack you here in the heart of Jewish West Jerusalem?"

"We are surrounded by enemies. All the Arabs want to kill us."

"Aren't you being a bit paranoid? Do they not know by now, especially after the Yom Kippur War, that you are one of the most sophisticated armies in the world? No one is going to carry out a surprise attack on you!"

"They want us to be pushed to the sea. They hate us."

"Do you know any Arabs?"

"No, I don't want to. I want to fight the enemy, not make friends. I am not your Jesus Christ."

"Aren't you worried that you might accidentally shoot your little sister while cleaning the gun?"

"Why would I? I've been trained to look after my gun, and no one has ever heard of anyone in Israel accidentally shooting anyone dead. If you think about it, we have very few gun crimes compared to the rest of the world, given the fact that every household has at least one loaded gun."

What Amos said was true. I often wondered why there were so few gun-related offenses in a country where brandishing guns was an integral part of the popular culture. And it was legal.

"Do you want to hold it?" said Amos, enjoying my nervousness.

"Okay," I said. I took the cold metal thing from his hand. The way I was holding it, I was pointing the muzzle at him. He moved swiftly to one side.

"You don't hold a gun like that! That's when you accidentally end up shooting your friend or your foot! Look where your finger is, it's right on the trigger! But I've put the safety on, here it is. You push it this way, now the gun is ready to fire."

"How many times have you used it? Have you killed anyone?"

"I don't know," said Amos, suddenly pensive. "I don't want to kill anyone. But when in an operation we are asked to fire and run by our commander, we don't go back to count the number of casualties. I haven't directly shot anyone dead. But I think I've wounded people when we carried out incursions in Gaza. The Gazans are the most violent of the lot. They definitely want to see us dead, pushed to the sea."

"Amos, if Arabs always wanted to kill you, then why does your father have such wonderful memories of Yemen, where his family came from?"

"He's selective about his memories. Anyway, he doesn't have any memories. He wasn't even born there. His memories come from our grandparents. They had a good life in Yemen, but not as good as that of the Arabs. They were still second-class citizens. They weren't allowed to wear shoes in public! Have you ever heard of such weird discrimination?"

"But your grandmother also says that life was good. Your grandfather was a high official in the government. Look how the Promised Land has treated him. He lives in a characterless shikun estate in a two-room apartment. Your grandmother said that back in Yemen she lived in a big village home with gardens, goats, and servants."

"You know, when people leave their homes, they always remember the best fruit, the best water. If everything was so wonderful for my grandparents, they wouldn't have left all the wealth behind and come here, would they? Why did they come here?"

"Because they thought it would be really like the mythical land of milk and honey! I never heard your grandmother talk about Arabs trying to kill her. Even today, so many years after being here, your grandparents still speak Arabic. Your father, who was born here, speaks Arabic with his parents. And you, a mixed Ashkenazi and Yemeni child, without your kippah you could look like any other Palestinian in the streets of Gaza."

"No, I don't look Arab!" Amos retorted.

"Yes, you do," I said distractedly, as I realized that I had started fiddling with the gun. It was well oiled and shiny. The trigger was cold and tempting. It felt as if I were crossing a certain boundary, from the periphery of innocence to experience. Once you've touched a killing machine, you are no longer clean. I ran my fingers around the cold muzzle and the trigger. I was holding a weapon for the first time in my life. It was like vertigo, feeling the devastating pull of gravity. I felt that I wanted to just go for it.

———

"Mummy, come on, this is our stop!" Maya pulled me as she jumped off the high seat directly above the wheels that she always sat on. Her schoolbag was already on her back. At age four and a half she had her father's perfect sense of navigation and she never forgot which stop to get off. In fact, she knew the way home even when we walked back.

Maya and I went home to pick up my recording equipment before going to collect Jeff. In the car, she started talking about Dudu again, the father of her friend. She said that she was very proud of Dudu, who protected the children from terrorists. I felt that I was living in a futuristic crime fiction like the Terminator series where there was a perpetual war and everyone was afraid of the collective enemy. Where there was a permanent army that was always ready to fire. I was living in a world where every child had seen a gun and every child had touched a gun and every child knew what an ammunition belt was for. When I was a child, I believed that guns were for criminals or the dark heroes in Bollywood films only, where it was okay for glorified gangsters and superheroes like Amitabh Bachchan to shoot greedy landowners. As a child, I thought that guns were also used by antiheroes and the proletariat army who wanted to take from the rich and give to the poor, like the Bengali Naxalites. I could not imagine seeing a gun held by an ordinary citizen like Amos. Or Dudu, for that matter, a family man. It was very hard for me to grasp that every Israeli teenager knew how to operate a gun, how to shoot.

The traffic was bad and we had very little time when we reached Jeff's house. As I rang his doorbell, I said to Maya, "You must use the bathroom, wash your face and hands."

"Would you let me hold the microphone?" she asked, pointing to my equipment bag hanging from my shoulder.

"No! I won't. Not this time."

"But you sometimes do!"

"Only when we do fun recordings. Like when we do wildtrack in the street or in a café. Today is serious and I need to talk to people just on my own. Is that okay? Please be the sweetest girl that you are. And *do not* speak Hebrew or call me Ima when we are in the refugee camp."

"Are there children in the camp who don't have much to eat, the children for whom I always have to finish my dinner?"

"I don't think the children at the refugee camp are malnourished. Palestinian kids suffer from a lot of things, but starvation usually isn't one of them."

"Where do *those* children live then who you say would be upset if I didn't clean up my plate?"

"What children?" I said absentmindedly as I rummaged through my bag to make sure I had enough blank tapes. It had been a long time since I recorded an interview.

"For *those* children, you always say I have to eat up everything for them. Sometimes you say they are in Africa."

"Well, in some parts of Africa. Many in India, Latin America, and in so many other places. Now, come and say hello to Jeff."

Jeff ushered us in and asked us to wait in the living room, while he "finished an important call to the U.S."

"So I don't need to eat more for the Palesti-ninian kids?" Maya persisted. She did not make any move toward the bathroom.

"Don't think so," I said distractedly. I was half listening to Maya, as I observed the living room and on its wall the framed black-and-white photographs of street children in the Old City of Jerusalem in the 1930s. As if to respond to Maya's curiosity about poverty, for a few moments my thoughts went back to the children of a totally different world, with narrow dirty streets lined with shacks built of collected junk, often by children; with women in rags in squalid markets collecting rotten, worm-infested discarded vegetables and fruit, children going around with handheld fishing nets from one overfished pond to another in search of a few shrimps or a lone catfish buried deep beneath the squelchy mud—just so their mothers could prepare one hot meal a day. Poverty that I saw around me when I was growing up was something people just accepted as a karmic reality. There was even some glory attached to it, when finally the long-awaited and well-earned meal was cooked over the firewood collected by tiny hands, when the family sat around it to eat. With the woodsmoke smell in the air, and the stomachs partially full, the children fell asleep in the open air. Poverty was there, right under your nose as a fate-destined way of life, and the believers in karma—the immutable effect on an individual's worldly life resulting from a past cause—hardly protested. There were poems written on this theme. One that readily came to my mind was by the celebrated Bengali poet Kazi Nazrul Islam:

Poverty,
You've endowed me with greatness.
You've equaled me to Christ.

Poems such as this could be written because, I thought, those impoverished Bengali children were not burdened with disposable food offloaded by the West. Most refugee camps all around the West Bank and Jerusalem were more than self-sufficient in food thanks to the world's food donations. It was often heard in this region that the availability of the donated food kept the status quo in place: the UN had a job to do, and the refugees had a point to make. There was the Israeli occupation and there were refugees.

Jeff came back to the living room where we were waiting and apologized for being so long on the phone. I turned my attention to my daughter and was confident when I told her that she would not see starving hollow-eyed, potbellied children in the refugee camp in East Jerusalem.

"Now, would you help me put these bags in the car?" I said to her. She always liked being useful.

After about a fifteen-minute drive north from the Damascus Gate of the Old City, we arrived at a junction called Anata. As we turned right, we saw that the road from there changed significantly. We had to drive very carefully, bypassing deep holes and stray stone barricades—remnants of a recent blockade due to an Israeli army raid. From the Anata junction around fifty meters along the road that led to the refugee camp, there was a checkpoint. We were closely watched by the soldiers, but they did not ask for papers. They did that only on the return journey to Jerusalem. I felt slightly nervous seeing the condition of the road and the curious eyes that watched our car and its passengers. I was driving a hired car with a yellow Israeli number plate. Maya was in the backseat, and Jeff was telling me about the already well-known fact that the Palestinians were not

allowed to build even a goat shed on their land without permission from the Israeli authorities. He was a frequent
visitor to the camp, and we were going to meet some of his
Palestinian co-activists, as well as the man whose house
had been demolished several times. This man had come to
international fame by Jeff's campaign that saw foreign vol-
unteers flock to Jerusalem to help rebuild his house after
each demolition. As I drove slowly toward the entrance
to the camp, our car was surrounded by a swarm of boys
between the ages of six and thirteen, all shouting things in
Arabic and laughing. But I was not going to give in to the
old prejudice. I was not going to represent the first world
with its covert fear of the East, of the claustrophobia of
crowded places among strangers. I was not going to be
the one who stood out as an onlooker in a bazaar, feeling
suspicious of everyone around me. I was from the East,
after all. Although in the Shuafat refugee camp, my heart
told me otherwise.

"Would it be okay if I took some pictures of the camp
from the main road before we enter?" I asked my radical
leftist Israeli companion in the car.

"Sure. I'll wait here with little Maya. But be quick," said
Jeff.

Followed by a trail of boys, I walked to the edge of
the road. From where I was standing, the sprawling camp
below looked as if it were assembled before me like a 3-D
puzzle. There were houses built atop one another, with
narrow, dirty alleyways dividing up the maze. There were
children everywhere. There was a wall of children between

Shuafat Refugee Camp

the car where I had left Jeff with Maya, and myself. They were touching my camera. I was smiling and was still adamant not to let the foreboding of the foreigner unsettle me. Also, it was too late for me to walk back to the car without taking any photos, as they had already seen the camera and they knew the purpose of our visit. I looked through the lens and the buildings jumped into focus, and for a moment I thought they looked like cardboard boxes with child-drawn roofs and the black water tanks atop like lice. I was amazed by the sheer number of water tanks that dotted the rooftops in this jam-packed refugee camp. I would learn soon that while there was no lack of food in Palestinian camps, water shortages were severe during some months of the year. Also, on occasion, following insurgencies or disturbances, the water supply would be cut off along with gas and other amenities. Hence the precautionary measure to store up as much water as possible in the numerous spare tanks that the Palestinians had on the roofs of their homes.

When I was satisfied with my pictures, I started walking back to the car with a jaw-stretching, painful grin that I had been holding there since we entered the camp. I was nervous but struggled not to show it on my face. I had to wade through a sea of children, holding my camera up to stop them from touching it. Some of them demanded to see the pictures I had taken.

When I reached the car, which seemed like ages, the window next to Maya was half wound down, and I saw Jeff saying something to her and offering her a handkerchief. As I pushed my way through into the driver's seat and managed to shut the door, he said, "You took the key and the automatic car window wouldn't close. But you have a very brave daughter."

"What do you mean? What happened?" My smile vanished immediately. I turned around to see Maya. At first I saw nothing unusual. But after the initial palpitations of my heart had stabilized, I noticed there was a very wounded expression on her face. She did not accept the handkerchief. Why was Jeff offering her a handkerchief when she was not crying? I tried to look closely, and before I could believe what I saw, she said, "They spat on my face."

"Who spat on your face?"

"Those boys."

"Those boys" now glued themselves against the car window on Maya's side, which I had wound up. Their faces were pressed against the glass, and the window frame looked as if it were part of a transparent box packed full of faces. Mocking faces. Laughing faces. Faces with their tongues out. Pressed against the glass, like a surrealist art composition.

"Why didn't you call me, my poor baby!" Suddenly I felt all my political correctness concerning the Palestinian issues waning, and I found myself cursing the boys, which they rebuffed by jeering loudly at me.

"I didn't because you asked me not to call you Ima in Palestine."

"Oh, you should have just called me Mummy, then. Why didn't you shout for help?"

"Because you said I mustn't be rude to Palesti-ninians," said my daughter, now accepting Jeff's handkerchief and wiping her face. My mind was disheveled for a moment, not knowing what to do next.

I felt Jeff gently patting my back and asking me to move off, away from the pandemonium on the street that we had inadvertently created. He helped Maya wipe her face. I opened a bottle of water and helped her wash her face, vigorously rubbing it with the handkerchief. "Move!" said Jeff again and took the bottle away from me. As I turned the engine on and started to drive away, shaking the children off the window, I heard him say to Maya, "It's okay, you are really brave."

"I'm okay, Mummy." It was now the brave girl's turn to calm me down. "But I didn't speak Hebrew. Why did they do it, then?"

"They still thought we were Israeli. Well, I am an Israeli," said Jeff.

"But Mummy said they have lots of food. They are not poor, so why are they angry with us?"

"Yes, they are poor," Jeff replied to her. "They are as poor as poor can be. Imagine growing up in a place with sewage-filled alleyways that became flooded every winter. Imagine seeing Israeli tanks entering your homes and taking your brothers or fathers or uncles away in the middle of the night. Imagine not being able to travel. These boys have never been out of these streets that are closed from all sides by checkpoints or high security walls. The lack of food is not the only thing that makes one poor."

"Yes, but it doesn't justify spitting on a child's face," I said.

"The weak always turn on the weaker. If they could, they would spit on me."

.8.

THE CURSE
OF THE "RAFAIMS"

"*It was so irresponsible of you,*" said Leo that evening after we came home. "Taking her to the world service in Bush House was one thing, but dragging her to a refugee camp full of unrest was not the right thing to have done."

"Well, why didn't you offer to babysit, then?" I said, knowing that he had a point, that I should not have taken her to the camp but refusing to admit it.

"So, why did you not offer to babysit?" I asked Leo again, with an added hiss in my voice.

"I told you so many times we need to get help, to get a full-time nanny. We have an extra wing in the house, it could easily be used as the nanny room."

"Why don't you look for one, then?"

"You won't like my choice. The last time when I found someone, you just rejected her."

"The Palestinian woman you brought didn't speak a word of English or Hebrew. How could I have told her what to do with Maya? How would she have communicated with me if there was something seriously wrong and she had to call me?"

"Well, you have enough Arabic to understand if there was an emergency. Besides, she could always call me. Don't you see you'll always find a way to blame me?"

"What if you were in Gaza or Libya or Cairo or Beirut and she could not reach you? I can't have an Arabic-speaking nanny who has no English."

"I am going to read Maya a story." He headed for Maya's bedroom, where she was waiting for her daddy.

"Please don't ask her anything about what happened today. I want to help her bury it for a while, until she is old enough to understand the humiliation, the pain that circulates around the conflict *in this country*." I relished saying the last words, to make the point that we could have avoided this experience had we chosen to be elsewhere. It was, after all, *his* bloody conflict. I did not know where the anger was coming from, but I could hardly suppress or defuse it. I was frustrated and wanted to right the wrong. But it was too late and unrightable. I, an irresponsible mother, subjected my little daughter to a terrible, unnecessary experience for the sake of my work. Somehow, all my efforts to stay behind to look after the children had been nullified by this one wrong move.

I sat in the windowsill feeling accused, blamed, and started crying looking at the dark carob tree outside, its

branches heavy with pods that, when boiled and their contents extracted, tasted very similar to cocoa. Before coming
here I had never tasted carob. My heart felt empty, riddled
with guilt, but I was too proud to admit it. Besides, Leo's
accusatorial tone did not help at all. A few minutes later,
after reading what seemed like a very short bedtime story
to Maya, he came back to the living room. He stood in the
middle of the room on the bare Hebron tiles with a puzzled
look on his face, not knowing whether giving me a hug
right now would be admitting defeat in this phase of our
argument. He was not ready to lose, and I was not ready to
concede defeat. The point was not that I had imprudently
taken Maya along to a rough refugee camp on a work trip;
I had no choice but to take her. I did not ask for his help because I knew that it would not have come—he would have
just said that I was trying to stop him from doing his job.
Funnily, though, it never crossed his mind that he might be
stopping me from doing my job by not sharing parental re-
sponsibilities more evenly and therefore perpetuating a medieval division of roles based on gender. Doing my job was
secondary, something I must do in my spare time, while he
was this noble peacemaker, a man with a mission to change
the Middle East.

Besides, I remembered the times when we first came
here, when almost every weekend we would travel somewhere that was useful for his work. We had spent many Sat-
urdays in ultra-right-wing settler outposts in the hills near
Nablus talking to them about coexistence, or had drunk tea
with Palestinian shopkeepers in the market of the old city of

Hebron while watching settlers—who had taken over and settled on the top floors of the market, throwing rubbish, including soiled tampons and nappies, down below onto the shops and homes of the Palestinians. These trips were fascinating and thought-provoking, but they were not anyone's ideal weekend getaways.

Of course he would argue that all his decisions were meant to be free of danger, born of better judgment. In fact, now that I started going through most of the one-day "weekends" in Jerusalem, a great many of them we had spent going on guided tours to "educate" ourselves on the workings of the conflict. We participated as a family in Finding the Green Line tour, Abandoned Palestinian village tour, Erased Palestinian homes tour, among a dozen others. Even as we went away camping, to zimmers, driving through tracks in the Judean desert in our little car that defeated 4x4s, we were constantly mapping the blurred contours of the world's most contentious real estate dispute. Everything was part of a mission to understand the Israeli-Palestinian conflict. We became slaves to the conflict. The long weekends of our English years, of walking in the moors or the Lake District or on grassy green hills, or cycling in the New Forest and stopping to have a beer in the village pub, became reflections from a distant utopia. And when we went to visit the neighboring Arab countries, we spent a lot of our time trying to fathom how willing the Arab population was for coexistence with Israel. They mostly weren't willing at all! One could just walk through any bazaar in Cairo to get this consensus among the majority—and Egypt was one of Israel's two peace partners. It was not that I did not enjoy all this, but somehow, life became a relentless race with the current affairs in the Middle East.

Leo came and sat next to me and put an arm around me. "You don't have to always feel so angry with me, I do nothing to spite you. I am just doing my job."

"I too want to do a job, any job. You told me when we came here that from now on we would be living as a regular family, no travels, or very few of them. I was not prepared that we won't even have proper weekends because Sunday is a workday here and you won't take Friday off because it's a workday in Europe. It would have all been fine had we been single, without children. But one of us has to be there for them, and it can't just always be me."

"I am sorry," he said. "I know it has been hard for you, but you have to give it some time."

"It's been a year here—I have given it ample time, the status quo remains the same."

"Maybe when the Gaza stuff is out of the way, I'll try my best to be around. At the moment I can't predict my movements so soon after the Israeli disengagement."

He spoke quietly, which should have softened my heart, but I somehow could not suppress an astonishing surge of rage. I felt used, manipulated. I stood and swung past him into the kitchen, shouting that I had no faith in him, that I regretted coming here to see my youth wither away, caught in a relationship that was so unequal.

"You have stifled my dreams, and from now on I am going to stifle yours. Since I can't just pack up and go to a hotel as you have done so many times, I'll make your life as difficult as possible by noncooperation. I don't want to spend an evening sitting next to you. I am sitting here at the kitchen table; I will cut my tapes and finish my package. You'll get a taste of what it's like to be living next to a mindless, working robot."

"That's why I go away, to escape your *j'accuse*. I was going to stay here this week, but I won't now. I am leaving first thing tomorrow morning. To Gaza," he said and hurried upstairs to his study.

This was so typical. If I remained sweet, he would say that he had to leave because he had a job to do. And if I was unsweet, by making an issue out of his erratic disappearances, he would say that he did that because I shouted at him. I no longer knew these days what were the tops and tails of our arguments. We had attached ourselves to a rotating cycle of doom; we just picked up an argument from where we had left off. There was no beginning, nor was there an end within view.

In these situations, the best thing would be to stay calm, let the moment pass and deal with it at a later stage. But my willpower would be crippled by my relentless frustration at his unilateral decisions to leave. I would not be able to stop my irascibility from taking over and wrecking the whole thing to pieces.

I noticed mysterious shadows dancing on the floor. I looked up and saw silhouettes of the cactus on the terrace above being magnified by the streetlights and filling the dimly lit kitchen through the skylight. Anger blinded me, I could not concentrate on the tapes that I had recorded in the refugee camp. I started stomping around the kitchen. My jittery eyes fell on the fax machine and the telephone set. I picked up both and dropped them on the floor.

These were his modes of communication to his colleagues in Gaza, so they had to go first. A little vengeance, not too big, but not too small either. He could run away, but until he did that, this was what I would be doing, I would be smashing up his world of communication.

Luckily Kiran was at his guitar lesson. I heard Maya begin to cry upstairs. Leo hurried down to the kitchen and looked at the site of destruction in disbelief. He started pushing me away from there, but I resisted. I pushed him against the wall and went for his glasses. I smashed them, too, on the floor.

"How dare you? They are my eyes. I am blind without them. You are obscene, you are out of your mind. Insane!"

"We'll see how you go to Gaza tomorrow. Without your eyes."

Maya's cry became louder upstairs. He held me tightly by the arm and started pulling me toward the sitting room. I struggled to wriggle out of his grip, but it became stronger. He said, "I am going to lock you up there until you've pulled yourself together."

"No, you won't, you are not my bloody master." My arm was hurting. I tried to get out but couldn't. I started kicking him in the legs. He pushed me away with a loud cry as if he had been injured. His sudden shove, together with the force with which I was already trying to pull my arm free of him, propelled me to the far end of the living room, toppling me off balance. I hit my knee against the coffee table and it gave like a mass of jelly, with an intense pain. It was my bad leg that I had broken before in the Jerash amphitheater in Jordan while playing with Kiran and falling off a Roman wall. The pain made me dizzy and sick. I must have suffered a few seconds' blackout, because when I opened my eyes, I saw Maya standing in the middle of the room crying hysterically.

"Daddy just went out. He said he was going to get new glasses. Are you okay, Mummy? Did you break your leg again? Mummy, I'll get you some water."

"Come here, I'll give you a hug. Come," I whispered to her.

"I am sorry, Mummy. Can you fix the telephone, because we have to call an ambulance."

"Don't worry, my love, it's not serious. It happened before. I'll have to find my knee brace somewhere in the medicine cabinet."

"I'll get it for you, I know where it is," said a sobbing Maya as she turned to go up to the bathroom.

"I'll go and get it. Come here and give me a hand," I said to her.

But when I tried to move, intense pain threatened more blackouts. I stayed sitting there on the floor next to the heavy glass coffee table, the legs and the base of which were redesigned from a Bedouin grain thresher that we had picked up in Jordan. I was lucky that the glass did not break. I sat there holding my child, trying to draw comfort from the warmth of her little body and her embrace, her tiny arms around me. It helped to calm my nerves. I was by then beyond any feeling of shame or guilt. I had desecrated the very idea of parenthood. Our daughter was providing me with security, something that I should have given her. Instead I had upturned her little world of trust in her parents.

Before I fell asleep in that position, I blamed the ghosts of the house in Emek Rafaim. They would not leave us alone. We had disturbed their continuity and they were intent on destroying ours. Our tottering marriage was supposed to steady in the new setting in Jerusalem, but instead it started to increasingly mirror the conflict around us. From the beginning the already shaky foundation felt even shakier, starting with the disappearance of the container with all our household things. Our stay here contributed to more strife rather than peace, for which we were unprepared. The house and the country were trying to make a point: that they did not need outsiders to come and settle here. It was haunted, the premises here as well as those of this city, if not of the whole country that persistently scared off meddlers: which showed why the international involvement here had been steadily rejected by the locals; why the 2000 Camp David Summit degenerated into a second intifada. And the Oslo Accords before that led to the creation in the West Bank of an administrative and bureaucratic mess of arbitrary lines around so-called Israeli- and Palestinian-controlled areas: A, B, and C, never to be reconciled since 1993. The ABC of our life as a family, which incidentally also began at the end of the same year when I fell pregnant with our first child, must now be divided into compartments of intense regret, passion, and self-pity.

———

Leo came home at some point; I did not dare to look at the time. Confrontation was not a good idea. I needed his help. He was walking stealthily, took Maya from my arms and put her back in her bedroom. From the corner of my eyes I saw that he had new glasses, nicer and trendier. They made him look older. I wanted to ask about Kiran, where he was. He probably realized that and said that he had picked him up from his music lesson and taken him to Yezan's house for a sleepover. Clever idea. I was too embarrassed by this latest mishap—one of a series that our son had witnessed as he was growing up—to stand face-to-face with him.

"Do you need to see a doctor?"

"Yes. I probably tore or twisted the same ligaments, they have to be put back in place."

"Can you wait till tomorrow morning? I'll take you to Hadassah after dropping Maya off at school."

"I probably can, but I need my knee brace. It's in the bathroom." I remained sitting there, trying to gain strength, as the slightest move was sending off dizzying pain to my brain, darkening my vision.

"Here, I got some strong painkillers for you."

I felt calmer, as always happened after an argument. Extreme antipathy was replaced by intense affinity, need for a passionate embrace, soft-voiced words of love. I knew how he felt and I knew how I felt and we both knew what we needed from each other.

He sat next to me and we hugged.

We sat on the cool stone floor looking at the dancing shadows and I cried. We felt serene.

The next day, on the way back from the hospital on my temporary crutches, I asked the taxi driver to stop by Orli's house. The previous night's brief serenity and warmth were already waning as I made the journey back from hospital on my own. Leo could not stay with me, to take me home. He did not discuss with me how I was going to pick up Maya from kindergarten. Fortunately Kiran was picked up and dropped off by the school bus.

"Who did this to you?" Orli asked.

"No one, it was an accident."

"What do you mean it was an accident?"

"I tripped over a coffee table."

"He didn't hit you, did he?"

"Of course not."

"What happened, then?"

"I just said!"

"He pushed you?"

"No! I pushed him."

"So he pushed you back? Men are not allowed to do that. They are stronger." Orli's voice sounded very serious.

"Why did you think in the first place that my 'accident' involved *him*?" I asked her.

"Oh, don't be stupid. Your face says it all. Why would you be here otherwise, at this hour when the kids are in school? What about your BBC report? You said you would be working on it today."

"I had no idea it was so obvious, you are able to see that we had a fight. But I started it. At least I think that I had started it, I made the first move."

I felt a strong urge to tell Orli everything. I was dying to lighten the load off my chest. I did not want to go back to the lonely house. I did not want the responsibility of picking up Maya—in fact, I had no idea how I was going to get her from school on crutches and spend another evening on my own, unplanned, unpredicted, unprepared for this latest setback. Another evening with two children, when I would have to repeat the same replies to the same questions from them:

"Where's Dad?"

"He's in Gaza."

"But he was there only last week."

"He had to go again."

"Why?"

"The think tank that he works for wants him to write another report on how Gaza is doing postdisengagement."

No, I would not say this in as many words, because I would not want to set off a barrage of questions from my daughter: "What's a think tank? Is it like a water tank? Do you sit there and think?" And from my son: "What's this disengagement thing? Yezan says it's just another Zionist trick . . ." I would not want to have another long evening with the children with too many queries that involved the absurd political realities of this place. I would pack them off to bed early so that I could sit in the living room facing the ghosts, who now permanently inhabited the souls of the dancing shadows and hovered over our Hebron tiles. I would confront them, "So are you happy now? Now that you are winning? I don't dispute that you have a right to disrupt the peace. But why couldn't you find a different home? I suppose this *is* your home and you have the right to ask why *we* didn't find a different house. Maybe we should move out. No one is happy here. Maybe I should give it a chance. Give our relationship a chance, please spare us from your mocking tongues."

Then I would plead with them, "Tell me, then, the ancestors of the rightful owners of these premises, what I should do now. Should I give up, go back as I did from Morocco six years ago and had found my life back in London although on my own with a child, or should I stay and see if this time we can make it work? Is it then not for me, not for us, the bliss of a family life? We met from two polar opposites: he with a solid family background, so he wanted to leave it behind, and I with no family wanted to cling to one—any family, half a family. Is that why we do not mix, we do not connect?"

"This is outrageous," I heard Orli say. It sounded as if she were speaking to me from a faraway island. A mug of oolong tea was steaming away before me and I was disoriented for a few moments and thought that I did not hear what she said next, but I heard her perfectly well and I was taken aback, although I would not deny that those

"Dancing shadows" on Hebron tiles in our first house

were the exact words on my mind on the way back from
Hadassah Hospital that made me stop at Orli's house. Leo
had called a taxi for me and said that he could not change
his plan and not go to Gaza. He had organized meetings
there and he could not "let them down." He could not let
the Palestinians down.

"This is unacceptable, this behavior. He has real chutz-
pah, after this, to leave you on your own with the kids and
go to Gaza for . . . how long did you say?"

"No idea."

"Do you know what this will be seen as, no matter
how much you try to protect him? Deliberate negligence

whereby a woman is left on her own on crutches to look after two children."

"Oh, no, I had already broken some ligaments in my leg a few years ago in Jordan; the knee just keeps going ever since. I can't cycle, I can't run very fast. This has nothing to do with our argument. I am just ashamed of myself for not being able to stop the argument when Maya could hear us. I am not sure how we are damaging her and, before her, how we must have damaged Kiran."

"And you still want to be in this relationship? Come on, we live in the twenty-first century, people do move on, you know, and they rebuild life. You can't continue to live like this. I can't remember—I have known you for a year— when you said anything nice about your relationship, except that you love him. He is never there for you when you need him, but you are always there for him whenever he just hollers at you to announce his presence, you just roll into his fold."

"Don't exaggerate, Orli. I love him because of our history, we have been together for a very long time. It's easy to break, but not easy to build."

"It sounds from what you are saying that you have built nothing whatsoever."

I was too tired to take it all in. I wanted comfort, not a judgment on my marriage. I thought of my friends in London. They would never say this in these words, even if that was what they thought of us. But life appeared to Orli from a clear-cut angle, where everyone was in her right compartment according to her idea of justice or injustice. For my London friends, life had a lot more gray areas.

"I have a lawyer friend," said Orli. "I should ask her to give you a call. Just have a chat. Nothing to lose. You should know your rights."

The oolong warmed me up and relaxed my muscles. I was not as shocked as I had thought I would be. These were the ultimate words of profanity in my idea of a sacred marriage. I stretched out my bandaged knee and said to Orli, "I know my rights—at least the rights that matter to me. I know I have a right to deserve empathy and sharing in the marriage. I have a right to leave this place if it is splintering my family into unbridgeable pieces. But I do not wish to punish my partner by any worldly law."

"That's interesting to hear from an atheist! So you believe in divine justice? Oh, God will punish him! What goes round, comes round!"

"Don't mock me, please. There's got to be some justice. There's always conscience. By the way, the oolong is lovely. Thank you."

"For some, there's no conscience. Some like to select their conscience, like we Jews did. If we were to be inflicted with pangs of some impractical moral sense, how could we live here, in Leo's Palestine? All the *non*-self-hating Jews had to overcome the bites of a guilty conscience."

"Here we go again," I thought. I definitely did not want to spend the morning bringing up examples of the Jews and the Palestinians and compare my life to their sense of guilt or nonguilt. The justice or injustice of the conflict. Is there life beyond Palestine and Israel? Beyond the conflict? I crutched up to go. It was a short walk to my house, I should be able to manage.

I was not expecting that evening, after I had had my session with the ghosts of our house, a call on my mobile from Orli's lawyer friend. I tried to stay calm, although my heart was racing. I was glad that Maya was in bed and it was safe with Kiran, as he spent all his time listening to loud music through earphones.

For the first time I felt annoyed with Orli. For the first time it seemed serious, the crisis between Leo and me. Never before had I arrived at a junction where it seemed final, our marriage irreconcilable. Although I should take responsibility for what had just happened, that I was on the phone with a lawyer who had been roughly briefed by Orli about some vague domestic disorder, which I tried to deny. But I could not get off the phone. She asked me questions about the financial situation, the sharing of homes and the number of joint accounts. I did not answer most questions, and when I did, I said that there was no problem in terms of our financial arrangements even in the aftermath of a calamitous separation. But she went on demanding that I tell her everything anyway, because things do change when couples separate. It was agonizing, the whole conversation, mostly her explaining my "rights." They included feminist issues as to how men should treat women and vice versa, and that any breach of that must not be tolerated by women because that undermined similar causes involving other women. If only, I thought, relationships could sustain according to a particular feminist or any other code of conduct! I never thought of what I did for my family as "women's duties," I said to the lawyer, which she did not like.

In the end, I managed to say one thing with real authority: that what happened the other night between my husband and me was not domestic violence and there was no chance of us going our separate ways, at least not for the moment. I did not want to blame Orli, because I had left it vague when she said she would get her lawyer friend to call me. I had not given it much thought because I believed she would forget about it. It sounded lame, this excuse, even to myself; part of me obviously was bitter and I wanted to let the situation take its course. But I was not prepared for what the lawyer said next: "I'll call again next week to see how you are doing."

"Thanks, I should be fine."

"One can never be sure, things happen fast, they can deteriorate beyond one's usual expectation. If any violent situation arises, just give me a call, here's my cell phone number."

I sat there feeling soiled. There was no violence, was there? I started the fight. I pushed first. Orli's voice would not stop ringing in my ears: "Yes, but he is stronger, and men cannot push women a little more than half their weight." I put my hands on my ears, I wanted to blot out the word "violence." There was no violence. Leo and I behaved like two teenagers, we never grew up, we fought like children without shame, without inhibition. There was no violence.

I was not prepared to have a legal, feminist discourse on my life, between Leo and me. Orli having an opinion on my life concerning Leo was one thing, but getting a lawyer involved was something I could not feel at ease with at the current state of my life. I thought of the children and I felt truly fearful of another call next week, which she probably would make as my irresolute plea to her not to call me was probably not sufficient to dissuade a lawyer.

I was not unprepared when the call came the following week, again the soft-voiced drone that I must know my rights. I was surprised that I still could not unequivocally say to her to stop calling, that I did not need to be told what my rights were, that I had no financial worries even if we were to separate. But I did not say any of these. I just listened, making myself seem like a small, vulnerable woman. I did not even decline when she asked me to stop by her office, which was on Emek Rafaim, so that we could informally meet.

But what I was not prepared for was an envelope through the door from the lawyer's office a few weeks later. I opened it with trembling fingers. I could not believe my eyes. It was a bill for a thousand dollars for telephone consultations.

I never believed that my friendship with Orli would ever come to a phase when I would want to avoid her, when I would not want to be confronted by her or to confront her. It was probably not a coincidence that I left the bill from the lawyer's office lying around on the telephone desk, which Leo picked up when he was installing a new fax machine.

"This is what you have been plotting with your *best friend*!"

"Don't be mad at me. It is unexpected for me too."

"You always liked to broadcast your woes to your so-called best friends and make me look like someone who beats up his wife."

He stormed off upstairs, leaving the lawyer's letter on the side table. In his fury he forgot to connect the fax machine. I did not feel guilty, nor did I take any responsibility for the lawyer's bill, but I felt that our private war had spilled over, out of the bedroom onto the public space. It was now recorded in the lawyer's telephone log, and in this age of computers and terabytes of online space for documents, the log would be there forever and ever until there was a cyber crash. That left me feeling very uneasy.

"We are leaving this house," Leo said a week later.

"Fair enough, we don't really want to live on a street full of English speakers in a house haunted by the ghosts of the past."

"Not just that. I don't want us to live so near Orli, a woman who so skillfully tried to insert a dagger through our marriage, our family."

"As if the marriage was without any thorns in the first place!" I said.

"Never like this. Never before did you feel you had to take a friend's advice to consult a lawyer to end our marriage. If we have to end this, we need no lawyers."

But you would never let me go, I wanted to say. Why was it, then, every time we reached a terrible breaking point when I really intended to leave that you turned back with all the love of the world and held on to me? And for a few days or weeks or if we were lucky, a month or two, we got on well before the vicious cycle repeated itself.

"Besides," Leo said, "she wants to take my children away. We have to move so that she cannot entice them again into her lair with her anchovy-flavored burgers."

Leo often accused me of trying to take his children away every time I said enough was enough. Sometimes I felt that the fear of being burdened with this particular accusation involving the children kept me tied to the marriage. I did not know why I felt that I needed to prove that I would never take them away from him out of personal revenge. The children belonged to both of us.

PART

TWO

A PIECE OF QUIET

"I asked Daddy what he did," Maya said as she dipped another strip of toast into her egg. Kiran was immersed in his usual about-to-be-a-teenager reticence. But after some months of much shouting and screaming while I watched in despair my baby boy turn evasive and recalcitrant, I gave up fighting with him. I felt that I could no longer argue with a child who before his twelfth birthday grew to almost 172 centimeters, an inch taller than me. So at the breakfast table Maya did all the talking and I was the sole listener, as it was not clear from Kiran's face whether he any longer lived in our world.

"So what did Daddy say?" I asked her, breaking an egg into the frying pan.

"He said he went to Gaza to talk to the Palesti-ninians so that they could have a 'piece of quiet.'"

"What's that?" I asked, trying to look serious.

"It's a piece of quiet. That the Palesti-ninians and the Jewish people need, my dad said. He said he was helping them with it."

I saw Kiran raise his eyebrows. So my about-to-be-teenage son did react to certain things from time to time! Especially when it came to lecturing his sister.

"Maya, it's peace *and* quiet. Not a piece of quiet. Quiet is not a soft-boiled egg that you eat with soldiers. And it's Palesti*nian*, not *ninian*, you idiot! You make them sound as if they're some kind of ninjas who came from another planet!"

"No! Daddy said it's a piece *of* quiet that he wants to give to Palesti-*ni*nians!" She emphasized the extra "ni."

It was incredible how meanly the two children who were nearly eight years apart fought.

"Okay, okay, you are my ignorant little sister." Kiran scowled at Maya.

"Mummy will make you packed lunch instead of lunch money from now on, because you've been horrible," Maya said. She, like her dad, had a way of always having the last word in any argument.

"I'll send you both to your rooms if you go on like this." I issued my warning, which never worked anyway.

"But I'm telling you the truth," she said this time with real conviction. "Daddy did say that he was in Gaza so the Palesti-ninians share a piece of quiet with Israel."

"Did he say so? How is he going to do that?" I asked her. I decided to distract her so she and her brother would stop tearing each other apart at the breakfast table.

"By going to Gaza," she said like a little pundit on world affairs.

"So Gaza has a reservoir of *quiet*, I didn't know that." I sat down with my coffee. Right now Gaza had anything but "quiet." The "disengaged," disgruntled settlers left the whole place in a heap of rubble like a postwar site, and it would take a long time to rebuild the strip even with international help. Leo always said he preferred Gaza to the West Bank. He thought the Gazan Palestinians were much more original and open-minded than their West Bank brothers (not sisters; women were hardly visible in the Palestinian public political arena except for one or two symbolic faces such as Hanan Ashrawi).

The school bus hooted and I hurried Kiran out the front door. I waved to Hassan, the Palestinian driver, and sat down at the kitchen table to finish my coffee, while Maya went to her room to get ready. She always took a long time in the morning. We never arrived at the kindergarten before nine, an hour and a half late. This was her last year there and I did not mind too much not being on time. I wanted to enjoy her company as much as I could. Her language was still full of unexpected surprises, wit, and mischief. I was sure that she had made up the "piece of quiet" story. I seemed to remember that she had heard it from her grandmother, Joy, the much-repeated story of Leo using the phrase when he was a little boy. She was very clever to plagiarize the expression to taunt her brother—and me too, to some extent. She was perceptive and sussed it out that I was unhappy with Leo's obsession with Gaza, his frequent departures to that strip of blazing strife and discontent.

My peacemaker husband. I sighed and sipped my coffee. During the past decade I had followed Leo everywhere along the stretch of the world called the Middle East: from Morocco to Palestine, from Egypt to Jordan. I did not chase any ideal, dream, or ambition in his Middle East. I, the ex-feminist, the seller of Trotskyite newsletters in the Underground in the early days of my life in London, had been totally and desperately like a Bollywood heroine, obsessed with a man who was in love with a piece of land that would never reciprocate his devotion. I spent days on end without him, living on my own with the children while he traveled around the region, the love of his life. He traversed the whole swathe of the land, from Lebanon to Egypt, Jordan to Iraq. On my own, pining for him, I tried tirelessly to befriend the Middle East, tried getting to know her by probing her, pleasing her; by learning Hebrew and Arabic; by agreeing, despite being in my early youth a fervent atheist, to have the religious coming-of-age ceremony for our reluctant son. By sending our daughter to a Hebrew-Arabic bilingual kindergarten.

———

We hardly communicated since we moved to our second house during our second year in Jerusalem, in a religious neighborhood in the west of the city near the president's residence. The Gaza disengagement had become Gaza engagement for my husband, and he spent several nights a month there.

Our new house had once been a freestanding bungalow surrounded by mature gardens. After the creation of Israel, the property had been abandoned for some time, probably until the 1950s. Following the mass migration of Jews into Israel from all over the world, ugly high-rises shot up, defying the biblical landscape; shikun estates spread across the skyline, hiding Jerusalem's steeples and domes.

Atop what once used to be a beautiful house surrounded by trees and fragrant shrubs rose a three-story estate, which was subdivided into flats with their different entryways. Fortunately we had the original entrance and, therefore, had the sole use of the gardens. It felt very cut off. Even the postman did not come all the way down to the front door; he left our mail at the main approach to the building. Because of the additional floors on the top of our house, the living room hardly ever got any sunlight, so it had a cave-like feel. The house had beautiful floor tiles in all the rooms, and a relief in original blue, green, and red mosaic, "the tree of life," on one of the bedroom walls. In the mellow light that hung in the room day and night, it looked like a cave painting.

We chose the house because of its wild gardens. But I began to feel a bit isolated, even missed the buzzing English-speaking cafés on Emek Rafaim. Since it was not as convenient just to roll out of the house and into a café, I would often find myself moping about, in my beautiful cave waiting for my Odysseus to come home.

But Gaza was important, even our little daughter knew that.

"When will Daddy come back from Gaza?" Maya would ask every time Leo went away, as going away became synonymous with going to Gaza.

"When there's peace in the Middle East," would be my usual answer. She would take me seriously and not notice the note of sarcasm in what I said, which I somewhat relished repeating out of my suppressed frustration at feeling left out of the more pressing political process in the region. Over the following months, however, things would only get worse in Gaza and the road to peace would seem longer than ever.

In moments of anger and discontentment at my accidental relocation to the Middle East, I would justify even more vigorously my antipathy toward the international community's arrogant chase after peacemaking. And it made me all the more exasperated, as Leo was single-mindedly involved in it as part of his pledge that he had once voiced so clearly to me in London on a beautiful April afternoon many years ago that he would never love anyone or anything more than the Middle East.

What if I, too, started to love the Middle East, wrote about the Middle East, devoted my interests to the Middle East? How would he react then? What would he do?

.10.

FIDA

We grew up at the cross-road of exile and exile
Where the roads came together childhood fell from our hand
as the wind knocks over an umbrella with one gust
this is my bow to what will remain

> —*Mourid Barghouti, "I Run toward*
> *You . . . I Run with You"*

"*Keif halek?*"

"*Ana mabsuta.*"

Fida burst into a fit of giggles at my standard answer in Arabic regarding my well-being.

"What's wrong in saying the same thing? *I am well.* Pretty good response to me!"

"You have to do some work on your Arabic. You could also, for example, have said, '*Ana majnune,*' I am mad."

"Mad? Why, at what?"

"Mad at the world, like I am, quite a lot of the time."

"*Majnune*," I thought. I already knew the word. Mad with love. In Hindi, in Urdu, and in folk Bengali. It brought back tales of a certain Persian prince called Majnu, who fell head over heels in love with a beautiful courtesan called Layli. I thought that I would not mind attributing my own state of being a lot of the time to this word!

If Orli was my facilitator behind settling in this place, then meeting Fida was like breaking through layers of memories to stumble upon a solid link to the languages that I once spoke. The bridge was slowly being shaped as I listened more and more to her Arabic and spent long evenings with her in Ramallah, where she worked and commuted to every day from Jerusalem. Now that I could converse in simple Hebrew, I was trying to cross the hurdle of Arabic thanks to my encounter with Fida. Arabic was no longer an insurmountable barrier.

On a balmy morning in June I came to collect her from her house in Ein Karem in southwest Jerusalem. She had been recommended by a friend. She had agreed to work as my interpreter and, in the BBC language, "fixer."

She was taking me to the northern village of Barta'a, where Israel and Palestine merge and where all its seven thousand inhabitants were related through intermarriage. This was an exceptional village, which was spared from the Israeli security wall that otherwise runs along the border between the northern West Bank and Israel. Fida had fixed an interview with the two mayors from either side of the village, one was West Bank Palestinian and the other Israeli Arab.

I found her gazing from her terrace at the lush valley below. The terrace hung over a fast road that skirted a deep drop into the valley of thyme and sage, with the most incredible 180-degree panorama of terraced hills and almond groves, abandoned by bygone Palestinians of the old village of Ein Karem. Dresses, sheets, jeans, and shirts were flapping about in gentle breeze on the washing line. I parked the car and walked up the steps when I saw her appear in various stages: with the first piece of washing removed, I saw her very long, thin arms; her long legs in low flattering jeans strode toward me. She was unusually tall for a Palestinian woman. When her face appeared from behind a faded orange sheet, it looked familiar. I had seen that long face with sleepy kohl-rimmed eyes and a melancholic smile before: the features that belonged to one of the best-known faces in the world. It was the face of a familiar icon, in dimly lit churches and decorated alcoves.

Fida had the face of Jesus. The same long droopy all-forgiving expression, framed by soft, long dark curls. She smiled kindly, before following my eyes to the nearby hills and the stunning view, saying, "Yes, what you see all around once belonged to us. I've come to reclaim it all!"

She brought me back to reality with a jolt.

From the jovial tone of her voice it was hard to tell why she chose such words to greet me on our first meeting. Did she not trust journalists? Did she want to feed the cliché and say what most foreigners wanted to hear? There was subtle irony in her voice, which I detected with much discomfort. The discomfort was related to the fact that my husband was Jewish. I could suddenly taste the insecurity that my son, whose middle name was Akiva, felt when the secret of his name was at risk of being revealed to his Palestinian friends. I could once again understand Leo's justification for not wanting his Palestinian colleagues to know of his religious affiliation. I thought I had better not say anything about the Jewish connection, as I did not want her perception of me to change. I wanted to get to know the strikingly tall, Jesus-faced woman and vowed that our acquaintance would stretch beyond the BBC packages that she was helping me with.

"Don't worry, I'll claim the land, this village, with peaceful negotiations," Fida said, and started to laugh.

I heard echoes in my head of Kiran repeating what his friend Yezan said to him: "When I grow up I'd like to lead a popular movement, a peaceful one, though, to claim my land back."

There I was, standing on the terrace of an old Arab house in the former Arab village of Ein Karem, facing a long-limbed woman whose face resembled the prophet of Nazareth, thinking how I should develop our new ties without saying the wrong word, without revealing what must not be revealed.

I was lucky that there was not much time, as we had to head off to the north. The conversation in the car was cryptic all the way through, tinged by what I thought was her quirky humor. Especially when she said, "Maybe Abu Mazen and Ariel Sharon should listen to *you*, since the Europeans have failed here. You could give us some of your

Gandhian techniques. We need a Gandhi here. Peaceful struggle, which drove the British out of India. We are sick of suicide bombers."

I was about to say, "Do you really mean that you want to drive the Israelis out?" Did she think of Israel as a colonial power as the British were in India? But I kept the bubbling thoughts to myself as I watched her straight posture and her dreamy eyes looking at the Arab towns and villages, now behind Israel's security barrier. As the car sped through the plains of the West Bank, I started counting the tall concrete panels of the "wall," illegal under international law, which not only put the Palestinians behind prisonlike enclosures, it further cut off Palestinian villages from one another on both sides, from daily contact between the people who were once neighbors. The wall of separation isolated the Palestinian villages from any kind of real contact with the world, from the nearest big Israeli cities with businesses, hospitals, schools, and other facilities, from the airport in Tel Aviv that was less than an hour's drive away. Beyond the wall, I saw tall Ottoman minarets in densely spread towns. I suddenly realized that by using this road, which cut through the occupied West Bank, I was in a way supporting an illegal land-grabbing program by Israel. When I said this to Fida, she said, "I could have taken a different route, but I wanted to show you this main north-south settler highway, also known as apartheid road 60, which runs bang through the middle of the West Bank towns and villages to connect the Jewish settlements that are dotted around on hilltops, as you can see, all those red-roofed houses."

Raja Shehadeh, the renowned Palestinian writer, claimed in one of his books that no one (no settler) could have a bigger claim to the hills (where the settler had settled in his fortresslike residence) of Palestine than he did. He went on to say that the European settlers had vandalized the land, destroyed the thyme and za'atar fields. How could they lay any claim to this land? In the very structure of the settlement building there was this "I am the monarch of all I survey" message. In order to create the hilltop settlements, the tops of the biblical hills were chopped off and there grew sprawling white concrete red-roofed cities, desecrating the landscape and unsettling the wildlife. Indigenous Palestinian villages are built in man-made terraces on the slopes of the hills, dispersed with olive groves and cacti fencing that enclosed gardens with seasonal fruit and vegetables. During my many tours with Leo of "demolished Palestinian villages," we were told to look for the mature cacti and fig trees that had once formed the boundaries of a certain village. The houses were matte gray or ocher, often moss-covered, with modest windows, not taller than two stories. Inconspicuous, they blended in a symbiotic way into the surrounding nature. There, the indigenous man did not trample the earth; he only made himself modestly comfortable on it, made himself at home.

"We'll soon take the intersection to Road 6, which runs parallel to Highway 60, and drive past the walled Palestinian town of Tulkarem, where my mother comes from," said Fida, bringing me back from the visions of a bygone era in Raja Shehadeh's books. "Road 6 there runs along the Green

Line, so you'll see how Israel snakes along like a possessive lover the entire swathe of Palestine. Zigzagging through it, intersecting it, and riding its borders, always making its presence known to its reluctant mistress. About your guilt over driving along this highway through occupied Palestine, I have no great sympathy, my dear. Feel whatever you like to feel, let your conscience torture you. For me, however, it is all Palestine, occupied or not, with or without the endorsement by your international plan."

"But you are using an Israel-built road meant for Israeli settlers! Your conscience should be at least as bruised as mine."

"As long as I can use whatever bits of my land that I can have access to, I'm not boycotting it! I can't boycott traveling through my country! That's for you, the foreigners." Fida paused a little, then said, "If and when the Israelis move out of the occupied West Bank, do you think they'll take Highway 60 with them?" She chuckled. "Like the way when they disengaged from Gaza they left the whole place in ruins, buildings bulldozed, greenhouses destroyed, and water channels poisoned?"

I remained quiet. This was more or less what Leo said the settlers had done before they were pulled out by force by the Israeli army.

It was a beautiful drive but loaded with history, with resentment and pain; and every now and then an eight-meter-high wall blocked the roadside villages from our immediate view. Green-domed mosques and minarets poked out from behind the concrete barrier to remind us that people lived on the other side. I felt there was a wall growing too between Fida and me, a wall of fear of misunderstanding. What if she did not want to keep in touch beyond this work trip? What if she did not trust me because I was the wife of a Jew, or if she thought of me as just another foreign journalist trying to live off the conflict? What if she did not think much beyond working for me as a fixer, and when this was over she would return to her terraced flat in the abandoned Arab village now annexed by Israel, and I to Jerusalem, to file yet another story on the Israeli-Palestinian divide?

"So what brought you here?" she asked, as she turned away from the high observation towers set atop the wall around Tulkarem, the village where Fida had earlier said she had gone to school.

"To follow my husband," I was about to declare but decided on saying instead, "Well, to work as a journalist."

"But you said you were freelancing for the BBC, so they didn't send you here?"

"You are right. I was on sabbatical from the BBC but decided to stay on after my leave was over and work here as a journalist."

"What a strange place to choose! Has the world not seen enough of this conflict? Isn't there a media fatigue? How much more can you say? Haven't you said it all already?"

"We probably have, you are right, but about this particular area there isn't really a readership fatigue as yet, that's why I still have a job! But don't you think today's story is going to be different?"

I tried to divert her attention so that she did not confuse me with questions that I did not know answers to.

"Well, it would be interesting, although in the end it's just another story of Israel arbitrarily putting barriers between people, creating sometimes funny situations such as the one we're going to see." She paused for a minute. "There's a dentist in this divided village, apparently he has two wives, one from Israel and the other from Palestine!"

When we arrived in the village, I found myself in a place that reminded me of the arbitrary border between two Bengals.

The village of Barta'a was home to one of the world's largest clans, the Kabhas, related through generations of intermarriage. But since the creation of the state of Israel, the villagers had been living under two different administrative systems: Barta'a West under Israel and Barta'a East under the Palestinian civil authority. Although the Kabhas continued to intermarry, the two sides were deeply affected by the realities of separation and the desperate longing to unite.

We were driving through Barta'a's bustling market amid throngs of people. Here, the two villages could meet more freely. Like in any other vibrant Middle Eastern souq, shoppers and traders were busy exchanging the usual market talk; the prices of local produce were being shouted out by vendors to attract buyers; giant watermelons, cauliflowers, and long white aubergines—the specialties of this region—were on display. But what made this market different from any other was that the Green Line, which under international law divided Israel and the Palestinian territories, went right through it, through shops, the main street and, in several cases, through residential homes, carving up communities and families at random.

"Right here, you have one foot in Israel and the other in Palestine," said Fida, standing next to a toyshop at the bend of the main street in the village. There were twinkles of sarcasm in her beautiful eyes. But I wasn't sure whether or not to laugh at what was, I by now understood, a characteristic wisecrack. Her comment contained one of the many painful paradoxes that perpetually disunited this land.

Colorful inflatable toys and beach balls were swaying from the front awning, from left to right, from Israel to Palestine, from Palestine to Israel. Fida was standing right in front of the shop, in two countries at the same time, heaps of cheap China-made toys hiding the Palestinian side of her leg. The image took me back more than twenty-five years, to the bordering village between two Bengals where I grew up.

There was a river, it was most probably the river Bhairab, although I could not be too sure, between East and West Bengal. We used to swim across the river to go to another country: the West being part of India and the East of Bengal an independent sovereign state, Bangladesh. Our carefree border-hopping days ended in the late 1970s when we were barred from crossing the familiar river. Our movements were restricted as a result of the deployment of the gun-toting Border Security Force on either side that did not hesitate to shoot at any living object. But I remembered as a girl crossing into the market town in West Bengal to buy trinkets and terra-cotta figurines of popular gods and goddesses, some of which traveled with me all the way to England and which I still carried with me. The idols, the silent bystanders of history, stared back at me from my desk in Jerusalem, constantly reminding me of the irony of fate—that almost three decades later I would be living in a place where the politics of division of my childhood would repeat itself, albeit to a greater degree. I would be standing in a village town in the Middle East, baffled by a preposterous border randomly drawn up by unseen hands of foreign bodies, who had absolutely no interest in the lives of those on the ground.

Fida and I drove through the market to the house of Ghassan Kabha, the Palestinian mayor of Barta'a East. We went to pick him up to bring him to the Israeli side, since he was not allowed to drive his Palestinian green-number-plated car into Israel. There was no fence or any visible division line here, but halfway down the market, the car number plates changed color and became yellow as the area fell in Israel. I wanted to interview him with his Israeli counterpart, who's also his cousin.

"I've already put one foot in jail," said the mayor, after the car that I was driving crossed the invisible border to Israel. "But my cousin, the mayor of the Israeli Barta'a, would *inshallah* make necessary phone calls to get me out!" One foot on the other side. I recalled what Fida had said a few minutes earlier, which for the mayor equaled one foot in prison. I did not know whether to take the mayor seriously. But as we would get to know him better during the course of the day, we would be acquainted with his extraordinary sense of humor, with which he had armed himself to get through the daily absurdities of life. In fact, I found wise-cracking a favorite pastime among the Palestinians. How else would one carry on with the occupation that had infiltrated deep into their lives?

The "Israeli" mayor, Riyad Kabha, greeted his cousin from behind his elegant black desk. He said that Ghassan's presence at his office would be seen by the Israeli authorities as illegal and that he was knowingly violating the immigration law, which, if imposed, would mean that even spouses of some villagers would end up being heavily fined or behind bars. I asked the Palestinian mayor whether he knew the dentist with two wives, and what would happen to him if he decided to spend the wrong night on the wrong side with the wrong wife! He laughed and said, "My own life isn't any less complicated or, for foreign journalists like you, less newsworthy! Here's a story for you: my wife is Israeli Arab, an ethnic Palestinian who was given an Israeli passport because her family is from the northern Arab triangle within Israel proper. So the children are 'Israeli' too, I can't pick them up after school, as it is on the Israeli side. I am not allowed to drive my car with Palestinian number plates into 'Israel,' which is the other half of the village."

"I suppose your wife picks them up every day?"

"Yes, then they come home to have dinner and sleep *illegally* in their Palestinian home!"

Barta'a's mayors on the Green Line (Courtesy Alban Biaussat)

The mayor said, "Do you know what happens if an Israeli citizen is arrested for going to the Palestinian territories?"

"No, what happens?"

"He is fined two thousand shekels, which is nearly five hundred dollars."

"So the total fine for your four children and your wife on any day could amount to two thousand five hundred dollars?" I asked the mayor.

"Yes. And not only that, we can't even travel together. A few times that we went abroad, I had to travel to Amman, the Jordanian capital, to board a plane from there, while my wife and children flew from Ben Gurion."

Following the age-old tradition, Mayor Ghassan Kabha had married a cousin, who was from the Israeli side of the village and was a cousin of the mayor of Israeli Barta'a. Straddled between Israel and the Palestinian territories, Barta'a's residents on either side were not technically allowed to visit their cousins, aunts, and other members of the family.

One of my earliest memories was of a wedding between a man from West Bengal called Shanti—we used to call him Shantikaka, Uncle Shanti—and a woman, Reshmi (which means "silken"), across the river Bhairab from Bangladesh, the Eastern half of Bengal. It was a secret affair because it was not only a marriage between two people of different nationalities but also an interreligious one, with Shantikaka being Hindu and Reshmi, Muslim. They first met in the village market where at the time there were no visible border police, amid the displays of terra-cotta idols and silken bangles. All the children knew about their secret dalliances in a nearby field of bright yellow mustard flowers, and I could still remember that in return for keeping our mouths shut, we received from the cross-border lovers handfuls of *batasha*, the sugary wafers that were traditionally offered to the temple gods, which the lovers would buy from the market to appease a bunch of godless little monsters before heading for the fields.

The village of Barta'a stood astride the slopes of a valley called Wadi Elmia. One day in 1949, the residents woke up to the new reality that they were no longer allowed to cross the valley to go over to the other side. The west of the valley now belonged to the new state of Israel, and the east, to Jordan. Along the valley the so-called armistice line or the

Green Line was drawn; it became the new border between Israel and the Jordanian-controlled West Bank. Overnight, members of the same family, friends, and relatives were torn apart. One of the villagers told me that he was then six years old but had vivid memories.

"I still remember that once we wanted to see our aunt who was on the Israeli side. My father tried to cut through the barbed-wire border fence to give his sister a present. But the Jordanian soldiers spotted and stopped us. He couldn't deliver the present and so we stood on a hill closest to the valley. My aunt was also standing on a high place across the valley on the other side, and we were frantically waving at her, shouting, 'Aunt, my aunt, come closer, we want to see you!'"

After the summer war of 1967, when Israel occupied the formerly Jordanian-controlled West Bank, the border fence between the two Barta'as was lifted and the Kabhas hoped that at long last they would be reunited. They were, but not for long. The first intifada, the Palestinian uprising in the late 1980s, led to tougher Israeli restrictions, which meant that free passage between the two villages was no longer permitted. And the second intifada in 2000 made it more difficult, almost impossible, to get permits for families who were caught on the wrong side of the border to visit relatives.

So, what would the ideal solution be for the Kabhas in Barta'a, so that the cousins could unite again beyond the borderline? I asked the Palestinian mayor, Ghassan Kabha.

"I want Barta'a to be one united village," he said. "It will not bother me to which country—Palestine or Israel—the village belongs. I'll be Palestinian wherever I am."

His Israeli counterpart and cousin, Riyad Kabha, expressed a more sublime vision for Barta'a: "I think the ideal solution would be for the village to become part of a union. One village, one local council, and it must be self-ruled. Let's say, it would become like a 'theme park' belonging to two states. Perhaps we could be a model for future for the entire country!"

This was one of the proposed solutions from the Bengali intelligentsia for uniting the Bengalis right after the partition of India in 1947, and once again after the creation of Bangladesh in 1971. But people on both sides had since moved farther and farther away from that dream, and now it would seem impossible from looking at the nationalistic politics in the subcontinent that Bengal would ever be reunited. Also, many from the older generation who kept the dream alive for many decades since partition hoping that one day they would return to the homes that they had left behind—the guava orchard, the white mansion, the fishpond in the backyard with an emerald body of water full of ancient carp—had already died or were too frail to go on dreaming.

"Come on, lady," said Fida (I would soon grow fond of her calling me "lady"). "We have to go and look for the doctor."

"Doctor . . . who?" I asked absentmindedly.

"Our Doctor Who, he has one wife here and one over there, across the valley." She laughed.

"Such a person really exists?! I thought you and the mayor were joking."

"Of course not!" said Fida. "Not only wives, there are places where the valley merges into the market, where people have homes with their bedrooms in Israel and the kitchen and sitting room in Palestine!"

"That must be taken as an example for a perfect one-state solution!" I said jokingly as I tried to grasp the bizarre reality in Barta'a.

Fida said, "Do you really believe the Jews want to share the same country, this country, with the Palestinians?"

"I think when the time comes they would be left with no choice. When you've demographically outnumbered them."

"When will the time come? They are waiting for the Messiah, then we'll all become Jews, you too!" Wisecracking again.

I became careful not to say anything that might give away that I already belonged to a Jewish family. I did not want to lose my friendship with this very special woman who with such extraordinary sarcasm challenged the political absurdities of her country. Because I felt (although later I would be proved wrong) that had she known my Jewish connection she would not so openly express her views about the Jews and the Israeli policy.

As we walked from the mayor's office along the valley toward the market, Fida said that even the shrewd Israeli politicians were caught in their own legal trap, as they did not know what to do with places like Barta'a where the law defies itself and enforcing it would be violating the most basic human rights such as taking children away from their parents—even the mayor of Palestinian Barta'a would not be exempt from it. She went on, "I was born and grew up in the northern Israeli town of Umm al-Fahm—it's not far from Barta'a, we can drop by if you like on our way back— but I live in Israel on short-term renewable visas. Because my father had married a woman, my mother, from the adjacent Palestinian town of Tulkarem in the 1970s before securing an Israeli passport. So we are all floating aliens in Israel. Like a tourist, I am required to renew my "residency permit" every year, the current one will run out in four months. And a Jewish lawyer friend of mine, Tamar, she is actually my flatmate, whose Tunisian father immigrated to Israel from France in the 1980s to fulfill his Zionist dream, represents me in court to get me proper papers so that I can live in *my* country. How do you find it, then, lady, an immigrant's daughter is representing an indigenous resident to secure her birthright to remain in her country! This is what will one day bring down the state of Israel, which is built on lies and biblical fantasy. If all else, I mean international pressure, peace protocol, etc., fail to move Israel from its current stance, this violation of human rights in black and white will lead to Israel's downfall."

.11.

FIDA AND TAMAR

Every cuisine tells a story. Jewish food tells the story of an uprooted, migrating people and their vanished worlds. It lives in people's minds and has been kept alive because of what it evokes and represents. My own world disappeared forty years ago, but it has remained powerful in my imagination. When you are cut off from your past, the past takes a stronger hold on your emotions.

—*Claudia Roden*, The Book of Jewish Food

The friendship that we developed in the divided village of Barta'a would defy all my fears of the first encounter that Fida would not want to know me beyond our work relation. A few weeks later she invited me to spend the weekend with her in Ein Karem.

The former Arab village in southwest Jerusalem had been gentrified in recent years and was now home to elite Jerusalemite artists, lawyers, and politicians. But there were

on the fringes still some houses left, unrefurbished and untouched since they had been abandoned by the Palestinian
refugees in 1948, which had subsequently gone to Jewish
refugees from the Arab world. Now the quaint little houses
were rented out to students and young professionals. Fida
shared a small apartment with Tamar, a left-wing Israeli
lawyer who was actively involved in representing Palestinians who the authorities said were not entitled, for "security
reasons," to formal "papers" to reside in Israel.

It was Friday afternoon and Fida was cooking the famous mouth-watering za'atar dough balls made with freshly
picked thyme from the fields. From where I stood in the
veranda, I could smell the wild herbs from the valley. The
apartment had one-meter-thick walls and a huge unkempt
garden with a hanging patio overlooking the vast wooded
valley and terraced hills. As I stood there leaning forward
supporting myself against the iron railings, a woman with
long blond hair came and stood next to me. She was smoking a cigarette and wearing hippie colors, bright and psy-
chedelic. We had already met a few weeks earlier, in a
popular liberal West Jerusalem bar called Dewan, where
Fida had invited her friends to a live music event by a Palestinian DJ. But this was the first time that I had seen her
in daylight.

"Who built these terraces on the slopes of these hills,
geometrically so perfect?" I asked, not particularly addressing either Tamar or Fida.

"The Palestinians, of course," said Tamar, a chain-
smoker, through a smokescreen, through which she looked

older. I already knew that she was several years younger than me.

"Traditionally the landowners, who were mostly Christian, lived atop the hills, and the Muslim farmers lived in the valley," Tamar continued, looking at the vista spread out magnificently before us. "They farmed on the rain-locked fertile terraces vegetables and fruit for generations, until we came. The European Jews didn't know terraced farming, and the Arab Jews who had settled in Ein Karem before the gentrification were not farmers. Jews who came from the Arab world were mostly tradesmen and tailors, as they were usually not allowed to own land. They knew how to make money, deal with gold and banking, but not how to sow seeds. Farming is relatively new in modern Jewish culture."

I looked more closely and saw that the old stones that had once lined the edges and kept the terraces separated from one another in a neat order of steps had come off in various places. The remnants of old almond orchards were visible where the stones still held on to the earth.

"No one picks those almonds. Every year they rot in the trees, before the trees bloom again. We, the Jewish settlers in these hills, do not know how to pick, dry, and process almonds," Tamar said, with the afternoon sun glowing on her face and in her flowing hair. As I admired her suntanned complexion and her unusually long, golden hair, she saw something in my eyes, in my silent scrutiny.

"I don't belong here, do I, with my hair, my blue eyes? Is that what you are thinking?" Tamar's lawyer's eyes looked directly into mine, as if she were trying to fathom my hidden reservations.

"No one has a monopoly over a particular piece of land in this world forever. It is about respect, so long as you don't vandalize what the bygones have left behind: the houses, monuments, mosques, and churches, so long as you don't desecrate their memories in these hills, I don't see any problem in either of us being here," I said, thinking of a particular abandoned "Hindu" house in Bangladesh with the ancient tulasi, sacred basil, now home to a Muslim family that continued to benefit from the basil as a medicinal plant, using the leaves to ward off colds. "So long as you don't obliterate the past, and in some way preserve the memories and the rituals of the people who had been here before, there's no need to feel you don't belong."

But then in a series of cinematic flashbacks, the senseless vandalism that had taken place after the creation of the Jewish state flickered before my eyes from many of my historical, "educational" weekend tours of Palestine: demolished houses, desecrated cemeteries, defaced mausoleums, neglected Muslim and Christian monuments. The Jewish state was exclusively for the Jews. The Promised Land for the Jews only. I looked at Tamar again on the patio against the background of the lush hills of olive, almond, and thyme. I felt enormous admiration for her, for having the courage to question her entitlement to this land.

Tamar, as Fida's lawyer, represented her in court proceedings that evaluated Fida's entitlement to citizenship in her own country. All Palestinians have a difficult status, but Fida's family has a uniquely awkward one. Her father, who was from the northern Israeli village of Umm al-Fahm, fled with his parents to Kuwait during the Arab-Israeli War of 1948. He came back after the 1967 Six-Day War when Israel annexed the West Bank, but he was denied an Israeli passport for fleeing to "the enemy territory" during the war.

I understood that Fida and Tamar's relationship was fraught with dependency, duty, and guilt. Fida needed Tamar to get residency papers so that she could go on living in the place where she was born. And Tamar needed Fida to overcome her guilt for living in an abandoned Arab house in an abandoned Arab village on confiscated Palestinian land.

"Fida is my justification for living in this 'occupied' Arab home," Tamar confirmed my conjecture. "I wouldn't be here without her. Look at this house, look how airy and cool it feels, compare this to the new houses built by the Jews. Palestinians knew how to build homes that would be cool in hot summer months and warm in cold Jerusalem winters. These thick walls retain heat. Once you've put the radiator on for a couple of hours, the heat is trapped within these walls for days. Why would I want to live in one of those flimsy new red-roofed European houses built by the Jewish immigrants who had no experience in living in such a climate? But then how could I, a Jewish human rights lawyer, have justified living in occupied Palestinian property? Because Fida is here, she keeps the balance, the memories of her people alive. The weight of guilt is lessened."

Tamar's voice was emotionally charged as she, as I understood, tried to make sense of what she had just said first and foremost to herself.

We did not say anything for a long time, the three of us just stood there trying to pull strands from our own interpretation of history, roots, banishment, and entitlement, and weave our own visions for life. I had my own pangs of homelessness, but they were wrapped in a romantic image that I had created for myself since I left Bengal. I did not want to live in a Bengali-majority place; I wanted to spread out and absorb the "other." Although at times it was tinged with a splash of self-pity, being a minority was also like belonging to a special status, which meant that I did not have to conform to the status quo, I could let loose my idiosyncrasies, and people would just say that I was a little peculiar and blame it on my alienness. I mostly enjoyed my unique place in various societies that I had lived in since leaving my Bengali home.

I did not envy the lives of these two new, very important friends, standing on either side of me on this beautiful terrace. One grew up as a refugee in her own country hating the settler-occupier, and the other, with the knowledge that she was a settler in the place that she called home. This knowledge took away the innocence of her youth that most of us elsewhere in the world took for granted. Barely thirty years old, Tamar worked around the clock, her phone rang constantly, and she would talk to her clients any time of the day or night. She was perpetually on call. They both had to grow up too quickly and, in the words of the Palestinian poet Mourid Barghouti, "childhood fell from their hand, before they became adults."

After a while Tamar said, "I have to go and see my dad, I usually have the Shabbat lunch with him. You must come one day to eat his famous couscous. He does it with chicken and merguez sausages. He's originally from Tunisia, by the way, well, via France." I watched Tamar in her multi-colored dress walk down the steps to her car, which was parked right below the house on the street that skirted the edge of the cliff winding down to the left toward the valley of thyme, za'atar, and rosemary, and to the right, uphill, to the Ein Karem village center with gourmet restaurants and boutiques.

The path from Fida and Tamar's roadside house wound gradually down right to the heart of the valley. In spring, with the blooming of the lupins, the meadows here turned into a sea of purple. In early summer, the purple turned to yellow; the fruit of the lupins were disk shaped, a great quantity of which could be seen being boiled in huge vats of brine at Jerusalem's Old City gates and at various junctions in the West Bank, bus stops, and checkpoints. Palestinians called them *turmus*, to which many were addicted. People walked in the street or waited long hours at Israeli check-points, popping the salty turmus in their mouths. After the falafel, the deep-fried chickpea balls in pita pockets, boiled lupin pods probably came second as a street snack.

Fida and I were walking through the lupin fields, toward the center of the valley where she said the za'atar thrived. She needed the herb for her baked dough parcels.

"This is the only place that I would call home. So, officially, I don't have a home," Fida said stoically and grappled for some moments with distracted reflections on the Great Loss of her ancestral land, before continuing. "Also, this land to me is no different from the produce of its soil. For me Palestine is synonymous to za'atar, parsley, sage, almonds, and olives. The Palestinian people are like the olive trees—no matter how much you try to prune them, uproot them, try to burn them down, the next season new shoots will grow and new roots will spread deep into the soft soil after the winter rains."

When Fida and I arrived at the first za'atar bush, she said in a trembling voice, "Each olive tree they uproot because of their security wall, and replant to decorate their road islands and roundabouts, the deeper our connection to the land grows. The uprooted tree will grow back in its new habitat, to replenish the memories of the refugees. And so even if the internationals, the peace industry, and the Israelis learnt to forget the Right of Return of the refugees, the ancient plants would rewrite on the Palestinian soil the stories of those people living in refugee camps and in exile all over the Middle East and elsewhere."

I thought it sounded extremely romantic. Her voice was euphoric. Nostalgia, pangs of loss created a mist of hope among the exiled, a longing to return to a homeland whose political entity no longer existed.

"How do you feel living in Ein Karem, as a tenant under a Jewish landlord?" I asked Fida. I knew I should have avoided or changed the subject, as the atmosphere was getting gloomier and politically charged.

Fida looked up to cast her dark, sad eyes over the terraced hills and said, "It is actually *Ain* Karem, *Ain* with a guttural Arabic 'Ain.' The European Ashkenazi Jews have adulterated the sound of *Ain*, which also exists in the original, old Hebrew alphabet. So now in modern Ashkenazi Hebrew the *Ain* is pronounced as *Ein*."

"Does it matter?" I said.

"What?"

"The names of places?"

"Yes," said Fida. "Why should *Ain* Karem be *Ein* Karem? Just to suit the European tongue?"

She made long strides among the bushes, and I watched her thin, elongated arms stretch over the young shoots of the wild herb; in swift movements, she pinched off the newest top leaves. Her black plastic bag was now bursting with the flavor of the valley.

"*Yallah*," said Fida, "let's go and make some food." She looked up and smiled. She tied the plastic bag and stretched her arms sideways and up as if to embrace a 180-degree vista of the hills and the valley.

The rest of the afternoon we avoided talking about land politics and concentrated instead on making za'atar parcels. She mentioned several times that this was an age-old recipe that she was following as she washed the leaves, crushed them, and mixed them with garlic, coarse salt, and olive oil. She prepared the pastry in swift movements, her elegant fingers pressing the dough hard and sprinkling salt and water in it, kneading the mixture until it became soft and elastic. There was a certain amount of urgency, nervousness in the way she kneaded the dough, cut out the pastry, and filled each parcel with the salt, za'atar, and garlic mix. There was something very ritualistic about it, as if she were stuffing the memories of the Palestinians who had once lived in the valley into those dough parcels. She glazed them in olive oil and egg yolk before putting them in the oven.

"This is how my mother folds them," said Fida.

"And your mother must have learnt from your grandmother," I said.

"She must have done." Fida went to the oven to turn over the first batch. The baked aroma of olive oil and marjoram filled the small kitchen.

"What is it about food, why do people keep their culinary tradition alive wherever they go? Why is food such an important medium through which to remember the past? The roots? Tradition? Home?" I said, not expecting a reply.

"Well, the memories of food are all that the displaced people have left. The best way to remember a lost world is to reconstruct the family dinner table. These za'atar parcels have a bit of the history of this valley trapped inside. Come, have one, close your eyes and tell me what you see."

Fida offered me one, very hot, fresh from the oven. I did not close my eyes but could easily visualize the ghosts of the recent past smiling at us from the alcoves of her Arab house. I could see the farmers who had just come home after tending the almond orchards and the olive groves, to taste the warm snack sitting by the kitchen fire with the rest of the family. In the late afternoon light that flooded Fida and Tamar's lovely patio, my thoughts went to many other immigrants and displaced people all over the world who remembered the life they left behind through food.

"Can I tell you about a famous English Jewish cookbook writer?" I said to Fida. "Her name is Claudia Roden. Her family came from Egypt. She wrote books on Egyptian and other Middle Eastern Jewish food, because that is all she says, is left to her of her ancestors who immigrated to Europe. Similar to what you've just said."

The current setting took a hold on my emotions. I told Fida that I had sort of a Jewish family and that my Jewish husband's whole life had been devoted to realizing a dream: that while the exiled Palestinians must *all* return, the Jews who are here should also have the right to remain.

.12.

THE LEGAL ALIEN

For almost two years we lived in this country on three-month renewable tourist visas, including Leo, because it was the easiest of the available options. He was of course entitled to make aliya, a Jew returning, under Israel's Law of Return, which meant that Leo, the children, and I as his spouse were entitled to live in Israel indefinitely. He, however, declined this privilege. "I cannot be part of the Israeli state until it is shared with the Palestinians as equals," had consistently been his position and so we did not go for the most obvious option: to become Israeli citizens. The second option was to get a work visa, and we were considering applying for it. The most popular option for Western Europeans and North Americans to stay and work on short-term NGO projects in Israel was to leave the country every three months in order to come back again. One could not just take the bus to Sinai in Egypt or cross the Allenby Bridge to Jordan, because one received only one-month visas at land borders. One was required to fly out of the country and return through Ben Gurion airport to obtain the three-month entry permit. During the past two years we flew to Cairo and Amman (Israel's only two peace partners in the region), to Calcutta and Dhaka (so that the children did not forget that they were half Bengali), and of course to London on holidays. The departures and arrivals were fraught with long, frustrating security procedures, which, despite being more bearable for those with Jewish connections, often left me angry and powerless.

The easiest way to get through airport security was to establish one's Jewish link right at the start, if of course one had any. The Israeli security at the time labeled passengers with various color-coded stickers, the colors changed every few months or so, so that people would not be able to guess under which category the system had logged them in its secret files. However, after traveling a few times during the first year, I came to believe that at least for that year the colors signified these specifications:

Pink: Jewish or those with Jewish connection, like our family.

Green: Jewish sympathizers and righteous gentiles.

White: Other foreigners not posing any security threats.

Purple: Foreigners who are potential security risks because they work in the Palestinian territories.

Orange: Foreigners posing possible security threats because they have Arabic or Arabic-sounding names, which may include Arab Christians. Or those who have stamps on their passports from any of the "enemy" states, such as Syria, Iraq, Lebanon, Sudan. (Once the children and I were given pink all-clear stickers, but Leo was held for hours with an orange because he had Lebanese stamps on his passport. He did not yet have a second passport for Israel only.)

Red: Palestinians. All Palestinians were considered collectively a major threat to Israel's national security.

Which meant that even the Palestinian chief of staff, who had a British wife, was strip-searched every time he traveled through Ben Gurion airport to visit his wife and children in England.

"If you are okay to allow me to go and see your prime minister Olmert when we have scheduled meetings as part of the peace negotiations and I am not strip-searched before entering the PM's residence, surely, you could let me fly without putting me through this?" Rafiq al-Husseini would routinely say to his interrogator while standing in a cubicle in his underwear. He said that he often traveled to Amman to fly to London from there, as that spared him the humiliation.

When our turn came to face the airport security, Maya usually did most of the talking, and it would be over in minutes. But sometimes I could not help poking at the country's absurd Kafkaesque security apparatus. Like the time when we were flying to England for Rosh Hashanah, the Jewish New Year.

The young officer had bright eyes and a professional smile. We were the last people in the long queue and our plane was leaving in forty minutes. To speed things up, he walked to us and asked, "*Ivrit ou Anglit?*"

He was asking whether he should speak Hebrew or English.

My daughter answered in her perfect accent, "*Ivrit.*"

The professional seriousness of the young officer immediately turned into a warmer grin.

"*Bemet?* Really," he said. "Where did you learn your Hebrew from?"

"In my school. We are going to London to see my *saba ve safta.*"

"Where do your grandparents live?"

"In Huish."

"Where is it?"

"In London."

To Maya, London and the UK were synonymous. I told the officer that Huish was a sleepy village in Wiltshire. He turned toward me and focused on the more specific standard "security" questions.

"So your family lives in England?"

"Yes."

"What are their names?"

After numerous passages through Ben Gurion airport, I was no longer surprised by these invasive questions about one's family because I knew what the officer wanted to find out. I dithered for a second. Should I delay the process, tease him and not come up with what he wanted to know? I told him their first names, which didn't give away anything.

"*Shem Mishpakha?*" Their family names?

I gave him their postwar names, which had no trace of Jewishness.

I enjoyed watching his expression change. He became more solemn, and the previously relaxed facial muscles tightened in pursuit of "the real truth" that Israeli security was so keen on finding out. The interrogator must establish his subject's ethnoreligious origin. I already knew what the next questions would be, and so instead of telling him what he wanted to hear, I prepared myself with meandering answers. This would delay the procedure, but I couldn't deprive myself of a little sport.

"Do your parents-in-law or you and your husband belong to a community?"

"Of course we belong to our community."

"No, I mean do they belong to a congregation?"

"I don't understand you."

But I perfectly understood him. He wanted to know whether we were members of a synagogue, a church, or a mosque.

"Do they go to the village congregation where they live in England?"

"They live in a sleepy English village. I don't think they have any congregation of any sort there. There's a village fair, though, every summer. And there's also a farmers' market from time to time. And occasional weddings. But most of the young people have gone to live in the city so weddings are far and few."

We had twenty minutes to catch the plane. But the course of communication that I had frivolously started, to wind up the interrogator, had gone too far. I felt that it was now too late to alter the course. I could have just said, "My husband's family belongs to the liberal Jewish synagogue in north London. I have been to that synagogue numerous times, on Yom Kippur, Rosh Hashanah, and Passover."

I looked around me and saw that the faces of the Palestinian passengers could hardly suppress their amusement at my deliberate noncooperation with the racist system. The interrogator would have ceased his questioning immediately had we satisfied him with our "appropriate" religious adherence to Judaism. I could not let my pride be crushed by the young Israeli security representative with bright penetrating eyes. The faces of those around me, mostly Arabs and some Filipino and Sri Lankan domestic workers who stood in long lines for many hours, stopped me from giving him the answers that he wanted to hear. As if the true answer would turn me into an opportunist in their eyes, although that would take me through the security checks without a fuss.

"Have you heard of anything called a 'Torah group'?"

"No."

"Where did you meet your husband?"

"In England."

"Where in England?"

"In London."

"Where in London?"

"Near Russell Square."

"In a particular gathering?"

"Yes, there were a lot of people around us at the university bar."

"So you met in a bar?"

"Yes."

"Which university?"

"London University."

"When did you move to Israel?"

"Two years ago."

"Do you belong to a congregation here, in Israel?"

"What are you getting at?"

"Try and answer my question." (They don't use the word "please.")

"Why can't you ask clearly what you want to hear?" I said in a low but firm voice.

"You tell me then what I want to hear." His voice was calm too, although I could hear a suppressed tremor.

"You want to know whether I or my family are Jewish. But you can't bring yourself to ask that directly, because it is not allowed under the 'democratic' charter that Israel reluctantly subscribes to as part of an international agreement. But . . ." I swallowed the rest of my sentence. "You are acting like a xenophobe anyway, you are waiting with a yellow star which, once you are satisfied with my answers, you will stick on my arm . . ."

The security officer's face hardened, but he was determined not to lose his cool. It was I whose voice was beginning to thicken and quiver, in anger and frustration at the sheer power that the young man standing before me held over thousands of people passing through the terminal. I could feel the powerlessness of the travelers who were held and interrogated for hours for possessing names such as Mo-hammed, Ahmed, Hasan, Salma, and for having any of the "Arab" countries between the Euphrates and the Mediterra-nean as the place of birth in their passports. The Palestin-ians were automatically the bearers of red stickers and were routinely searched, stripped, and questioned. But I was also thinking of all the other people with Arabic-sounding names, which included Arab Christians and even many Sephardic Jews who originated in the Arab Middle East.

There I was, standing with my half-Jewish daughter who spoke fluent Hebrew, and we held the unwanted privi-lege to pass through security without such humiliation. Without having to strip or to wait in the queue for hours. I was lucky that I did not, nor did my daughter, possess names that would place us on the list of "threats."

"Do you or your husband's family belong to a religious congregation in England? Like a synagogue, church?"

Ah! I thought, he had at last come around to what he had all along been waiting for. He finally shook off his cloak of formality. I felt calmer. I had won.

"My daddy takes me and my brother to the synagogue in Jerusalem on Shabbat," announced my daughter as I looked him in the eye, the claimant to democracy in a para-noid regime obsessed with racial profiling.

"What's the name of your synagogue, *hamouda?*" The interrogator asked Maya, in a softer tone. The muscles on his face had relaxed and his eyes had widened to make room for a smile.

"I don't know the name, but I made a honey pot there for Rosh Hashanah. We put real honey there. My daddy cut apples to dip into the honey."

My daughter's Jewish heritage was impeccably confirmed and the interrogation stopped abruptly. We posed no threat whatsoever to Israel. The helmsman of "Jewish democracy" escorted us through the second phase of security checks. We had less than fifteen minutes to run for the plane, but I knew that we would not miss it, now that we were proven members of the Great Jewish Family. I did not show any sign of satisfaction or gratitude as he said, addressing Maya, "Little one, did you pack your bags yourself?"

"My mummy did when I was asleep."

"That's fine." Then he turned toward me. I saw his sharp Ashkenazi eyes. They stared at me fiercely, as if to reprimand me for subversive behavior.

"Do you understand why I'm asking these questions . . . to make sure that no one has put anything in your bag that might be a bomb. Did you pack your bags yourself? Has anyone given you anything to carry as a present for someone?"

"You are asking if Mummy has a bomb in her bag? Why should anyone put a bomb in her bag?" Maya asked. She looked shocked. I could feel Kiran behind me, struggling not to kick his precocious little sister. He was asked by the officer to take his headphones out of his ears and he was furious that he had to listen to Maya.

"Yes to the first and no to the second question," I said to him and waited. But he was satisfied with us and did not need to continue with this line of questioning.

"Take your bags straight to the fast bag drop counter. You haven't much time before the plane leaves," said the officer as he put white stickers (our *yellow stars*!) with specific numbers that embedded a secret code, which dispelled all security risks, on our suitcases and passports. The security officer, however, made a point this time by giving me a white sticker: "other foreigners not posing any security threats," instead of pink, which was given to those with Jewish family connection. I wondered if it was a mild warning, for challenging the interrogator and wasting his time. He yelled at an attendant to supply us with an "all-clear" tag. He then moved to the next person in the queue and opened a booklet of stickers that contained color-coded labels for ethnic profiling.

"Do we not have to have our bags X-rayed?" I asked, rather bewildered, as I felt guilty proceeding toward the bag drop desk when so many others were queuing up at the X-ray machine. When rows of "suspicious" bags were lifted and placed on a long bench to be opened and hand-checked before their owners were authorized to check in.

"No, you proceed straight to the fast check-in counter and pick up your boarding cards," said the first officer, who shook hands with Maya. "Bye, *hamouda*, it was great to have met you. Look after your mummy."

The people in the queue, some of them presumably with names like Mohammed or Ahmed, looked at me with blank eyes as my children and I, displaying the correct stickers, dragged our bags and our legs toward the counter. I no longer had the courage to reject the special status that had been bestowed upon us. My brief show of rebellion had been defused by the selfish worries of an opportunistic traveler who could not bear missing her plane.

There I was, a South Asian alien, passing through Ben Gurion airport without having to go through even standard security measures. This time I played my cards well, thanks to my babbling half-Jewish daughter.

.13.

THE STREET OF
THE JEWISH
BATTALION

My days in the cavelike house on Hagedud Ha'Ivri, the Street of the Jewish Battalion, were turning gloomier now that the brief winter and rain had descended over Jerusalem. I decided to do no more than one feature a week for the BBC so that I had enough free time to do some writing. I was also taking private Hebrew lessons and had enrolled in an intensive Arabic course at Al-Quds University in East Jerusalem.

I found myself staying in more, and I started to feel the dampness around me, which intensified as the weather grew colder and wetter. Winter in Jerusalem is treacherous, as the houses are not geared to fight the freezing wind, rains, and even occasional snow—we had three inches of snow when we first arrived. But at the time we were living in a more comfortable and much grander house with central heating in Emek Rafaim. Our house on Hagedud Ha'Ivri, just half a kilometer south of Emek Rafaim, was more modest and older. Leo wanted to go to a place with more rooted "local" people. Our new neighborhood was moderately religious. We felt guilty driving on Shabbat while the streets around us were thronged with families and children in their best white clothes going to the synagogue. The house at first had seemed enchanting, and throughout the summer we had lots of garden parties. When the weather turned really hot in August, the cave with its lovely mosaic on the wall and the flower-patterned tiles on the floor was cool and sanctuarylike.

Leo was locked in his study in the far end of the house writing reports on the Hamas takeover of the Palestinian Authority, while I wrote, did my weekly feature for the BBC, bathed, washed, and put the children to bed. We had very little private interaction. In a way it was good, as we both wanted to forget the incident with the lawyer and the fallout from our dispute with Orli. Her name was not to be mentioned in the house in Leo's presence, even the children knew that. Although I had made new friends through work, and through Fida, I became cautious about how much information about my family I shared with them. I kept my distance with the new friends.

On a usual day, Kiran would take the bus to school by seven thirty and I would leave the house a little later with Maya. Life seemed static, without a buzz. The "cave" needed artificial lighting twenty-four hours a day and I felt that I was living in a timeless zone. I would run my life around a ticking clock, as it was not possible to tell the time of day sitting in my "study" in the corner of the bedroom.

The kitchen and the sitting room were even more devoid of daylight than the front of the house where my study-bedroom was. I started skipping lunch, as it depressed me to walk into the darker chambers of the house where I would be startled by the sound of my own footsteps. The whole place echoed, and the heat emitted by electric radiators was not enough. I worked with my daughter's hot water bottle on my lap and two radiators on either side of my desk with the door firmly closed.

Until three. Then it was time to run for the bus to arrive at the YMCA in time to pick up Maya. That was the highlight of my day, to sit with her on the bus and during the half-hour journey to hear her story, or stories. After almost twenty months in this city she was as vivacious as ever, full of questions and contradictions concerning the place where we lived and what determined the fate of our little family and influenced that of the entire world in one way or another.

Amos, Leo's cousin, came to babysit from time to time. He had finished his compulsory service in the army and had also completed the "normalization" holiday— traveling for three months in South America. He was looking for work but could not find any or did not know the kind of work he wanted to do. He had been trying various things. Through fellow Israeli soldiers posted in Gaza, he had started an ingenious business: he employed

Palestinian women in Gaza to knit kippah, which he sold
in the markets in Jerusalem for probably ten times the
price they cost him. But after the Israelis moved out of
Gaza following the summer disengagement, his business
collapsed. In November, just before Sukkot, the Feast
of Tabernacles, he had a temporary business: importing
palm fronds (used on this religious occasion) from Jordan
and selling them at an extortionately high price in Israel.
He made a fair amount of money there, but all his projects were short-lived or seasonal: the kippah business collapsed because of political changes, and the importing of
palm fronds was for only the one week of Sukkot.

So he called babysitting a transitional job before finding
a new business venture. I liked Amos, there was openness,
total transparency about him. While he loved his country
and would give up his life for it, he had no illusions about
the army. He openly admitted that as an individual in the
army, he had carried out commands that would be seen as
violations of human rights. He did not deny that he inter-
fered in the basic privacy of ordinary Palestinians by raid-
ing their homes in the middle of the night, terrorizing the
children, who would be rounded up and interrogated while
his colleagues would search for "terrorists." He did, from
time to time, question his actual conduct but did not have the
courage to challenge the order of his commander. The call of
duty was ultimately greater than his sense of social justice for
the Palestinians. His primary duty was to the state of Israel,
which, contrary to his moral scruples, he believed God had
assigned to the Jews. He liked talking about his operations

in the army. He said that during incursions into the territory, say, Nablus, he would never touch personal belongings of a family. He said that there would be radios, personal computers, jewelry all lying around under his very eyes but neither he nor his colleagues would touch any. He said that he even shared, during a long siege, food with the family, with the father or brother or uncle or son of the elusive terrorist.

I, however, heard different stories from the besieged men and women in the Palestinian territories. I heard constant complaints about raiders taking small and portable valuables; they also trashed the place, throwing things everywhere, breaking plates and pots and pulling out vegetables in the garden. Amos described himself as a good soldier. He only did his duty, he said, which did not include trashing the house of the suspected terrorist. He told me that during one of his operations, after he was ordered to empty all the contents of a chest of drawers for clues to the supposed terrorist's whereabouts, he caused laughter among his fellow soldiers when he started folding the suspect's clothes and putting his papers and things back in the drawers. I liked to think of Amos as the "good soldier Švejk."

By having Amos babysit I was also trying to maintain a regular link to my husband's cousins. After all, they were the only family we had in Jerusalem and it was important for the children to know them. Kiran was very fond of Amos, who was a master of card tricks that he said he had learnt and practiced during "those long night shifts in the army when keeping alert needs the self-control of a yogi. But I had my cards!" he said.

With Amos in the house in the evening, I was able occasionally to escape from the house on the Street of the Jewish Battalion in the neighborhood of Katamon. Fierce clashes had taken place here during the War of 1948. "The battle of Katamon," as it came to be known, saw the overthrow of the Palestinian fighters who from the surrounding houses (probably from ours too) were putting up a bloody resistance to the Jewish Legion. Soon after the battle was won and over, all the names of the streets around where we lived were changed and renamed after the leaders of the Jewish terrorist cells that sabotaged trains, bombed hotels (including Jerusalem's landmark King David Hotel), and killed those who they thought resisted the creation of the modern world's first Jewish state, including the UN peace mediator.

Amos's presence was important as it gave me some freedom of movement outside school hours. Once a week I went to Ramallah to visit Fida, who had stopped commuting from Jerusalem after an unfortunate but inevitable falling-out with Tamar. She was sleeping in the house of her new boyfriend, Mahmud, who worked in the office of the Palestinian leader, Abu Mazen.

The dreariness of the winter in my cave house, Fida's departure from Jerusalem, Leo's frenetic work and absences, and the fast-emerging sense of purposelessness set off a lethargic weariness inside me. I did not feel as upbeat as I did in the beginning of my BBC freelancing. Somehow it seemed that I was pathetically trying to put back together my professional life that was shredded to hopeless pieces. I was not happy.

So when Fida called one evening to invite me to eat with her at Darna, one of Ramallah's best-known restaurants, I jumped at the opportunity to escape the gloom of the house. I felt free in Ramallah—from moral dilemmas and the repetitiveness of my vindication of the choices I had made, from the niggling question why I was still living in Jerusalem in an unreachable marriage. If I was feeling so pathetically depressed about it, why didn't I just pack my bags and leave? The short drive—just twenty minutes from my house to the checkpoint—took me to a totally different world. The drive into Ramallah was in itself an experience of the unique, frustrating dynamic—the lack of communication between the Israelis and the Palestinians.

At Al Ram checkpoint, the Israeli border guard asked me, "Where are you going?"

"Ramallah."

"Why?"

"To have dinner."

"Dinner?"

"Yes! Do you have a problem with that?"

"Strange!" said the young soldier. He called his female colleague, who had fierce eyes (female soldiers made me more skittish than their male counterparts), and said, "Look, this lady is going to Ramallah *to have dinner*! Why, don't we have good restaurants here?"

"You don't have stuffed pigeon and arak-filled nargila," I said, to their amusement.

"Have a good day, madam."

The soldier waved me through. I cast a furtive glance at his female companion and felt nervous again seeing her face expressionless and hard as a meteorite, perhaps only a hydraulic drill would succeed in digging up some sparks.

One time on my way to Ramallah, just as I was about to leave the house, Amos too had expressed curiosity and disbelief at my going to the Palestinian city to see friends, socialize, and eat.

"Do they have fun there?"

"What do you mean?"

"I mean do they have any restaurants, bars where you can drink?"

"Of course they have bars and restaurants and coffee shops, and the streets are full of people at all hours of the day or night. The streets there are livelier than they are in Jerusalem's city center and people lead a more normal life. You don't see as many fanatics as you do here. Palestinians in Ramallah know how to have fun. And they don't come to restaurants in army uniform with AK-47s dangling from their sides."

"It's strange," said Amos. "I can only think of the Palestinians as I see them at checkpoints. My only contact is through the barrel of a gun."

Ramallah, so near and yet so far, Amos would often say, the city that he could visit only as part of an incursion, as a soldier. Israelis were banned from going to the West Bank following the grisly lynching in Ramallah of two soldiers a few years ago.

Lion Square, Ramallah

"And you don't even have a choice, since you are banned from going there. You can't, even if you want to, speak to the people beyond the wall," I said to Amos. "You can try, but you'd risk a heavy fine. If there had been freedom of communication between you and the Palestinians, the Israeli government with its policy of segregation would be redundant. Because if the Israelis could taste a bit of Ramallah's night life, they would never want to point a gun at a Palestinian again. The Israeli youth would dismantle the checkpoints and there would be free-flowing cross-border movements of revelers."

But I knew that what I had said to Amos was just wishful thinking. It was not so simple. The accumulated anger and hatred of the past sixty years was not going to go away so easily. Both sides needed a healing process, and I was not sure how long it would be before the two sides could forget and forgive in order to start afresh.

"I don't think the Arabs would ever let us stay in this country if we don't put them in their place," Amos said, and I thought he probably believed this. "But it would still be nice to visit this friend of yours, Fida, in Ramallah one day. May be you could smuggle me in."

"Maybe intermarriage is the answer. Shall I be the matchmaker?" I said to Amos. "Your father can then speak Arabic with your Palestinian bride."

"You must be out of your mind. My father would never accept my marrying a Palestinian girl. By the way, why do you outsiders always think that you have a solution for us? What makes you think that we might want to listen to you? Why should I believe that anyone without any connection to this land can solve our problems? Why doesn't the world just let us be? We need no matchmakers!"

"Because you've created a South Africa here with a well-established policy to deprive the indigenous people of their rights, even the most basic right to reside in the land of their ancestors, the land on which they were born and lived. And this has happened in the middle of the twentieth century! In a so-called democratic nation. I am not talking about the days of the colonies when the Aborigines and the Maoris and the Native Americans were wiped out from the face of the earth by white settlers."

"We are not settlers! We belong here. We were here before the Palestinians. This was our land! For thousands of years we prayed to come back here. We are not settlers."

"You are kind of settlers. The Hindus of the Vedas—the Aryans—traveled from Central Asia four or five thousand years ago and settled in India. Does that entitle them to claim the geographical entity called Central Asia as their ancestral homeland?"

"But we longed to come here, we prayed every year for three thousand years, *next year in Jerusalem*. Why can't the Arabs give us a piece of land? We have nowhere else to go. They have the entire Arab world, from Morocco to Libya, when we only have Israel."

"Amos, the Arab world has twenty-two nations. They are all different with different accents, dialects, complexions, and cultural traditions. Imagine Palestinians going to north Sudan and saying that it is just like their country!"

"You don't understand," said Amos, looking somewhat distraught. "The Jewish connection to this land is different from anything else that may come to your mind. We are the only people who always wanted to come back to the land we had been exiled from. You won't understand. The outsiders won't understand our pain."

So it all boiled down to Jewish exceptionalism that the Israeli state preached in its schools, and through the education system hammered into every child's mind that the Jewish question was a different one, an exceptional one. That the Jews had a legitimate right due to their exceptional suffering to claim everything that was Palestine.

Eretz Yisrael Sheli My land of Israel
Ve yesh lanu etz, ve yesh lanu kvish, yesh lanu gesher . . .
We have a tree and we have a road and we have a
bridge . . .

Maya still sang this popular song, only now she did it to annoy her brother.

———

After Fida and I had dinner in Darna's lovely setting with live oud music, she said that she would come back with me to pick up her clothes and a few things from Ein Karem. She was now semipermanently living in Ramallah and was only a few steps away from closing the Jerusalem chapter for good.

The checkpoint soldiers at Qalandiya said Fida did not have permanent residency in Israel proper, and while her application was being considered at the Interior Ministry, she was not supposed to have been in the West Bank at all. She could not travel out of Israel or live anywhere else other than her address in Ein Karem until her permanent status was sorted out. It was raining again, making the concrete and metal terminal building and the high wall that blocked the entry to Jerusalem look bleak, out of a disaster film set. Fida screamed at the soldier, in Hebrew, "Please let me get through. I live there. I am Israeli. I am more Israeli than you! Israel is my home."

I was not sure whether it was yet another of her wisecracks or if she was really pleading with the soldiers. There was this seriousness about her, but she could also have been mocking the absurdity of the situation. The soldiers handed over my passport to me and said, "*You* can get through, but not with *her*," pointing to Fida. "She can't cross into Israel."

"But her home is across this checkpoint. She was born and lived there all her life. Her clothes and books, her toiletries, her dog . . . her entire life is there. What are you talking about that you won't let her go home?"

"Sorry," said the soldier. "She can't cross through there. This is an international border, and according to the rules that apply to those who want to cross, she doesn't have a valid passport or permit to enter Jerusalem."

"But she could easily have taken one of the settlers' roads and passed as a settler," I said. Fida and I had crossed into Jerusalem via one of those roads many times before and nothing happened.

"We are only passing through here because it's quicker. What you are doing is really absurd. Can I talk to your superior?" I said to the soldier. I felt my voice was growing louder, tetchier.

Fida looked amazingly serene in the face of such a bizarre spectacle. She tapped on my shoulder and said, "Don't argue with them, you might be held for hours. Some stupid child soldier might want to take out his own personal revenge on you for answering back. They are like robots, programmed to say the things they are saying. There's no point. I should have taken you through Hezme, used by Jewish settlers. I usually always cross from there, as with my Hebrew and unveiled face I easily pass as a settler coming from the nearby Beit El settlement."

She then said that she was too tired to travel all the way to Hezme. It was late, around one in the morning, and the rain was incessant and depressing. She wanted to stay in Ramallah. I turned back from Qalandiya and drove her to Mahmud's house, which was not far from the checkpoint. Mahmud was the son of a well-known PLO leader who had been assassinated by the Mossad in Tunis in the 1980s, where the Palestine Liberation Organization was based at the time. He was standing in the balcony when we came back. He stepped out unsurprised, as if he had been waiting for her. Fida hardly said goodbye to me before running inside with him. It was not the rain that made her run, I knew. I sat in the car for a few minutes, ashamed of having the privilege now to go back to Qalandiya and drive straight through, with no teenage soldier wielding his bayonet-pronged rifle stopping me. Before I turned the engine on, I saw Fida come out to the balcony. She had a forced smile on her face, underneath which, I knew, shame, rage, and powerless frustration were brewing to a calamitous cocktail, the kind of smile that sent me the message that she would burst into tears the moment I was out of her sight. She would not express her shame before me, a foreigner, the impostor-resident, the unlikely settler in her country.

It was this quotidian humiliation in public places that would one day drive the golden-hearted woman out of her country. Fida would immigrate to Canada in two years' time. Tamar's voice echoed in my ears: "This is exactly what Israel wants, to intimidate and humiliate on a daily basis, until the occupied people flee of their own free will."

Just before I drove off, I wound down the window to wave goodbye. Fida, who was usually so talkative, barely lifted her right hand before turning round and disappearing behind the French doors. I saw Mahmud gently put his arms around her as they went inside. I felt slightly happier. At least there would be a pair of arms to hold Fida when she cried, until her anger and shame subsided.

As I had expected, getting through was easy. When Amos opened the door, I saw that his kippah had fallen off to the side of his head as the grip that usually held it in place had become loose. He must have been sleeping.

"Someone called," he said.

"Who?" My heart leapt at the possibility that it might be Leo.

"At around one thirty, someone called Makhmud wanted to know if you reached home okay.

"What did you say?"

"I said I was your husband's cousin."

"You didn't, did you?" I was horrified.

Amos laughed. "Just joking! I knew this Makhmud was from Ramallah. I didn't want to complicate your life, so I just said I was the babysitter."

"Thank you for that! Under normal circumstances it would have been fine, Amos, to reveal your identity to my

Palestinian friends. But not tonight. By the way, you didn't call him 'Ma*kh*mud,' did you?"

"I can't help my Israeli accent."

"Yes, you can. You are the son of your Yemeni immigrant father who still speaks Arabic at home. You can try and pronounce it correctly, 'Mahmud.'"

"But I was brought up to pronounce the 'h' as 'kh,' like a real Ashkenazi," Amos said. He rearranged his kippah, put on his jacket to go. Before leaving he hesitated by the door for a few seconds. Then he said in a contemplative voice, "I was very happy to talk to your Makhmud. It was brief but a normal exchange of words. You see, my only words so far with someone called Ma*kh*mud had been '*Jibne hawi-yye!*' Give me your ID! This is the first time I spoke to a real Ma*h*mud as an equal. It was strange. It was kind of nice."

I noticed that Amos pronounced the aspirated 'h' this time properly, as he said the name Mahmud again. After all, he was the son of an Arabic-speaking Yemeni. Amos had a big heart. He was my good soldier Švejk. I felt good having him around.

.14.

DISENGAGEMENT

"Shall we get married?"

"We are married."

"I mean shall we get married properly?"

"We are properly married."

"I mean beyond the registry office business, a wedding with a big party as we talked about when we first met."

"That would be wonderful."

"It would, wouldn't it? Where?"

"We'd hire a farmhouse in a kibbutz. You'll wear a sari. We'll find a Hindu priest and a liberal rabbi who'll marry us."

"Under the chuppah you'll break a glass like a proper Jewish groom," I said as I hugged Leo.

"And you'll wear a red sari with a red bindi on your forehead, like a proper Bengali bride."

The entire evening I dreamt of wearing a flowing red sari with my long hair blowing in the sweet crop- and dung-smelling kibbutz air.

Sometimes he could say things that felt so good, I would be swept off of my feet, be left speechless in a deluge of emotion, even after all these years and the chronic personal conflict that we had suffered.

I said, "Next weekend, shall we take two full days off, go stay in a kibbutz? We can ask around for a wedding venue. The kids can run around. We can leave on Friday afternoon after school and come back on Sunday afternoon."

"I can't take three days off—Friday, Saturday, and Sunday!" he protested. Weekends had been exasperating from the very beginning. Israelis worked on Sundays. Kiran's school had the Christian-European weekend, Saturday and Sunday. Maya was in an Israeli kindergarten, so her weekend was half day on Friday and Saturday full day.

"No, but we could expect you to take the Israeli weekend off at least, Friday and Saturday?"

"But I often have meetings on Fridays."

"Take Sunday off, then. At least you won't have to answer to your bosses in Brussels and Washington."

"You know it's difficult. It's the first working day in Israel."

"Does that mean we can never go away for a long weekend?"

"I'm around a lot, my office is here."

"Precisely. I see your back when you are in your office, in front of the computer, twelve to fourteen hours a day. I wish your office was *not* at home, you would then at least come home to be with us."

"You know I have a demanding job, a very demanding boss. Have some understanding."

"Tell me, then, when do you want to do this, spend a long weekend away with us? If by some fluke we do decide to have a kibbutz wedding, don't you think we'd need to set aside at least two full days for that?" I said dispassionately, trying to defuse the tension that was building between us.

So the most beautiful moment would be tarnished by sudden, unpredictable arguments such as this several times a month. There was no Orli in our lives anymore, but we still argued. In fact the bickering turned darker since we came to live in this house. After or during each argument he would leave the house with his laptop, accusing me of creating a war zone at home. It was becoming increasingly true that I could not keep my exasperation under control, which would make my otherwise perfectly valid case void of reason. He would pack his little suitcase and go to his favorite place on earth, Gaza. Sitting in the house in the dimmed glow of the yellow floor lamps that we had on twenty-four hours, I would ask myself, "How did I come to this? Am I turning into one of those frustrated, bitter, morose wives of ambitious men?"

It was not that I could not have a buzzing life in Jerusalem. The city and the place as a whole offered a great deal. I could, if I wanted to, go out socializing or dancing with Tamar and her friends in Dewan on most nights, I could go party with the internationals on most weekends, go hiking in Mount Hermon, or with our more adventurous acquaintances I could venture out to the canyons of Mitzpe Ramon in the southern desert. But my heart wasn't in any of this, at least not at this particular phase in my life. I missed Leo. And I was faced with the huge responsibility of bringing up the children often without knowing when their father would be coming back or, even, where he was. I was constantly finding myself on edge. I was too scared to breathe deeply in case I missed being vigilant. I knew that I was being unreasonable, but I became paranoid and feared that if I went out too often enjoying myself, something terrible would befall my children and I wouldn't be there to protect them from it.

There was no mention for a while of the kibbutz wedding with a rabbi and a priest. The Israeli disengagement in Gaza and the aftermath with the Hamas takeover had also seen Leo's slow disengagement from the family; he became more obsessed with the place and even ignored the Second Lebanon War. He was either in Gaza, writing about Gaza or, when he was in Jerusalem, he would be talking about Gaza. He was a great believer in that overcrowded strip of land, which offered, as he put it, fantastic hospitality to any guest. He felt, he always said, more at ease in Gaza, that the Gazans were a friendlier people than their West Bank counterparts. Gaza had the answer, he said, how to resuscitate the deadlocked peace process.

"What's amazing is that you walk 150 meters and you are in the Arab world."

"Which 150 meters?"

"The no-man's-land between Israel and Gaza. You cross it and you are in the greater Arab world."

"Why should it make Gaza any greater than the West Bank?"

"The West Bank is such a messed-up place. It has become so *Israeli*. The way it works, the way its system works, is completely Israeli. Often it is hard to tell where Israel ends and the West Bank starts."

"So Gaza is bigger."

"Yes, you have to go to Gaza to feel the bigger spirit. The Arab world runs there continuously, since the disengagement. No Israel in Gaza to carve it up like it has done in the West Bank. There are no ABCs of separated areas controlled by Oslo bureaucracy."

"What happens then, after the 150-meter walk?"

"After you've passed the Erez crossing, a short walk away is the Arab world with no Israelis manning any checkpoints, there are no walls, gates, or road barriers. Poor West Bankers, they don't know what it is like to move freely."

I would try to argue, but I knew what he was saying was true: someone from Ramallah could not travel to Bethlehem or Jericho and vice versa without crossing multiple Israeli checkpoints, without having to go around hills and valleys, as they were not allowed to use the direct routes meant for Jewish settlers. The "settler roads" were built with state money to create direct access between various West Bank Jewish settlements and link them to Jerusalem, bypassing and often bisecting Palestinian towns and villages. I knew what Leo meant by "a continuous Arab world" in Gaza.

"They don't have to worry about speaking or not understanding Hebrew at *machsom*, the checkpoint, facing interrogation by Israeli soldiers," Leo would say. "They are less nervous and less afraid. They are not as shortsighted as their West Bank brothers."

"And sisters."

"And sisters."

But then, after the initial euphoria and optimism following the Israeli disengagement from Gaza, Leo started to have doubts about Israel's real intentions. Although he was happy that there was no Israeli presence in Gaza, he was no longer sure about the "unilateral" nature of the disengagement process. He expressed his skepticism often. I was impressed by the brilliant job that Israel had carried out by pulling some of the fanatic settlers out of Gaza and ceding Gaza to the Palestinians (the media coverage of this was dramatic, spectacular: religious settlers putting up a fierce resistance against the soldiers who in many cases used physical force to subdue them). I saw in the disengagement a promising sign that I hoped Israel would continue to follow in the West Bank—by dismantling illegal outposts and settlements in the near future. I believed that Israel's "unilateral" move had brought the possibility of peace a little closer. But Leo now said that he thought differently.

"If anything, this might push the possibility of peace farther away. It is the *unilateral* business that I am not happy with. Why do you think the Palestinians sent only a qualified welcome to this 'groundbreaking' move by Israel? Why weren't they overjoyed? Why weren't there all-night parties with nationalistic frenzy?"

Leo said that Palestinians were quite rightly cautious about any Israeli move. It was hard to believe that Israel would do anything to their benefit after four decades of occupation. Gaza, a hotbed of resistance, poor, with a very low literacy rate, with warehouses full of crude Qassam rockets . . . Without the Jewish presence it would be so easy for Israel to deal with Gaza, just close all the borders so no one was allowed out. Turn it into a prison, collective punishment for throwing a few homemade rockets into Israel. With the various interclashing clans roaming about, things won't get any better in Gaza and the Qassams won't stop being launched into Israel. But now Israel could take real actions against the rocket throwers. Israel would now be able to go into Gaza with all its might, cut off electricity, water, gas— *with* the Jewish presence there all these would have been impossible. And with so much power in the hands of the clan lords, Gaza might risk becoming a rogue state without any international support and cut off from the rest of the West Bank.

However preemptive his predictions might have seemed at the time, they would become ominously true in a few months' time, when Israel would shut off a lawless Gaza from the world. My former editor from Bush newsroom, Alan Johnston, would be kidnapped by one of the clans; Hamas would control Gaza following its landslide victory, engage in bloody clashes with the warring clans in order to secure Alan's release. The international community would stop the much-needed aid and resources going into this sliver of land inhabited by a deprived million, boiling with rage and hatred against Israel, the rest of the world, as well as one another.

"Are you writing about these predictions in your reports? I wonder what the world would think . . ." I said to Leo.

"We're supposed to support this disengagement. I just didn't like the way Israel handled it, pulling out the settlers using force rather than negotiation."

"How else would Israel have moved back to the west side of the 1967 borders if they didn't throw the fanatics out by force?"

"By leaving the settlers where they are, if they don't want to leave voluntarily, Israel and the Palestinians can actually accelerate the peace process."

"What do you mean? Apply the Algerian model?" I said. Tamar always talked about applying the Algerian model to find a solution to the settlement issue. When after eight years of bloody war France and Algeria signed a peace treaty, the withdrawal of the French from Algeria was going to be completed in phases. The French were given three years and the option to choose between taking up French or Algerian citizenship within those years. Since Paris did not forcefully pull out the colonial settlers, it was not under any obligation to pay compensation to those who voluntarily returned to France. Most of them did return, although around twenty thousand French settlers decided to stay in Algeria as dual nationals.

"In that way Israel won't have to pay the kind of huge compensation that the evacuees from Gush Katif settlement in Gaza had received," I said to Leo. "But why do you think the Palestinians would want those zealots—who insist the West Bank, the biblical Judea and Samaria, was given by God to the Jewish people—to live among them? Can you guarantee that there won't be revenge attacks considering what the settlers have done to the Palestinians for decades?"

"If they really can't or won't move out, then they just have to live with Palestinian passports. And about stopping a massacre from happening, we need to have a sound treaty, which would give substantial compensation to the Palestinian refugees," Leo said, his voice clear, full of determination.

"If peace was something that Israel really wanted," I said, "it wouldn't be continuing to build the concrete separation wall looping in many of the larger West Bank settlements."

Once more, I felt that I did the right thing by coming with him to the Middle East to witness firsthand the many twists and turns of this age-old conflict. Leo was so driven and with such noble ideas for this troublesome dot on the world map that I admired him for believing that he could at least *try* to make a difference, while many of us had long ago forsaken our lofty ideals to make the world a better place.

His organization believed in a two-state solution, but Leo wanted a binational reality shared between the Jews and the Palestinians. Leo felt that a crude partition might only perpetuate the conflict. He believed in including

Gaza—boycotted by the international community and Israel—in the peace process and speaking to Hamas as an equal political entity.

The internationals advocated bypassing Hamas until it recognized Israel in its political manifesto. Many of Leo's contacts in the diplomatic community did not protest the international boycott of Gaza following the Hamas takeover after its sweeping victory in the Palestinian legislative elections in 2006.

Leo always said that the international community should not make a huge fuss over Hamas's reluctance to "recognize" Israel, as it was only a resistance strategy and that some members of Hamas were actually interested in taking part in discussing peace.

I was not so open-minded about Hamas and its dubious Islamist standpoint in Palestinian politics, but I was not totally displeased with the eventual Hamas takeover of Gaza. Because it seemed at the beginning that the party would have the popular support to crack down on Gaza's powerful clans and bring in some sort of unity rule. And also because Hamas did manage to secure the release of Alan Johnston after almost four months in the hands of "the Army of Islam." We all shed silent tears during those months, in particular on the day when one of the groups claimed that they had killed him. His release by Hamas's political maneuver reinstated my previously wobbly faith in the Islamic party. But it did not last long. Soon after its spectacular election victory, Hamas started disfiguring and massacring its Fatah rivals in Gaza.

Despite all his fine ideas about the political future of this place, Leo was stuck with an organization whose views he did not fully share. And I was often merciless, especially when he would be disengaged from the family during those weeks of writing "the latest report." I would harangue him that he produced volumes of lies, that he did not believe in his own recommendations. I would lash out at him, saying he was bigger and better than that. I believed that he came to the Middle East not to provide what the internationals wanted in their Middle East reports but to do something that the people in the street wanted.

I should have been more understanding and discreet. I should have been more diplomatic, empathetic. But my personal estrangement from Leo resulting from my gradual disconnection from his frenzied life and the political weariness of the place had already left me resentful and hardhearted. The disquiet in the region seeped so deep into our lives that there was no escape from it. I did not want to sacrifice my family to his "cause," to conflict management in the Middle East.

.15.

LIVING APART
TOGETHER

I did not want to go on living under the same roof with him and not have a proper break, a laugh. I could not go on, in the semidarkness of our house, living what felt like a Penelopesque existence day after day, month after month.

So after about two years of "living together apart," I started thinking of giving "living apart together" a go.

But something happened in the meantime, or rather a series of steadily deteriorating events that somehow brought forward with a devastating pull our breakup. The first happened when, after another hysterical row, he packed a suitcase and went to stay in a hotel in Haifa.

Of course, I assumed it would be temporary, as it had been so many times before. This time, though, something inside me announced that I absolutely could not live with these departures anymore. Whenever a situation did not suit him, he would leave the house for as long as he liked. Then, after the storm had abated, he would come back with a bunch of red roses or send by post beautiful long stems of feathery mistletoes to say he had missed me. I had accepted everything, and all these years I had been good and stable. I was always there for him whenever he came back from his adventures. Even after the Iraq War, where he went without discussing with me his decision to cover the war, I had remained a good wife staying behind with our children. I had accepted, albeit with passive resentment, our separation when the children and I were evacuated from Jordan and we had had to settle back in London, waiting for Leo the war correspondent to come home.

This time, after his departure for Haifa, I also packed my bags and took the children for a long weekend to Bethlehem, to clear my head. We stayed in the Franciscan monastery, where Maya befriended Father Servino, a Polish monk who had lived in Bethlehem almost all his life. Father Servino babysat the children the whole weekend—filling up Maya's pre-Christmas stockings with chocolate bars and Kiran's with DVDs of some of his favorite films. There, in my room in the monastery, in the shadow of the Church of the Nativity, I found the real taste of an innate reserve of willpower. After being a stable and committed wife and mother for so many years, I was finally strong enough to break the family. I wanted to find a different kind of life, free from obsessive love and emotional dependency. I felt free of guilt as I prepared to take the first step toward separation.

After the long weekend away in Bethlehem, I came back to Jerusalem with a new, solid resolution.

It was quite late when we arrived home on Sunday night, as the children wanted to have their evening meal at the monastery's restaurant and therefore taste once more Father Servino's famous spaghetti pomodoro. I carried little Maya, who was fast asleep, from the car down the steps and entered our dark garden. Kiran dragged the small suitcase behind me. Balancing my sleeping daughter in one arm, I fished out the keys from my bag in the dark. I opened the door. We entered our cave.

He had not come home. A very small part of me irrationally still wished that he had.

The first thing I saw when Kiran turned on the lights was his washing on the rack that I had left to dry in the living room before going to Bethlehem. The room smelt of damp clothes and washing powder. I saw his shirts and his pants and trousers. Despair took hold of me again, making me unsteady momentarily. My resolve was crumbling, even though I felt strongly that I should fight against such tumultuous emotions. Standing in the room, I thought I would have given us another chance even this time, even after having taken a vow to move on, to not moan or groan over his absences anymore. If only had he been home when we came back.

With the cave gloom around me, the damp clothes of an absent lover, the children asleep in their beds, their heavy breathing filling up the house and accentuating my aloneness, I soon came back to my senses, to my vow taken in the Franciscan monastery in the shadow of the church that held the grotto where Mary, the single mother, gave birth to a prophet.

I started folding his clothes. His stripy shirt, his blue pants with white stars on them, the orange trousers that he refused to wear in public during the Gaza disengagement because orange was the color of the settlers and their sympathizers who were against the Israeli plan.

Snippets of the bitter argument that had taken place before he left for Haifa came back to haunt me. I felt so soiled by the shameful pettiness of the repetitive bickering that it made clear once again the distressing reality before me. It forced me to pick up my eroding resolve. I folded up his shirts, trousers, and pants, put them in his wardrobe, and closed it. It seemed like closing a chapter.

<hr>

Not quite yet.

The framed pictures that we had stored behind the sofa in the living room when we moved into this house had stayed in the same place for months. I grew tired of seeing the bare walls, so one day I went out and bought a stepladder. It was soon after my Bethlehem trip, on the day Leo came back from Haifa and said these words, "Give us, our family another chance," after I told him about the vow that I had taken in the monastery.

I did not need much more. I was already weary of my resolve, of the daunting task of moving with the children to a different house. I felt that I had been thrown by the god of destruction into the stormy sea on a sinking boat; I was tossed around in an acute state of seasickness that blurred my decisions and the options that had only a few days ago seemed plausible.

One more chance, I wanted to give us one more chance. But I did not know then that there were no chances left to try. That I should just leave now when there were still some sparks left in the wreckage of our marriage. But instead I hung on until the final blow struck us.

"Let's go to Tel Aviv, to the beach tomorrow," he said, and the children started jumping up and down. I acquiesced with a thawing heart, indulging in a warm feeling of well-being.

"But it's cold!" said Maya.

"It's cold in Jerusalem, not in Tel Aviv," Kiran reassured her. The sea in Tel Aviv wouldn't be warm now, but we would be able to dip our feet, splash the water, and walk on the beach barefoot. The sun would be out, and Tel Aviv was ten degrees warmer than Jerusalem.

In the evening, energized by this impromptu happy turn in our life, I stood on the stepladder and started putting the pictures up one by one. The space for a picture above the door was slightly higher than I could reach from the highest step on the ladder. I was standing on tiptoes and trying to hammer in the nail when the ladder wobbled and so did I. I fell on the side of my bad leg and the barely healed ligaments snapped again.

Luckily I still had my old crutches, and I bandaged my knee using the same wraparound support that I had left over from the previous fall. I did a good job putting it on, and after strong painkillers overnight I felt well enough the next day to walk using just one of the crutches. In the afternoon, when I said that I could manage the planned trip, we drove to the beach in Jaffa, as it was wider, cleaner, and more private than the adjacent swathes of overcrowded sands in Tel Aviv.

The beach was deserted except for a picnicking Arab family: grandmother and mother in full head-to-toe djellabas sitting around a display of dips and bread, olives, bottles of Coca-Cola. The boys and men in shorts and T-shirts were, to our children's great joy, actually swimming in the calm waves. We stopped right on the beach car park. There was a low climbable wall if one wanted to get down to the sea quickly, otherwise there was a path that skirted around the car park. Leo and the children of course climbed the wall; I, on my crutch, started to hop along the path. When I arrived at the outermost edge of the beach, I realized that it was impossible to walk on the soft wet sand using a crutch. I stood there one-legged, not knowing what to do; the others were by then throwing themselves into the cold waves and they looked at me quizzically, wondering why I was still standing there. I pointed to the sand and my crutch, but they were too busy enjoying themselves to pay attention to what I was trying to say. I kept my smile, although I felt that the test to keep my spirit high was getting harder. The painkillers were wearing off, and I needed to sit down to reach my bag to take some more. The bottles of water that I had packed were with the children in their beach bags.

At one point Leo understood why I was still there leaning against my crutch, and he came back to help me walk to our beach umbrella. I hopped, holding his shoulder. I sat on the sand—it was uncomfortable with a knee that I could not bend. I watched them splash and play. I lay down and watched the cloudless sky through the bamboo slats of the straw umbrella. The sun was strong even in December, but the wind was chilly. I read for a while. It was getting late and the children came back wet, shivering, and hungry. Leo said that we should go to one of the fish places on the beach for dinner.

"But I can't walk on the sand," I said.

"We'll help you."

"It's really difficult to hop, not comfortable. Can we drive somewhere?"

"You'll be fine."

"No, I won't be, I am in a lot of pain."

In the end we walked to the car and drove around for half an hour from one restaurant to another, none of which appealed to Leo. "Let's go to Old Jaffa," he proposed. The old city of Jaffa was pedestrianized, and when the car stopped I slouched in the passenger's seat feeling tired. A jabbing pain around the knee unsettled me. I fought against it. I could not see myself hopping again, on hard stone steps this time. Kiran and Maya were hungry and they were now fighting in the backseat. I started to cry—whether out of frustration at it not being understood that I was not fit to join an excursion when one of my legs was out of function or because of what I felt was a total lack of empathy on Leo's part, I didn't know. He did not like illnesses and disabilities.

He avoided visiting sick relatives. He had never been able to deal with any allusion to my physical unfitness, fatigue, or inability to cope with a particular situation. I was also crying out of embarrassment and guilt that my physical condition was stopping my family from having fun. But I could not move out of the car. I told the children that I would wait here while they ate their dinner in Old Jaffa.

Leo insisted that I come out and that he would help me walk. I told him categorically that it was too much for me and that I could not reach the restaurant. He said that I was making a big deal out of nothing and that I should at least try.

That set off a familiar feeling of being in jeopardy and not being heard.

A hysterical argument followed. A very upset Leo started driving away from Jaffa toward Ayalon, the ring road around Tel Aviv. "I am in a lot of pain," I said through my tears.

"Maybe you should see a doctor." Leo slowed down and parked the car along a dark, dilapidated neighborhood of south Tel Aviv. The streets were scattered with litter. "I'm calling an ambulance," he said. But I didn't wait for him to finish the sentence. I felt suffocated in the closed space of the car. The ugly row had poisoned the air between us. I opened the passenger side door and stumbled out. "Stop," said Leo, "you are not well."

As I stood leaning against a lamppost I felt that I was being watched by many eyes from the multistory shabby estates that lined the street. Maya and Kiran too came out of the car and stood with me under the dim streetlight. A few minutes later an ambulance arrived on the scene. The doctors were kind and asked me what happened and where it hurt. After their assessment they said that they didn't think it was necessary for me to go to hospital.

Then something unimaginable happened.

A police car appeared suddenly with blue flashing lights. Some feisty Ethiopian girls who had been watching the sad spectacle from the balcony of the roadside estate came down quickly when they saw the police. Whatever they said, their testimony made things worse. We were asked to follow in the car to a nearby police station.

I was baffled by the bizarre turn of events. I pleaded with the police that it was not how we had intended to spend the evening and that the situation got out of hand after a terrible argument, but they said that they wanted to ask Leo some questions. I wasn't permitted to go home with my husband.

I left Tel Aviv with Kiran and Maya at midnight, Leo refusing to look me in the eye when I wanted to talk to him before being escorted out of the police station to the car. I could hardly drive with tears welling up and obscuring my vision. We sat in the car for some minutes until the painkillers started to kick in. I felt a great heaviness in my heart, ashamed of us for being such undeserving parents to our children.

I drove back slowly using my good leg—luckily it was an automatic car—to our house in Jerusalem at two in the morning, only to realize that I did not have the house keys. I had left them on the dining table as Leo locked up behind us. I did not think I would need them, as we were going to come back together. I lay my sleeping daughter down on the garden table and asked my sleepy son to watch her while I called on Amos's house. Thankfully his family lived nearby and they had a set of spare keys.

The following day Leo rang and asked Kiran to meet him at a certain place. Our son was instructed to bring him his little case with some clothes, his toothbrush, and his laptop. To Kiran he explained that he was leaving home for a while. He did not want to speak to me. He told our son that he would arrange to see him and his sister in the weekend.

———

I knew, as he must have known, which was why he could not face me when he came to take his things, that for both of us there was no turning back. We had reached a solid, impenetrable barrier and, for some time, possibly for a long time, we would have to skirt around it before our paths might cross again.

I picked up with a firmer grip my forgotten resolution and started looking for a house. I found an exquisitely beautiful place on the edge of the Green Line on the West Jerusalem side. The golden Dome of the Rock was right before my mesmerized eyes when I walked to the bottom of my street. I moved out the same week and settled myself and the children in our new house with an abundance of sunlight flooding all the rooms with ten-meter-high ceilings, where I could breathe high and free. I was able to see the shameful triviality, our petty dissatisfactions from an altitude and feel that life could be loftier. Freed from the continuous rows, the false expectations, and the slow death of youth, hope, and self-esteem, I felt more composed. It energized me to think that we finally broke the vicious cycle dynamic of our relationship.

Every evening I walked down my street with Maya to have a glimpse of the magnificent Dome of the Rock. My new house offered me the much-needed space for reflection without Leo's shadow hovering over me, and my pathetic, unrequited dependency on him shaming me.

PART
THREE

.16.

THE PALM TREE
OF MUSRARA

We did not come to this country from a country
we came from pomegranates, from the glue of memory
from the fragments of an idea we came to this foam
Do not ask us how long we'll stay among you, do
*   not ask us*
anything about our visit.
                    —*Mahmoud Darwish, "Guests on the Sea"*

It was strange that I should still have wanted to go on living in Jerusalem, a place that was supposed to have contained us as a family. We came here to be together, not to live apart. But when the breakup happened, when we fell apart, it did some strange things. It inexplicably unburdened me of the unfulfilled expectations of the family.

I felt de-mossed in my new place, recharged with new hope. I created a stone wall around me that successfully barred the negative energy, spite, and paranoia that usually followed any separation from entering my life. I felt safe inside, within my walls. I would not let Leo or anyone invade that space, where I moved untouched by the past trauma and started instead chronicling my life and time in Jerusalem.

I was no longer enslaved by pining for a family with Leo and myself as the center. There were no distractions of despair and regrets. I shut out the old desperate world and created a self-sufficient parallel one, empowered by dignity and creativity. It seemed farcical, my past, our joint past, full of absurd rows and self-debasement. Like the tall and ancient palm tree in the garden of my new house, I felt free and wise.

For two months Leo and I contacted each other mainly for things related to the children.

He was astonishingly regular picking them up on Friday after school, and then they would stay with him the whole weekend, often until Sunday afternoon. In the beginning I did not know what to do with so much free time on my hands. On Sunday evening at dinner I would hear from the children that they had been doing exciting things: staying overnight on the sandy Eco beach in Achziv, camping on the shores of Lake Tiberias, walking in the woods of Bet Shemesh, and most important, he was cooking for them dishes that heralded a hidden chef in Leo.

"What did you have for Shabbat dinner?" I would ask the children, exhilarated and exhausted after their weekend excursion.

"Daddy cooked fish soup with lentils and tomatoes in it. Kiran and Daddy also made a cake. A chocolate cake," Maya would proudly announce.

As before, here too, almost as soon as I moved in, I could hear the house speak to me. Or perhaps it was I who started to see the house personified, and for the first time in our third year in Jerusalem, the house became my refuge, my friend. It rejuvenated me and I felt protected. It too was an abandoned 1948 Palestinian home, but the ghosts here were friendly, or perhaps by now, due to my circumstantial relocation to yet another Arab house, the ghosts had given up on me, they had become instead intrigued by me, this persistent settler. This time I spoke and they listened. I told them that I would rather live with the pre-1948 ghosts than in the soulless post-1948 homes devoid of mystery. The walls of my house were one meter thick and trapped inside was a certain geniality, which defused petty accusations that previously ruled my life.

One day, during a stroll with Maya around the Damascus Gate in the shadow of the Dome of the Rock, I was overwhelmed by the weight of antiquity around me as the afternoon sun shone on the magnificent dome, Sultan Suleiman's city wall, and the surrounding areas, illuminating several millennia of history. I came home and started counting the grooves on the palm tree in my garden.

It was a neighborhood landmark in the area called Musrara. "Once you've passed the high wall along the Ottoman mansions and the pedestrianized section, follow the path to the tall palm tree until you've arrived at a blue gate . . ." went the directions to my house in this quaint complex.

I heard that one could tell the age of a palm tree by counting the grooves on its trunk, each groove signifying the passing of a year.

There were one hundred and twenty one.

The ceilings in my house were so high that I could never find a ladder high enough to change the lightbulb in the bedroom, which had gone out during the time of the previous tenant, Chris McGreal, who was a correspondent for the *Guardian* newspaper.

Before Chris, Suzanne Goldenberg, also from the *Guardian*, lived here. And before that, the *Los Angeles Times* correspondent Barbara Demick, a single mother whose baby was born in this house. I was inspired by the spirit of the past writers, the tireless journalists, the observers and the chroniclers of the Israeli-Palestinian conflict over the past fifteen years. I felt that I did not even have to try very hard, because I could feel their presence around me when I stayed up late, writing down the annals of my own journey through the Middle East's hottest conflict zone.

Soon after I moved to my house in Musrara, my career took an interesting turn. I was doing an illustrated report for BBC Radio 4 on the victims and survivors of honor killing in a central Israeli city near Tel Aviv. I came to know a mother who had just testified in the Israeli court that her eighteen-year-old daughter was killed by one of her sons, who was only two years older than the victim, in the name of family honor. Through the mother I came across a long, dark history of girls and women being murdered by their brothers and cousins in a Bedouin-Arab neighborhood, an act that for many years had been covered up by the community for fear of revenge from the killers, until the mother came out and unleashed a hornets' nest by her open testimony. I saw how big and visually powerful the story was. I was not happy with just a short BBC "package"; I wanted to make a full-length documentary film. I felt so sure of the idea that within a few months I interviewed and put together a crew with a Palestinian cameraman, who lived on Via Dolorosa in the Old City, and a left-wing Israeli editor who had made aliya from the former Czechoslovakia. She was a child of the Velvet Revolution and yet disillusioned by it after it had failed to stop the inevitable split of her country. I was doing my little coexistence trial, getting the crew from the both sides of the divide to work together on my new project. Later on this would stretch to my recruiting a Christian Palestinian translator, a Muslim Palestinian narrator, and an American Jewish sound editor to work on my film on honor killing among Israel's urbanized Bedouins.

My relationship with Leo also took an interesting, surprisingly mature turn. In spite of everything, and our breakup, I did not waver from my old resolve that I wanted to *live* the Middle Eastern experience, by being, as much as I could, part of it; by agreeing to bring up the children, as my husband wanted, as Jews or half Jews; by learning the local languages myself and encouraging the children to do the same. Leo and I lived apart, but my position on this remained unchanged.

After two or three months, when we could face each other as friends without the desire to settle old scores, we agreed to observe Shabbat together, lighting candles, saying the prayers, and eating dinner in Leo's house in Nachlaot, near the Mahane Yehuda market. When he moved to what he called the politically correct neighborhood of Nachlaot, which had always been in Jewish hands and had not knowingly been owned by the Palestinians (the residents therefore did not have to bear the "guilt" that many Jewish owners of the "Arab" houses did or should, according to Leo), I avoided for a while going to the market, which I loved so much. But that initial bitterness born of the pain of separation did not last long. I embraced Leo's invitation to spend every Shabbat with him and the children in his house.

It was, nevertheless, disorientating living in two houses. Our two homes: one in Musrara, an apartment in a grand Ottoman mansion near the Damascus Gate of the Old City; the other in Jewish Nachlaot, one of the first neighborhoods that were home to impoverished Jewish immigrants from the Middle East—Iraq, Syria, Turkey, Kurdistan. Now the third or the fourth generation of their descendants lived in grungy cell-like, close-together, low-ceilinged apartments, often eight families in a modest two-story building. It was a different world, just twenty minutes' walk from my house.

The double existence only added to the schizophrenia that Jerusalem generated over loyalty, guilt, and identity.

I did not recognize my life or the lives of our two children in this strange setting. I was getting to know myself as well as Leo and the children in relation to the tension that was stored up in the crevices of the city's famous stones. I was going in and out of multiple identities, and the children had to drag along.

It was like being an obscure mass of matter, formless on its own but flexible enough to mold into any shape. And so, on a usual day, I could see myself shift from being the calm mother of two half-Jewish children living in Jewish West Jerusalem into an angry Palestinian sympathizer heading for the Gaza border to demonstrate against Israel's decision to cut off electricity in the strip. I would find myself fuming at Israeli shortsightedness, the policy to collectively punish the entire population to smoke out a few Qassam-throwing Islamic radicals holed up there. Then back in Jerusalem, the children and I would attend the long and elaborate Shabbat service at Yakov and Michal's house, with the illustrious painting on their wall of the Temple Mount without the Dome of the Rock.

.17.

THE UNLIKELY

SETTLER

"*Why did Kiran throw smoke bombs?*"

"Because he was just messing about."

"He said that he was throwing them at the settlers."

"He shouldn't have done that."

"Who are the settlers?"

"People who settled on the Palestinian land."

"You mean people who *took* the Palesti-ninian houses, like the one we live in? Daddy says you and I and Kiran live in a stolen Palesti-ninian house."

"Does he?" I said to Maya, not surprised that Leo had discussed such complex real estate issues with a five-year-old. We both did: we talked about the politics of the conflict in front of the children all the time. Children grow up too quickly here.

"You could say we are also settlers, but we didn't take it by force. And our house is on the land that is legally

Israeli," I said to my daughter, searching for the words to explain that the Arab house we lived in was on the right side of the Green Line. We were not violating the legal, international border between the two communities. But how could I explain the Green Line, which ran along Road 1 only one hundred meters from my house, to a five-year-old? I had already said enough and used complicated ideas such as "land that is legally Israeli."

The riddle that gave me great food for thought around this time was who the "right" settlers were on this land. Our children, especially Maya, continued to be obsessed with the settler issue, and from the snippets of conversations that Leo and I had these days, I understood that he too was busy doing a report on Jewish settlers in the West Bank and how they defined their identities. His view on leaving the settlers where they were to let them decide whether they wanted to be Palestinian citizens when a Palestinian state was born continued to fascinate me. I found myself preoccupied with the fine line between "legal" and "illegal" settlers. According to Fida, all the Jews who came here with the dream of Zionism were settlers. Tamar would go as far as saying that all European Jews, regardless of whether they were left wing or right wing, were settlers, so that made Israel, she would rephrase the Gettysburg Address, "a country of the settlers, by the settlers, for the settlers." But I heard more controversial things than this view of Tamar's. A left-wing friend of Hungarian Jewish origin once said to me that all European Jews were illegally living in this country and that Israel was the most successful colonial enterprise of the twentieth century. Amid all this, my own special status as a reluctant settler did not seem significant anymore.

"The question is how one chooses to settle and live here," Hamoudi, my cameraman, said one day when we were walking through the Old City.

"What do you mean?" I asked him.

"You see, Jerusalem has always welcomed travelers. It's all right to settle here, the question is how you do it. Everyone is an immigrant."

Hamoudi was born and grew up with his ten siblings in a two-room house just off Via Dolorosa. He knew all the alleyways and dead ends and which lanes led to the Al-Aqsa Mosque and which rooftops had the best view of the Dome of the Rock. He wanted to show me the Mughrabi Gate of

Entrance to a typical Via Dolorosa house

the Al-Aqsa and the Dome of the Rock compound. The Mughrabi, or the North African quarter, was the closest to the Western Wall before 1967, when the Old City along with East Jerusalem came under Israeli control. He wanted to show me where his family had settled when his grandfather immigrated to Jerusalem from Tunisia in the early twentieth century.

"So I shouldn't feel bad about living here, then?" I asked Hamoudi. After I learnt about his family's origins, I began to see in his long dark face traces of North Africa, where I had spent a year with Leo about nine years ago.

"You definitely shouldn't. You have as much right to be here as I do. I am only the third generation Palestinian from my father's side, but I feel that I'm totally part of it. I'm living here, not occupying it."

"But I probably am!" I said to Hamoudi. "I live in an Arab house that has a Jewish landlord, the original Palestinian owners are probably rotting in some refugee camp or in forced exile. I asked my landlord, but he said that he didn't know who owned the house before 1948."

"Well, did my grandfather pay any compensation for settling in our house on Via Dolorosa to the 'original' Palestinian owner?" Hamoudi's comment made me laugh.

"Come on, you know exactly what I'm saying. Your family didn't because I don't think the owners were evicted by force or intimidation."

"Still I think it shouldn't be a problem to settle anywhere you like."

"How do you do it, then?"

"The way travelers over the centuries did. My Tunisian grandfather had a vision one day, that he should travel to Al-Quds—you know, the Arabic name for Jerusalem. So he came, found a spot in the Al-Aqsa complex under an olive tree. He spread his prayer mat and settled there. I'll show you the place where he used to sit every day until the day he died. He moved to the Mughrabi quarter next to the mosque, near the Wailing Wall. Their house was demolished after Israel occupied East Jerusalem and the Old City in 1967."

We had taken the left fork at the bottom of the stairs that came down from the Damascus Gate. After a few hundred meters, the road branched out to the left again and became Via Dolorosa. It was midday on Friday and on my right there was a flurry of activities in the Muslim quarter. The street became the main thoroughfare for the throng of Muslims going to the Al-Aqsa Mosque. It was also the shortest route to the Western Wall. Among the Muslim worshippers rushing to join the Friday prayers were some Jews, settlers, accompanied by heavily armed Israeli soldiers. There were children: boys with payots and girls in long black skirts and black stockings. I tried to make eye contact with some of them, but they kept their eyes straight ahead and down, fixed on the butts of the rifles that their protectors were carrying. Even the children were not distracted by the rows of toyshops and mounds of colorful sweets in roadside stores. What indoctrination must have filled these children's hearts with such self-control? What zealous faith forged these boys' and girls' minds with such self-righteousness? That they were not supposed to look at Palestinian toys, that they were not supposed to look at Palestinian colors of the market: the vegetable sellers, the trinkets, the rainbow sweets that they were walking past on their way to the Western Wall.

As I made my way through Che Guevara T-shirts, wooden Madonnas, and inflatable Spider-Man figures, I could not help thinking how unfortunate these boys and girls were. These poor children in all-black nineteenth-century Polish garb were walking as fast as they could being guarded by soldiers through the buzzing Old City without showing the slightest awareness of the present. They lived in the past to please their parents, the religious Zionist education and the Zionist dreams that had been thrust upon

Haredi march through the Muslim quarter

them by the closed yeshivas (I never thought the Jewish study seminaries were any different from the Islamic madrassas in terms of their power to radicalize the youth) that they attended, where they spent the best part of their youth.

Hamoudi and I hovered around the Mughrabi Gate. It was impossible to enter the compound, today being the Friday prayer and only Muslims had access to the mosques on this day. I felt the buzz of the people around me, devotees: men in mostly casual clothes and women in all-covering robes and head scarves entering the mosque, as the Israeli soldiers checked their bags.

"We never asked the Jews *not* to come to Palestine. We just didn't want them to snatch Palestine away from us. This is our country, as much as they think it is theirs," Hamoudi said pensively.

I vaguely remembered Fida talking about the same issues. She said that she would never accept a two-state solution from the Jews. "Who are they to divide up my country? Historically this has been one Palestine and will remain so. You must be joking," she had emphatically pointed out to me. "Do you really believe any Palestinian wants to see his country cut up into two and the Jews to enjoy the better half? The moment we've accepted a solution based on two states, we've lost Palestine forever."

"So why are your leaders then sitting at the negotiating table? Aren't they just wasting time? If what you said was on everyone's mind?"

"They are buying time. The longer we spend pondering this Western idea of creating two states on the land of

Palestine, the more elusive it would become. I mean the two-state theory would lose its momentum."

"All this is very strong, my dear Fida," I had replied, "but has it ever crossed your mind that the Israeli leaders are also doing precisely the same? They also don't want to give you an inch more in case you'd take a mile!"

"Maybe, but time is on our side. Their claim is based on religious books, while ours is on the recent history. We preserve the immediate historical continuity of this place. The world will stop being blind one day and see that the Jewish state in its current shape is not viable. Israel would only survive in the long term by being a modest and *non*-Jewish secular democracy."

"How can you live with so much resentment?"

"Hate breeds hate, I am afraid," was Fida's reply.

"Where have all the saints gone? Once upon a time this land had produced saints and selfless, compassionate prophets," I had murmured to myself.

Hamoudi, too, did not want to give any concession to the Jews.

Fida did not want to live in a Jewish state.

Tamar would not want peace with Hamas-led Palestine even if there were democratic elections.

And these were the moderate faces of Israel-Palestine. What would then be the views of the zealots on both sides? I felt tired and confused, not knowing how the two sides would ever compromise to have a middle ground.

As I stood with my back to the Mughrabi Gate, I saw just a few blocks away a fortified structure with armed soldiers pacing back and forth on the rooftop. I saw a huge menorah erected on the roof, with the Israeli flag flying high from the flagpole. I saw Jewish children with long sideburns playing on the nearby rooftop as armed guards stood on alert. The giant Hanukkah candelabra was brazenly imposing from whichever angle one looked at it. I wondered whether the Muslim devotees bowing down in prayer five times a day inside the Al-Aqsa and the Dome of the Rock mosque compound could also see it.

"That house with the Jewish candle stand, do you know whose house it is?" Hamoudi asked.

"No," I said.

"It's Sharon's house."

"You mean Ariel Sharon?"

"There's only one Sharon, the mastermind of the Sabra and Shatila massacre in Lebanon. Now lying in hospital in a coma, while his legacy stands high here, too, in the Muslim quarter in the Old City," Hamoudi said. We noticed that the crowd had thinned a bit, as most of the devotees had gone in for prayer. I could hear the verses of the Friday prayer through the mosques' loudspeakers: *Allahuakbar*, in chorus.

I envisioned the worshippers, bowing down, and each time they would raise their bodies in unison, they would see the menorah. I thought of thousands of people facing the Dome, praying. During Muslim prayers there was one point when the worshippers turned to their left and right shoulders to greet the unseen angels. If they turned to their right shoulders, I imagined some eyes, especially of those praying in the vast courtyard between the two mosques, would see Sharon's menorah, they would see the fortress walls of the former prime minister's own personal settlement. What emotion that would stir in them! What dissension the unwelcome glimpse of the Hanukkah candelabra might release onto their unforgiving hearts. What sense of vengeance might they feel against the settler who changed the skyline and the dynamic of the Old City, where, ironically, under the Jerusalem municipality rules no one was allowed to build arbitrarily, in particular no one was allowed to build anything that would seem incongruous with the architecture of the Old City. Unless of course it happened to be the house of the now-comatose Israeli leader, Ariel Sharon.

Muslim quarter with Sharon's menorah

.18.

FILMMAKING

I had begun making my first documentary film on honor killing soon after Leo and I moved to our separate homes, when things were still too raw between us to be reconciled. So even though the separation as we both understood was going to be for a trial period and we were not supposed to talk about it and to still meet and go to our children's school meetings and etc., in reality all this had proved to be difficult at first. It was extremely painful for me, and although I had spent the weekends without the children being busy writing and working on my script for the film or planning my BBC packages, there would be moments of emptiness when I would sit on the balcony staring at the dark garden and the lone palm tree.

Hamoudi and I started working together around this time, when I was nothing but a bag of nerves and nothing would take my mind off my personal woes. When we traveled to Ramle (or Ramla, in Arabic), in central Israel, which was the location where nine women were killed by their brothers and cousins over seven years, Hamoudi was at first reluctant to be involved in anything that would portray the Bedouin Muslim society in a negative light. Then I asked him to do the shooting on spec, to see if he would want to continue with the project.

I would pick him up at eight thirty in the morning from East Jerusalem and we would drive through the so-called racist traffic lights where cars coming from the Palestinian part of the city were reportedly held three times longer than the ones that came from West Jerusalem bound for the largest West Bank settlement of Ma'ale Adumim.

It would take us sometimes twenty minutes to get through these lights, and at one point I too started to believe that there might be some truth in the racist traffic lights theory. I would be swearing away at these lights, before turning right to Road 1 toward Tel Aviv. Ramle, where the gruesome killings had taken place, was not far from Tel Aviv, the modern Israeli city on the Mediterranean with skyscrapers and overcrowded beaches, a city that offered respite to the conflict-weary liberal youth and a vast number of nonreligious academics, analysts, and activists. Only a fifteen-minute drive from Tel Aviv was Ramle, which was apparently the oldest Arab settlement, the capital of the Arab province of Filastin dating back to the early eighth century. After the Naqba of 1948, when the original Palestinian residents fled the city, the desert dwellers or the Bedouins from the southern desert moved in. There was a steady exodus of the Bedouins from the Negev, as it was taken over by various Israeli research institutes on solar energy and such, and so the Bedouins, the original wanderers of the land, dispersed farther up north, settling in various urban centers. Ramle was one of the bigger cities close to the dunes of Tel Aviv, where many of them had settled.

The Bedouins in Israel occupy an interesting place from the point of view of citizenship and tribal loyalty. They are Israeli citizens who serve in the Israeli military; they are also Muslims and so find themselves in awkward situations when appointed at Israeli checkpoints, where they are seen by their fellow Muslims as collaborators. There's also deep prejudice among the Palestinians against the Bedouins; they are considered ignorant (one of the terms for a certain tribe of the Bedouins in the Judean desert is *jahalin*, which literally means "ignorant") and thought to carry with them dark desert customs from before the birth of Islam. When I discussed honor killing among the Bedouins with my Palestinian friends, they said almost unanimously that "those people" still lived in *Ayame Jahalia*, the Age of Darkness before Islam.

The family I was dealing with had originally come from Be'er Sheva, the largest city next to the Negev. They now lived in a poor neighborhood of Ramle called Juarish, where there was a kind of desert lawlessness, which most of its residents were complacent about. The flying debris and open sewage were the first of many shocks that would unsettle an unprepared visitor. There were a few extravagantly decorated houses, which everyone knew were built on drug money. In the absence of the traditional goatherding in the desert, the Bedouin youth in Juarish turned to the underworld and reportedly operated the drug-dealing belt in central Israel. They also revived the old custom of killing women who were seen to have defiled their family "honor." They practiced both the drug dealing and the killing under the very nose of the Israeli police. I was told by the authorities—it was surprising for a police force to admit that they were defeated by the Ramle drug lords—that even the ambulances sometimes did not dare enter Juarish. You could not order a taxi; the streets of Juarish were eerily deserted.

After multiple murders of women—on average three every year—in the name of family honor, Juarish rose to notoriety when the mother of the latest victim, a seventeen-year-old girl called Hamda (whose bullet-riddled body was found in her bed, and whose brother was seen leaving the house a few minutes later), spoke out to the police and the media against her family, which she said had been behind the killing of nine women in seven years. Following her testimony, word of many of the past murders surfaced and took Israel by storm.

When Hamoudi and I arrived to do our first day of shooting, the streets were, as usual, deserted. We chose a spot outside the mosque to park our car, as Hamoudi thought that would be the safest place in case there were problems from the men if they found out that we were here to speak to the women of the community.

In Juarish, I saw the otherwise marijuana-induced relaxed mood of Hamoudi change. He looked more serious and alert. He went inside the mosque where we were meeting the sheikh who had agreed to be interviewed on the murders to explain that Islam had nothing to do with the desert code of conduct in his neighborhood. But when I followed Hamoudi into the mosque, there were neither the sheikh nor any worshippers. People started milling around where we parked the car. I came back to the car and sat inside nervously. Hamoudi came out a few minutes later and suggested that we visit the mother of Hamda, since the Bedouin sheikh, who condemned the murders, was not there yet.

We left the car outside the mosque. He took his camera bag, but we thought walking with a tripod would not be a good idea, so we left it in the car. There were rows of mature flame trees along the road that led to Hamda's house. They were all in bloom and the sky seemed to have been sprayed with scattered bright red paint. I thought of Hamda's body drenched in blood, and it felt as if in death her soul had merged with the crimson blossoms.

Later on, Hamda's grief-stricken mother, Yamama, would show us the wall next to Hamda's bed, which she said had been splattered with her daughter's blood. Hamda was shot nine times.

"My son did it. My son too died for me on that day when he shot his sister. How could my own son, whom I gave birth to and breast-fed for three years, commit such a vile act, kill his sister for talking on the telephone to a man?"

"Who was she talking to?" Hamoudi asked.

"She wasn't talking to anyone," Yamama said, contradicting her earlier statement. "It was a lie, her brothers made it up to kill her because she rejected her cousin who wanted to marry her. She was too young to marry. My beautiful daughter, my youngest child, they took her life just like that."

The wall next to the bed where Hamda had spent her final night was pockmarked with bullet holes, which Yamama would not let anyone plaster over. It had been a year since the murder and she was still mourning. She spent most of her daylight hours sitting by Hamda's grave.

"This is my new address, Hamda's resting place," she would say to the camera, sitting by her daughter's grave at Ramle's Muslim cemetery. This stirred strong emotions in Hamoudi.

I became obsessed with the story, disgusted at the nonchalant attitude of the community and the Israeli police to a whole series of unresolved, horrific murders of young women by close family members. The police chief of Ramle

Yamama praying at the murdered Ramle girls' graves

said to me, on the record, "This is what the Arabs do, this is their custom! We can't do anything about it, we can't change them! When we arrive at a murder scene, everyone is silent, even the mother, all the forensic evidence—the blood, etc.—had been cleaned up." This was how several other police officers in central Israel defended their impotence when it came to incarcerating the "honor killers." This came from the same police force that was capable of intercepting the most sophisticated security crime against the Israeli state.

Sometimes to wind down after a disturbing day of filming, I would indulge in Hamoudi's special remedy. To soothe my nerves I would share a joint with him, driving back to Jerusalem. He would roll it perfectly while I drove and hold it in the inside of his palm while I slowed down before the checkpoint on the Tel Aviv–Jerusalem "settler highway" 443 that passes through the West Bank. The soldiers would not notice anything unusual to stop us and would wave us through. I could not stop feeling nervous every time Hamoudi had a joint hidden in his hand as we approached the road barrier guarded by heavily armed Israeli soldiers, but he would nudge me to keep the usual checkpoint smile fixed on my face.

"Why do you unnecessarily risk this?"

"Risk what?"

"What if they could smell it?"

"Then I would ask them to join in! It happened to me one or twice. It was not the joint, which they took without a fuss, but when they found out that I was Palestinian, they got really fidgety. They thought that I was trying to get them stoned to pass through the checkpoint with a consignment of Qassam rockets! So they opened the boot and found my camera. They thought I was an investigative reporter, secretly capturing the soldiers smoking hashish. They became so paranoid that they took the whole roll of film out of the camera and destroyed it then and there. Bastards!"

"I wouldn't risk offering a joint to a checkpoint soldier."

"As a Palestinian I'm always risking my freedom, my every move is monitored by the state. In a way this little silly defiance, smoking a joint while passing through a checkpoint, is my way of saying, *fuck Israel*."

So Hamoudi would be rolling while approaching or crossing the checkpoint with perfect ease, while I would be worrying about my reputation in the unlikely event of being caught. Then I thought, sheepishly, if that happened, I could use my "connection" here to get out of trouble. I silently went through the much-rehearsed verse, "My husband's cousin lives in Katamon. Her name is Michal. Her husband is Yakov." These two names—they are Amos's parents—Leo and I often used, and they worked like magic to get through checkpoints, airports, Allenby Bridge. In the past two and a half years in the country I passed through Ben Gurion airport and some of the other border crossings umpteen times to renew my visa. Whenever the interrogators became too heavy-handed, I dropped these names and I was immediately issued the correct color-coded stickers on my bags and passport. Sometimes, I would furtively look at the cubicles where they took "terrorist" suspects like men with long beards and in dishdasha or wearing the keffiyeh, veiled women, foreigners with names like Rafiq or Ahmed, and unusual but suspicious elements such as Hamoudi who had long hair, smelt of hashish, and was called Mohammed in his passport, to be questioned for hours. Such travelers were required to arrive many hours before departure to go through airport security. Hamoudi said he arrived four or five hours before his flight so that after all the strip searching and interrogation he did not miss his plane. He was a very disturbing element for the Israeli security. He wore his long hair in a ponytail. He did smell of intoxicating grass (but fortunately he would not risk carrying any while passing through airport security). He was a resident of the Old City of Jerusalem. He was soft-spoken and would obediently wait for the interrogator in the cubicle having already stripped himself down to his underwear. Once a female officer was apparently so distressed seeing a weird long-haired, half-naked Arab that she set off the airport's alarm system. When asked why he was sitting there in his underwear, he replied that he had passed through the same airport for the past ten years at least three times a year (to help his brother's business in Germany), and he could not remember a single journey when he went through security without being strip searched. So he said to the security personnel, "I just wanted to make your and my life easier by doing beforehand what you would ask me to do anyway."

The adventure of our drives to Ramle to hunt for the honor killers, the show of Hamoudi's quiet rebellion against the authorities, and the sharing of the Lebanese hashish created a temporary mist of much-needed respite from the recent upheavals. Of course very often the mist would be lifted and life would seem all exposed, and I would feel helpless having to cope with the two very unalike children with different needs, different languages, and contrasting political awareness. But the fascinating pace and liveliness of their growing up kept me tuned to my life in the Middle East's most disorienting city.

Despite being an extraordinarily close friend and colleague, Hamoudi kept himself totally disengaged from my private affairs. The ache of separation was visibly imprinted on my face at the time, and I would throw in comments every now and then to ease the load and also for him to understand my tense and edgy behavior. Once or twice I barked at him for being late for our eight thirty appointment when I would be waiting in the car with a scorching Middle Eastern sun on my face. He had an incredible ability to handle such situations. The whole journey he would not say a word, just smoke and stare at the shadows sliding off the windscreen. To get him to talk I would stop at the roadside gas station in Bet Shemesh and buy two double espressos and sweet cheese borekas for the journey. He would say thank you but still not confront me verbally, that I should not have been angry at him. He would still not tell me that he just overslept a little because he had a late night. We would not talk for the rest of the journey. This kind of Gandhian disengagement, quiet resistance from a Palestinian, left me in awe of him—for the very reason that he was beyond the stereotyping of the Palestinian resistance as suicide bombers or Qassam throwers.

Hamoudi never asked any personal questions regarding my family situation. He met both the children, and Maya was particularly fond of him and practiced her Arabic with him, calling him a *hamar*—donkey, and a *batikh*—watermelon. He even met Leo on several occasions in the popular East Jerusalem restaurant Askadinya, where he liked to hang out. But at my house he did not see Leo and never asked where he was. I felt so intrigued by his apparent lack of curiosity regarding my private life that one day while driving back from Ramle I told Hamoudi that I did not live with my husband. He did not look up, did not stir. After a long, frustrating pause, he said, "I knew there was something. You always look so sad, and often you are struggling to hide something by being superexcited by things when there's nothing to be excited about. Like when we stopped by the old roadside fountain on Route 443 to fill up our bottles and buy fresh figs, you started shrieking in ecstasy. I was surprised, because the figs were not even ripe!"

Nothing more. Hamoudi did not ask any more questions.

.19.

MAYA STARTS SCHOOL

In September 2008, Maya started school. On a Monday morning, Leo and I arrived early—separately—at the Lycée Français de Jerusalem to enroll our little girl in the first grade. We were undecided for a long time whether she should continue with the Hebrew system and start her first year in an Israeli school or we should look for an alternative. At first we seriously considered an Israeli school, as moving house under the new separate family arrangement was traumatic enough and we did not want her to go through any more major changes. She should be with her friends from the kindergarten and go to the same school as them. But then we thought about her future. If we went back to London, to Europe, to India, what would she do with her Hebrew education? Or Arabic, for that matter?

Despite our disagreements over other issues concerning the children, Leo and I managed to agree to send her to the French school. The Anglican school was known for its happy clappy note; it was so systematically transmitted to the young children of the primary section that a smug face of Jesus was permanently imprinted on each of them. Luckily, Kiran was in the secondary school, where the school authorities did not try too hard to brainwash the older, more skeptical students. Also, most of the secondary school teachers were Jewish American or Jewish English—all Israeli citizens—on local salaries, as the school could not afford to bring in "Christian" teachers from Britain or America, and so it was harder to persuade Jewish teachers to educate the children with the evangelical message.

The French Lycée was a reputable organization with a strict academic policy. The fees were the same as in local Israeli schools, unlike the Anglican, which collected private school fees.

But most important, the lycée had a secular education system, the same system as in France and in the rest of the francophone world. And in this land of religious frenzy where everything was determined by raw ritualistic, ideological, politicized, and intensely religious doctrines, we wanted the children, at least while in school, to be away from it all. The lycée provided that sanctuary. Its students did not sing hymns to Christ in the assembly as they did in the Anglican school. Yezan, Kiran's Palestinian friend, told me that the assembly had been the most uncomfortable half hour for him and other fellow Muslim Palestinians during the primary school years. They had to stand in silence, as there was no alternative service for the non-Christian children.

What also helped determine our decision for our daughter was the fact that 70 percent of the lycée's students were Palestinian. The school being in close proximity to Arab East Jerusalem and the fees being affordable, many Palestinian parents sent their children there for better education and better prospect for the future; they hoped that one day their children would get the opportunity to study at the Sorbonne and leave the rotten conflict behind.

Despite being an international school, the lycée in real terms functioned as a "local, state" school. More than half of the students came from East Jerusalem, Ramallah, and Bethlehem. They were the children of ordinary Palestinians, unlike those in the Anglican school whose parents were diplomats, ultrarich Palestinians, or politicians (the former Palestinian prime minister Salam Fayyad's children were among the school's star pupils).

The question that had been niggling me was why I thought that way, why, when I looked at schools, I noted how many children were Palestinian, how many "international," how many Jewish (very few were Jewish, as Israelis were discouraged by the state from sending their children to non-Jewish or secular schools that did not teach the basic tenets of Judaism). I would not go into a school in London and start counting how many children were black, how many white, how many Muslims, Christians, Sikhs, or Hindus. If I visited a school in Bangladesh, I would not start assessing how many of the children were Muslims and how many Hindus or Buddhists. I would not do that anywhere else in the world. But it was different in this land of claims and counterclaims over whose god was greater. God was Great in Islam, *Allahu Akbar*; but God was even Greater in Judaism, as *He promised the land to the Jews, His chosen people*; and the Great God was no lesser entity when *He gave man His own son, Jesus Christ*, to seek forgiveness on behalf of all Christians.

All our liberal values broke down in futile endeavors in the face of such intense religiosity about this place, where everything, each individual action, was weighed on the celestial scale against the personal or political vision of one's religion. Where every face you looked at, you would be thinking if this face was the face of a Christian, a Muslim, a Jew, an Armenian, a Greek Orthodox, a Catholic, an Ashkenazi, a Sephardi, a Shia, or a Sunni.

Even in the French school, the seat of secular education, I would worry about what I packed in my daughter's lunchbox. Whether it would be politically and religiously insensitive to put in her sandwich German salami (which would probably offend her Muslim and Jewish friends) or in her pasta a few prawns (which might not be pleasing to her Jewish teacher who was observant and ate kosher). In this land it was the hardest thing to be somebody without a visible religion, creed, or custom.

When we visited the French school, we were moved by the Palestinian children singing, in perfect accent, "La Marseillaise." While in classrooms they were not meant to use their mother tongue, the language of the playground was pure Palestinian Arabic, and that made Leo ecstatic. His daughter would be speaking four languages fluently, including Hebrew and Arabic, which he himself had studied and used during his entire work life. That was enough for Leo to make up his mind and I had already made up mine: I began to think that I did not want our daughter to be in the Hebrew system where she could be taught that the country belonged to the Jews only. Our daughter would not learn a single word about half the population of the country, let alone their language or culture. The lycée of Jerusalem was probably the only choice we had for our daughter, so Leo and I, for the time being, happily settled for it.

After a few weeks in her new school, Maya was coming home with Arabic swear words in perfect Palestinian accent, *tahaltizi*, lick my bum, and *kusummek*, your mother's vagina. Fortunately, she did not know what either of them meant. The playground Arabic kept me amused for the most part of our after-school time together. Once in a while I would ask myself: What about Bengali, the language that I grew up speaking as a child, the language that was spoken by more than two hundred million people? I had stopped speaking to her in Bengali quite early on because I did not want to confuse her. She was already struggling to cope with two Middle Eastern languages and now French; I did not want to impose one more, despite the fact that it was close to my heart. So apart from bedtime rhymes, which I still sang to her in Bengali, and the "terrible" words (*shaitaner bachha*, devil's child, being one of them) that I hurled at her and her brother (and her father when we were living together) when I was angry, she had very little connection to Bengali. Although she pestered me almost every day to speak to her in Bengali and in Hindi because she wanted to understand Tagore's songs and Bollywood films, I had no patience. Drowning in the soup of other languages, soon Bengali would become a familiar but distant tune in our ears. More and more her French homework for which she needed my help took over our time, which would otherwise have been reserved for learning Bengali.

One day after we came home from school, Maya went around the house collecting all the various statues and icons of Indian gods and goddesses and arranged them on a low coffee table, creating a shrine where she put fresh flowers and bowed her head holding her palms together the way she saw Rama and Sita do in the film *Ramayana*. It was not hard to understand that she was trying to please her mother, who she felt was on her own, squeezed between the Semitic faiths.

After I saw this, I decided to leave her to her French and her Hebrew, her playground Arabic, and of course English at home. That was enough on her poor little soul. I stopped playing Tagore's songs too often. No need to learn Bengali in Jerusalem.

Because I hoped she would do it anyway one day. When she was older. She would visit Bengal in search of her identity. In search of the other half of her identity.

.20.

ONE HUNDRED YEARS
OF SECLUSION

On Rehov Hanevi'im, the Street of the Prophets, where
Kiran's and Maya's schools were, there were many churches
and other Christian establishments. It was a long stretch,
the lower end of which joined Road 1 while the upper end
merged with Jaffa Road and the Mahane Yehuda market.
Along Road 1 ran the undefined east–west Green Line, beyond which was the Damascus Gate. It was called Damascus Gate because in olden days traders and pilgrims from
Jerusalem left the city through this northern gate to embark
on their journey to Syria. My new house was at the bottom
end of the Prophets' Street, on the edge of the west side of
the Green Line. An area that was also called the Russian
Compound.

Elegant churches with magnificent steeples and grand
architecture dotted this area. The Anglican school was originally a mission hospital in the late nineteenth century before

the thusly named missionaries established an educational body there to promote Christianity among the Jews. Here, one could forget that Jerusalem was currently fought over by the Muslims and the Jews. Here, one was faced with a different past: nine centuries ago Jerusalem was the hub of a violent military campaign by Catholic Europe against Muslims, Jews, and pagans. Although the churches on the Prophets' Street were built in later centuries, they reminded the visitor that Jerusalem was once a very Christian city. They told a different story of a not-so-distant past when crucifixes, not Stars of David, adorned the streets. Tamar and my other left-wing Israeli friends often joked about an interesting twist in this Christian tale of Jerusalem. They said that it was the Crusaders who had first established a fortress city here. From within the fortress they ruled Jerusalem for one hundred years. My friends' theory went like this: Israel was following in the footsteps of the Crusaders by building the separation wall, creating a new ghetto for the Jewish people to fortify their seclusion. The same fate might befall Israel; it too might sink in its own arrogance and short-sightedness, just as the Crusaders did after one hundred years.

"Oh, well, we have only forty years to go before Armageddon," Tamar would say with a relishing chuckle.

I had not seen Tamar for many months while I was recovering from the latest domestic turmoil, while I was searching for my own place in Jerusalem without Leo. In fact I had not seen much of Fida either, but for different reasons. As I settled more into my house and my work and felt confident that I was ready to dissociate myself from the pain of separation, I went to see Tamar in Ein Karem. She was preparing to leave for the United States later in the year, to start a postdoctoral degree on Israel's administrative colonialism. Her goal was to one day take part in the political policy making of her country, to help stop what she often joked about, Israel's decline into an Armageddon-like chasm created by a ghetto mentality, to stop the same fate as that of the Crusaders from befalling the Jews. "This is the only place that I call home," Tamar told me almost every time I saw her, "and I would so want to share that home with the indigenous Palestinians and the others who are here, the internationals, the Ethiopians, the children of the Vietnamese boat people. Believe me, there's enough space for everyone. How wonderful this country could be, if it only swallowed its xenophobic ego. I don't want to go and live in France or Tunisia! I belong here."

She had been living on her own in Ein Karem since Fida moved out. I had yet to find out from Fida and Tamar why they fell apart and how that happened so suddenly. From the snippets of past conversations with Fida, I smelt that there had been a rift between the two women. Something terrible happened, which seriously rattled Fida and she just would not make up with Tamar. She would not even discuss what had happened because the very thought of it, she had said to me, disgusted her. She was badly hurt.

"If you left, who would stop it?" I said to Tamar, sitting in her terrace inhaling the scent of thyme and za'atar from the valley below. I missed Fida. Ein Karem was not the same fragrant place without her.

"Stop what?"

"The Armageddon in forty years."

"I am coming back! I'll only be away for four years. Anyway, do you want to hear what I've been thinking lately about how to stop our collective downfall? Intermarriage. Impose mandatory orgies for the Hamas and the Haredi to relax their bottled-up frustration and rage." Tamar laughed, but I knew that she was not joking. She did believe in diluting all races, religions, colors, and complexions until the world could no longer be divided into ghettos of color-coded peoples. "The world family," she would cry out sometimes, after sleepless nights smoking too many cigarettes over a complicated case, "belongs to you!" Pointing at my children, she would say, "They are the future. A mixed-race future for the world."

Fida's view on this was no different from Tamar's: "If only a mullah could be found to issue a new fatwa that it is a divine order to have sex here and now, that one does not have to preserve himself for the 206 or so houris, beautiful enchantresses in the afterlife, the world could be such a relaxed place!"

When I relayed this to Tamar, she didn't laugh. She said, lighting a cigarette, "Do you know that Fida is now living in Bethlehem?"

I said to her, "Fida doesn't care what would happen in court when her case is due for a review in a few months if the judges decide to take her ID away."

"Under her special status she must have an address in Jerusalem," said Tamar the lawyer, "but she is spending hardly any time here."

Tamar looked tired. I told her that I had seen very little of Fida lately and now I would be seeing less of her, Tamar.

She was due to leave for Princeton in a few months' time.

"Four years is a long time," I said to her.

"Yes, I know, but I hope Princeton will help normalize my life a bit. It will help me live my life as a young PhD student and not as an overmatured lawyer whose sole purpose in life had been to challenge and rectify the racist Israeli legal system. I am not a saint," Tamar said.

"But it must also be wonderful to be wanted. To be needed," I said.

"Yes, but sometimes I feel, for example," said Tamar, "that I've strangled Fida by giving her too much. I scared her away. In my life as an activist I could never have a normal relationship. I am tired of this place that grew me, maybe in five years' time I would feel differently. But I do need a break now. Jerusalem is merciless."

"You remind me of Oz."

"You mean Amos Oz?"

"Yes, he talks about the same ruthless Jerusalem in his memoir, *A Tale of Love and Darkness*."

"Where his mother commits suicide."

"That's right."

"You see what Jerusalem does to you? It 'squeezes lover after lover to death,'" said Tamar, quoting from Oz's book. "Don't fall in love with Jerusalem. This is just a place for a stopover and I managed to spend all my life here. Even after a hundred years, the city squeezed out the Crusaders, remember?"

[285]

And, I thought, it also squeezed *love* to death, not just the lover. The person I loved for sixteen years had become a stranger after we moved here. Something that even the long separation during the Iraq War could not do.

But I did not say this to Tamar. I felt ashamed of thinking of my little personal tragedy when Tamar was about to jump into her mammoth new future, a worry-free, Jerusalem-free future. As she sat there on the terrace with a cigarette perpetually burning between her forefinger and her thumb, her mobile phone rang every three minutes. She picked up some calls and ignored most. "My clients," she said, "they all want to know who will represent them in my absence. Some of them don't know that I'm leaving, so they are calling with new cases. Do you see why I want to run away for a bit from all this? I am dying for some solitude. I would go anywhere, just to escape from this phone ringing continuously from six a.m. till midnight. I've been woken up so many times in the middle of the night by tearful clients because their husbands or their sons or their nephews or their other loved ones had been taken away by the Israeli army after late-night raids. They called because they didn't know where they had been taken to, which prison, to which part of the country. Terrorist suspects. Administrative detainees. No trace, no rights. A normal day for me would begin with such a call or calls from desperate relatives, I would begin my search to locate them in the country's numerous prisons, which would involve long travels, from Kiryat Shmona near the Lebanese border in the north to the Negev in the south."

Tamar was calm, but there was an inner, suppressed agitation that leapt out from time to time, when the cadence of her voice changed to a louder pitch before descending to a very low, melancholic drop. "I am tired," she said softly.

I felt so sad for her. I wanted to give her a hug but restrained myself fearing it would be a bit too cinematic.

"But you will come back, won't you?" I asked.

"Of course."

"When?"

"First two years on the Princeton campus and then there are choices. If I manage to finish my second year successfully, I'll have to go and do some fieldwork. A year here in Israel, a year in India."

"What's your fieldwork?"

"I'll be comparing colonial memories between India and Israel, more precisely, Bengal and Jerusalem."

I was fascinated. How enlightening it would be, I thought, to get to know Tamar's future research. My thoughts went back briefly to my own truncated PhD in Oxford. "For family reasons," I wrote to my fabulous and disappointed teachers at the time, I could not continue my research on oral history of undivided Bengal.

"And when you finally come back here, will you join politics?" I asked Tamar, feeling hopeful about this place.

"That's the plan."

"This place needs people like you. With you as a future leader, your theory of Armageddon could be postponed for an indefinite time." I smiled and added, "So there'll be a bit more time to ponder permanent peace with the Palestinians."

"How can you be so sure about my role? And what makes you think that I would be accepted as a politician?"

"Things will change in four or five years' time. People on both sides are fed up. They are desperate for a political solution," I said to her.

"Well, I do want to do something about putting an end to the fast-spreading Jewish supremacist creed in this country—the most bizarre phenomenon of the twentieth century!" Tamar said without a trace of vacillation in her voice. Her extraordinary self-confidence and clarity impressed me. When she made a statement, she did so with conviction. The listener was convinced that she believed in herself. Wasn't it what a politician needed?

"But I don't want to be part of a political party," she added. "I want to run a government office and change not by words but by deeds. I don't want to be a politician on the front page of the national newspaper or on TV news."

"How would you do that? How would you run a government office?"

"Since I'll have a PhD in administration, I believe I would be able to run a ministerial office. Manage the office and work from within the rotten system. Well, we'll see."

"How will you change the system from within?"

"I have plans," she said softly but with an assertive smile.

"So am I seeing before my eyes the future leader who would herald the perfect 'one-state' solution, pave the way for peaceful coexistence in a binational state? In fact, according to your dream theory, a multinational state for the Jews, Palestinians, internationals, Vietnamese boat people, the Ethiopians, and so on?" I said. She had better come back before the keys around the necks of the refugees became too burdensome. Before they had taken them to their graves in strange lands.

As if she could read my mind, Tamar said, "I'll have to come back while the dreams of the refugees are still alive."

"You had better hurry up. They are old, most of them are in their seventies or eighties, the ones who remember the Naqba."

"I hope they will hang on for another five or six years," Tamar said.

"I hope so too," I said to her.

Another beautiful evening had descended on her terrace. A pleasant herb-fragrant rush of air brushed against our faces. I felt a touch sad. We were still young, and yet despite the intoxicating breeze blowing against our sun-kissed skins we were laden with duties and despair.

"I have to come back," I heard Tamar continue with a sigh, from over the ocean of many more unknown, premature worries, "to tear down the wall of seclusion. To free Israel of the ghetto complex. Israel must understand that for the sake of its survival it cannot bar an enemy that it had created in the first place, by erecting a physical wall around itself. Hamas is Israel's own Frankenstein's monster. In the '80s, you must know it, Israel had provided arms and funds to empower Hamas to fight the PLO."

"I know that you'll come back. With so much pain and passion for this place, you won't be able to stay away too long," I said to her.

"I think that it might be healthy for me to stay away for some years from my country's obsession with seclusion. I will come back to have a fresh start."

I felt privileged to have known Tamar so closely, the future politician who would bring in the much-needed new dynamic. I believed in her.

"If only the Princeton selection board knew who they're about to take on"—I laughed, to lighten up the heaviness that had descended on the terrace amid all this long somber talk—"the future leader who would reshape Israel, who would put an end to the past six decades of isolation."

"We have to stop looking toward Europe and turn instead to the Arab world if we don't want to meet the same fate as the Crusaders!" Tamar smiled, musing on her famous theory.

Tamar had less than six months left before she was due to start her course in the United States. I wanted to make the most of the time that we had together. There were also many unresolved questions on my mind: What really happened between her and Fida? They broke up. I was still struggling to come to terms with that. When Fida came to collect her things from Ein Karem—I had brought her here in my car—Tamar deliberately stayed away. It was some four months ago, and they had not exchanged a single word since. What was it that so embittered Fida's heart? I wanted to understand, for it was Fida who did not want to have anything to do with Tamar.

I started thinking of what could be one of the possible reasons.

"Fida once said to me that you slept with some of your Palestinian clients. Did you really? Is that why she is upset with you?" I said, and felt somewhat embarrassed by my audacious conjecture.

"With some of them," said Tamar, not registering my unease. "The cute ones. Yes. Why, do you have a problem with that?"

"Professionally, do you not think that it is wrong?"

"No, I didn't work with my Palestinian clients as a so-called professional lawyer, which means that I mostly worked for free, as they couldn't really afford to pay."

"So they paid with sex?" The words slipped out of my mouth. But it was too late.

"No," said Tamar, without rising to what must have sounded like pure provocation. What a perfect lawyer, I thought. "They were intrigued, so was I, we had mutually agreed sex."

"But deep down, wasn't it a very unprofessional thing to have done?"

"I fought in court against the Israeli government on behalf of the Palestinians for access to their relatives in prison, free of charge, because I felt strongly. But it would have also been nice to be paid for my time and hard work. The way I worked was hardly professional, I was driven by my politics and my vision for my country. I was a political lawyer. What you said is wrongly phrased, maybe Fida's been filling you up with this misinformation. I didn't sleep with my Palestinian *clients*. I had mutually consented sex with some of my Palestinian *friends*, some of whom I happened to represent. What can you do about that? Every Palestinian in one way or another has to face the all-powerful state: for permits to stay in the country, to build an extension to their home, to leave the country, to put an extra water tank on their roof, to study, to go to school . . . Every Palestinian needs a lawyer to walk from A to B. What can you do? I am a lawyer, you may say that all Palestinians are my clients. Fida too was a client. Was it unprofessional, then, having Fida, my client, to live with me in my house? Go dancing with her in Dewan? Drinking with my client Fida, was it the right thing that we did so often? Fida was an eye-opener for me. She made me see new twists in the Israeli-Palestinian friendship, how carefully we have to tread, so that our eagerness to help is not seen as patronizing. They are justifiably a proud lot, the Palestinians."

They surely were, I thought. Fida in particular, of all the people I had come to know here, epitomized this pride.

When I contacted Fida again, I discovered that during those few weeks that we were out of touch, she had stumbled upon a big break: she was headhunted by Bethlehem's landmark hotel, Jacir Palace, to work as their sales manager.

I went to see her in Bethlehem. I did not recognize her, she had straightened her hair and it had been cut short to her earlobes, exposing her long neck and her sharp chin. I was led by the receptionist to an elegant conference room where Fida, wearing a brown suit, was talking to business executives about an upcoming meeting in the hotel with Tony Blair, who was visiting Bethlehem that week.

.21.

THE

JESUS-SMELLING SEA

Leo wanted to take the children away for the weekend. He said I could come too. But while I was happy to have Shabbat dinner on Friday nights with the family in his place, I was not ready to go away with him yet. I very much wanted to but did not know how to handle being in the closed chamber of a tent on the shores of the Sea of Galilee for a romantic long weekend only to come back to our separate homes in Jerusalem. So he left with Kiran and Maya.

I still felt purposeless, so many months on, when I was separated from them in the weekend. After the initial bafflement at having two whole days all to myself, which I did use creatively in the beginning, I was increasingly running out of ideas. The weekend began to feel too long and I did not know what to do with so much time. I had by now tried everything that was possible in Jerusalem to keep myself interested in the city. I had done most of the well-known walks, visited almost all the restaurants and most of the cafés. I was at a loss facing again another long forty-eight hours when the children would be camping with their father.

In the evening, Hamoudi's telephone call broke the spell of silence in my Musrara house.

"*Yallah*, *Taali*, come, we have the world's best steak here. Come to Askadinya."

"I don't eat steaks," I said to him, when I arrived at the restaurant in East Jerusalem. "I was vegetarian until recently. I am eating bits of meat now, but not yet a steak."

"Yes, yes, yes, I've spent three months in India. You worship the cow and we love eating your god!" Hamoudi chuckled.

"Ha-ha, you know all about India!" I said. Whenever people here made comments about the Indian pantheon of deities or Indian customs—always sounding condescending—I felt uncomfortable. It would be futile to try to make any sense to the Israelis or to the Palestinians of what the sacred cow or other ancient customs and rituals meant to many Indians. I found it particularly difficult to explain these to the adherents of the Semitic religions, whose cultures theorized that monotheism was a natural progression from idolatry. So often I angered my Jewish friends and relatives by suggesting that not eating food off the plate that had touched nonkosher meat was just as strange as Hindus not eating "the sacred cow." Even nonreligious Hindus sometimes avoided eating beef—it was part of an age-old custom which, if one had been brought up with it, was hard to give up. Similarly, many nonreligious Jews would not touch shellfish because they were not accustomed to the taste. It was interesting that despite their history of conflict, the Semitic belt—Judaism, Christianity, and Islam—had its own code of alliance among its followers. For example, under Islamic law a Muslim could marry a Jew or a Christian, but not a Hindu or a Buddhist or a Zoroastrian unless they converted. Islam called believers of the three Semitic religions "the People of the Book," since Islam recognized the Bible and all the prophets who preceded Muhammad.

I would offend many people by saying I was an atheist—in this region worshipping a sacred cow was better than being a nonbeliever. That left my "declared" Hindu position a bit precarious—no one was sure how to try monotheism on me. But that also meant that I was left alone a lot of the time and was seen as someone with an exotic, primitive faith. At least once a day I would hear Hindi songs being sung to me in the streets of West Jerusalem, the alleyways of the Old City.

So I thought I would ignore Hamoudi's comment. He ordered a bottle of merlot and said, "You have to try the Askadinya steak. It is the world's best. Believe me, even your god would be pleased that he tastes so good and that people are so happy being fed by his succulent flesh."

"That's verging on sacrilege." I laughed.

"You must try it. Just break the taboo—this is a good place to do it."

"I broke all the other taboos. It didn't feel good when I saw my friends cutting through their steaks and blood oozing out staining their potato mash."

"You can have it medium, still succulent but no blood. Also, here it will be halal meat, less bloody than the European version. Trust me, you would never forget the Askadinya steak. Okay, how about a deal? I'll work for you free for a day if you try a steak here tonight."

I was surprised by his persistence. It was getting ridiculous. I did not really have any taboo-related objection to eating steak. It just always looked very heavy and a lot of meat to be consumed by a skinny human being like myself.

But when Hamoudi took my silent smile for a yes and ordered a steak, I knew that it was too late, and in a few minutes I would become a serious carnivore, because once I had eaten the Askadinya steak, before all these people, I could not really pretend to be a vegetarian again. Having resigned myself to my fate, I silently sipped my wine.

"And this merlot is specially chosen for the steak," Hamoudi said and poured me some more.

Instead of a huge chunk of meat that I thought would come on a mound of mash on my plate, there was a small piece of charcoal-smelling, seared neat flesh presented alongside two florets of crunchy broccoli and two small boiled potatoes dusted with tangy pink sumac. The edge of the plate was also sprinkled with sumac with a few red chili flakes. The most interesting part of the dish was a pile of quick-fried coarsely chopped fresh green chilies and garlic on the char-grilled meat, drenched in a generous drizzle of extra-virgin olive oil. I'd never seen such beautiful presentation of a piece of meat. It looked like an offering to the gods, after all.

"*Tafaddali*," go ahead, said Hamoudi and waited for me to start. I held a serrated steak knife and smiled. Somehow the beautifully arranged platter before me resembling a divine offering helped me to go ahead. Hamoudi had an identical platter in front of him, and he waited for me to start. I cut a thin slice of the forbidden flesh. It was pink and juicy but not too bloody. I smiled nervously before putting it into my mouth. I waited. I chewed. I swallowed. It was not earth-shattering. I was not struck by the wrath of 330 million gods and goddesses. I did not turn into a base incarnation as a result, a rat or a hedgehog, for example.

I even liked the taste. Chili, garlic, sumac, olive oil.

We were sitting at the bar, and everyone sitting around us clapped. I had no idea that Hamoudi was waiting for this moment of victory. I saw the chef's head poking out the kitchen window, smiling contentedly. With a black mole on his left cheek, he reminded me of Robert De Niro.

The excitement of eating the steak and the sweet numbness that the merlot had created started to wear off as the night grew older. It was odd that I did not need to look at the clock, that there was no babysitter waiting for me to get back so that she or he could go home. In fact, I had no reason to get back home. I did not know how to handle the reality when I was not summoned by the needs of my family. My thoughts went to the children, who were camping with their father on the shores of the Galilee.

After our delicious meal that we washed down with the appropriate wine, Hamoudi and I went outside to smoke. There were many others also enjoying the fragrant evening breeze under the loquat, askadinya tree, talking and smoking. We sat on the edge of the pavement. There was a full moon, and perhaps it was the lunar spell that caused a torrent of emotions to churn inside me. I was missing the children. I was uncomfortable with the weekend arrangement. I was desperate to call to find out how they were, when my mobile phone rang. The inscription on the little screen, LEO, leapt up before my opaque eyes and disconnected me from the present.

"Hello?"

At first I could hear only the sound of the waves. The sound of the Sea of Galilee. Popular Hebrew songs were playing on a crackly sound system in the background. I knew those waves, I had seen and swam in their folds. He was trying to hurt me by camping on the beautiful spot that reminded me of our escapades in the past.

"Can you hear the waves?" he said in a trembling voice. I could hear my heartbeats. I felt dizzy.

"Yes."

"Hear them again." He held the phone to the edge of the sea. I was left with a vision of a great mass of water at the foothills of Nazareth. I was adrift in memories from a previous life.

We wake up early. I watch him pack. The tent. Utensils for cooking. Fire lighters. The barbeque. I watch with envy.

He packs tins of food. He packs a tray of fresh eggs. The children are excited, Maya more so than Kiran. He knows how to organize a perfect camping trip. He knows how to pitch a tent in the dark. He knows how to get food in the middle of the night in unknown places, how to light a campfire. We arrive at the

Kinneret, the biblical name for the Sea of Galilee, and he lets me sleep on a blown-up mattress. He pitches the tent in the dark.

In the morning he boils eggs and opens a tin of baked beans that he cooks in the tin on the campfire and brings me breakfast to bed. Maya can't stop talking about Jesus. He's been telling her the story of Jesus's life in the hills above.

On the shores of the Sea of Galilee, we hear Maya talk about Jesus, how he came down from the hills of Nazareth and had a dip in the sea.

We swim in the Kinneret where Jesus swam. The children are excited. We wake up early and roll into the cool green water, we swim in the sea full of St. Peter's fish. "I can smell the smell of Jesus," says our angelic daughter. "Jesus came down from the mountains"—and she sings, for no plausible reason, "She'll be coming down the mountain when she comes, she'll be coming down the mountain when she comes"—"and stood beside this lake. Daddy told me."

I close my eyes and contemplate on the Prophet of Nazareth. I swim in the Jesus-smelling sea. I breathe in the fish-smelling air. "Thank you for bringing me here," I tell Leo. I go up to him, I put aside a half-eaten egg sandwich. I hug Leo and tell him, "Thank you for bringing to me this overwhelming taste of history."

I jump into the sea. Next to him, side by side, we swim together.

"Can you hear the waves?" Leo whispered.

"Yes."

"I would like to swim with you."

"I would like to swim with you too."

"Jesus of Nazareth swam here," he said, sounding just like Maya.

"I swam in the sea where Jesus of Nazareth *walked on the water*. With you."

"I want to swim with you again."

"I wish I were with you."

"Can you hear the waves?"

"Yes. I can. I can."

I was about to add, I ate a steak. I was about to say, I broke the taboo. I was about to say that I was unable to contain the bubbling emotions inside me, unable to sustain the unpredictable course of events over the past months.

"What's up?" asked Hamoudi. We were still sitting outside the restaurant.

"Nothing," I said, suppressing my wild tears.

"What's up, *habibti*?" Hamoudi put an affectionate arm around me. I so wanted a hug, but I could not accept his. I missed Leo's arms, his strong embraces.

I swim in the Sea of Galilee. Only with him.

"What's up? *Shou? Shou sar?*" asked Hamoudi again. "What, what happened?"

I could not tell him what happened, what was happening. That I was possessed by a reckless longing for Leo.

"*Yallah*, let's cheer you up a bit," said Hamoudi. "Let's go for a walk."

"Where?"

"In the Old City. I'll show you something that will make you forget all your worldly troubles."

We walked together to Via Dolorosa. About one hundred meters into the narrow street, we found some steep stairs to the right. We walked up those stairs, and Hamoudi showed me a pair of iron doors, painted blue, that stood out in the light of the moon against the white stone façade.

"It seems the monuments are very near to where we are standing," I said to Hamoudi. I remembered this route, this was frequently taken by the Friday prayer worshippers. One of the gates of the Dome of the Rock complex must be just beyond those blue doors.

"Come on, then." He pushed open the doors and we arrived on an open terrace. We were suddenly bathing in moonlight, but it was more than just moonlight—I could feel the presence of some wondrous magnificence somewhere nearby. I was disoriented for a few minutes. When my eyes became accustomed to the light, I saw Hamoudi's face, the same victorious face as when he watched me eat the steak. He had rolled a joint, which he was now lighting as he stood next to me.

"Close your eyes," he said. He guided me to walk up a narrow passage. My eyes were still closed, but I could sense the light becoming brighter.

Hamoudi helped me stand against what seemed like one of the domed Old City roofs.

"Now open your eyes," he said.

My face was turned toward the source of light. It seemed the moon was within my reach. I opened my eyes and saw the dome. It was so near that I could almost touch it. The moon reflected off the golden cupola onto our faces. Hamoudi passed me the joint. I could not take it; I thought if I moved, the moon-washed monument would disappear. What I saw before me was an illusion.

Dome of the Rock from Hamoudi's roof

It was so near, I could see the ridges between the gold panels. I could see the exquisitely ornate green mosaic below. The octagonal base, which was built over "the rock" from where legends say Prophet Muhammad ascended to heaven, from where he circled around Earth riding the celestial horse called Burak and flew to the seventh sky.

I felt so privileged being so close to the magnificent monument and the hottest symbol of conflict on the world's political map that I turned and smiled at the bringer of this incredible vision. My eyes were filled with tears. I heard his voice echo through this unearthly beauty, *"Habibti, ma Tiklakhi, Kul ishi rahekun mniih,*" Don't worry, dear, everything will be all right, while I cried, thinking of Leo sitting at a campfire on the banks of the Tiberias. *I swim in the Sea of Galilee on a moonlit night. While the children are asleep in the tent. We are bathed in the moonlight. We swim in the Jesus-smelling sea, with a shoal of St. Peter's fish.*

.22.

THE HAREDI
AT THE BUS STOP

He was standing at the bus stop at the top end of Jaffa Road. He was wearing the full Orthodox Jewish garb, with black tailcoat and white tzitzit hanging from the sides, and a black hat. A very young face, partially hidden by the darkness that hung like a dusky drape over the bus stand with four red plastic seats.

"Do you have a cigarette?" he asked.

I was surprised. But it did not click at first why I was surprised.

I stopped and fumbled through my bag. I found the packet and offered him one, held the lighter for him while he lit his cigarette.

"*Mi efo at?*" Where are you from? he asked.

"*Mi London,*" I said, slightly surprised. I was not expecting someone like him ever to talk to me. Men like him, the ultra-Orthodox Haredi, would not even sit next to a woman on the bus, and they walked to the other side of the road if a woman accidentally crossed their path.

"Would you like to have a drink or something?" He quickly switched to English, hearing my accent in Hebrew. He was American.

"No, thanks, I must go home."

"Would you give me another cigarette to keep for later?"

"Sure." I gave him one more.

"Is this a strong brand?"

"I smoke only lights."

"Sure you don't want to have a drink?" he persisted, casting furtive glances here and there, above his and my shoulders. He took a puff, looked around, and started fidgeting with his tzitzit.

"No, thanks."

I walked away from him and came to a more raucous part of Jaffa Road. I realized what I did not register before, that he was *smoking*. He was an ultra-Orthodox Jew in black. He was smoking on Shabbat.

He was young, an American immigrant. He most probably wanted sex. Was it okay for them to have casual sex with non-Jews? Was it kosher? Did he think that I was a woman of the night, walking in a long black dress with a turquoise flower brooch looking for an Orthodox Jewish client?

The night was chilly. I walked faster, my long dress flapping around my numb legs, its pink lining showing. Was it the pink, then, which gave the lonely young Haredi man—he could not have been more than twenty-four—the hope that he would find company tonight? What could have been going through his mind when he approached me?

Perhaps he thought that it was okay to take a cigarette from a woman of the night, a *sharmuta*, on Shabbat. Halakha applies only to halakhically "included" people, attested by the Talmud, the Jewish law books. Since I didn't look like one of them, it was okay to do an un-Talmudic act outside marriage on me.

When I said that I was from London, a visitor, he turned more nervous because he probably realized that it would not be possible after all to have what he wanted. Was that why he then suggested that we have a "drink" instead? Where would he have taken me? I slowed down my pace, I felt stupid. Why did I not accept his offer and go for a drink? I was intrigued, but I could not really turn back now and say, "By the way, I've changed my mind, I don't have to go back to my lonely home, I would love to have a drink with you!"

———

I was walking back home from Leo's place in Nachlaot—a politically correct, historically Jewish area, where he lived in a newly refurbished ground-floor apartment with Syrian/Iraqi/North African Jewish neighbors. It had always been part of his dream to live close to the so-called Arab Jews. In his view, before the creation of the state of Israel,

Jews in the Arab world lived in near perfect harmony with their Muslim neighbors. In Nachlaot, when he spoke Arabic to the "Arab" Jews, he was warmly invited into their homes for elaborate meals with the paraphernalia of the Middle Eastern Jewish hospitability that comes on a platter of stuffed vine leaves, kubbeh, almond rice, and fluffy flatbread.

The day had started off as a nice relaxing Saturday. I had walked to his bright sunny house after my morning coffee. We were invited to have Shabbat lunch with his Syrian neighbors, with the traditional *hamin*, a dish with rice, cracked wheat, whole potatoes, chicken, meat, and eggs that had been stewed with saffron, cumin, and other spices on low heat since sundown the day before. There was Esther, the head of the household, mother of twelve children—seven boys and five girls—who were all present around a long table that occupied most of the narrow room that served as a living room–bedroom on other days of the week. Tall and taut at seventy-nine, Esther looked stunning, in better shape than many fifty-year-olds. She was the heart of the house, serving everyone and at the same time sitting next to everyone, moving around the table. Men were drinking vodka and women wine. I realized that this was not a strict religious house. One of Esther's sons was playing the oud, a melancholic and haunting piece of music. They were switching between Arabic, their mother tongue, and Hebrew, the language of the Promised Land, where Esther had immigrated to from Damascus when she was a young bride. There was a framed picture on the wall of her late husband, who had died the year before. He had a kind, very Eastern "Arab" face. Throughout our meal everyone talked a lot about the absent member of the family, the oud player did renditions of a number of his father's favorite tunes, most of them in Syrian "high" Arabic. Leo looked so happy, this was his ideal world: Jews and Muslims spoke each other's languages, prayed together, ate together, and lived in the same country together. He said, pointing in the direction of the men drinking vodka and playing music while Esther put the kettle on, "The Sephardi Jews were never as strict about Shabbat and kosher rules as the Ashkenazi. There was always room for odd deviations and changes. Music in an Ashkenazi home on Shabbat? Unthinkable. Religion should be fun, like this, it should bring people together. The Ashkenazi Jews practice Judaism as if it were a divine punishment. So Christian, their version of Judaism."

Just as he finished whispering these words into my ears, some of the women went outside to smoke. Another Shabbat mitzvah or prohibition that this happy household played around with. I smiled at the women and they beckoned me to join them outside. I realized that the house had only two rooms with a kitchen and a small patio. I asked Esther if she'd always lived here, and she replied that all the children were born here. I thought of Hamoudi's two-room house on Via Dolorosa, where his parents brought up his ten siblings. I was ashamed of our current privileges, which came at a great pain, as privileges often do in one way or another. Somehow we needed to justify our good fortune by inviting conflict, to balance it out. Having two houses and nine rooms between Leo and me and our two children—thanks to the rent that we received from our family home in London—I was too shamefaced to ask Esther how she had managed to raise them all in this small place: Where did they all sleep? Where and how did the children do their homework? Did she and her husband ever have any private space? How did they make love?

———

I reached the bottom end of Jaffa Road. Watching the raucous crowd of the "modern" Israeli youth spilling out of various bars and late-night joints, I thought again of the ultra-Orthodox Haredi man standing in the shadow of the bus stop, in his black cloak and black hat. As I walked away from his invitation, I thought that I had no idea of that world, caught between medieval practices and semi-contemporary lifestyles. What did those men do to pass their days? Their nights? The ultra-Orthodox did not serve in the army, most men did not work. Their wives produced babies every year as well as worked, the men received substantial state subsidies. What did they do apart from studying the Torah? How did they fill in the void between successive studies? Was it all repentance and bitterness to be healed by continuous Torah reading? How did they spend their evenings? Did the man who just wanted to have a drink with me have a wife at home? Children? Did he make love to his wife through a hole in the sheet as says the popular myth? Was his wife American too? Pretty? Did he kiss her? Or did he just perform his duties implanting a baby every year into her womb as he was required to do? Was that why he wanted to have a drink with me, to have a laugh, a temporary release from Talmudic restrictions because his wife did not have time, after taking the children to bed, to sit with him in the evening and just talk about nothing? Did he stop me to talk about nothing? He wanted to feel the lightness of being, something he had scarcely tasted. A scene from the delightful Syrian Shabbat that I had just experienced probably would be beyond his imagination.

The more I thought about the dark bus stop and the strange ultra-Orthodox Jew standing there mournfully, the more I regretted not accepting his offer for a drink. What would have happened? What would he have said? Where would he have taken me? Surely not to Mea Shearim, the ultra-Orthodox quarter not far from the top end of Jaffa Road, where he would be under strict neighborhood scrutiny, where he was watched day and night by his fellow men and rabbis and there was not a remote chance for a man in black like him to be seen enjoying himself, having a drink with a stranger, a woman.

Would he have taken me to a hotel? But he did not seem to have any money, he had asked for an extra cigarette for later. Did he want me to buy *him* a drink?

But I missed my chance. I would never know, I might never again have such a close encounter with an ultrareligious Jew in black tailcoat and tall hat, black trousers, black shoes, and white tzitzit hanging down his sides with 613 knots, which represented the number of mitzvot or Talmudic commandments.

.23.

COMING-OF-AGE

Kiran came of age in the spring of 2008. He carried himself impressively through the bar mitzvah ceremony. Prior to the actual event, which would be conducted entirely in Hebrew, he surprised us by taking his lessons regularly at the synagogue, memorizing the bits from the Torah that he was required to read. It was an occasion for a get-together for Leo's vast extended English, American, and Israeli families. It was daunting for me. My son, even at the age of thirteen, showed the kind of diplomacy that I could strive for, for the rest of my life, but would not succeed in mastering. Throughout the bar mitzvah preparations, he said that he was doing it to make everyone happy and that he would never consider himself Jewish or of any other religious denomination. His public show of allegiance was needed for family reunion. If only we could learn from his prudence and tactfulness, our marriage would not have been in such a bad shape.

We had the party in my garden, and part of the family slept in Leo's flat. Before the pain and unresolved issues of the breakup could settle, we were thrown back together with the bar mitzvah celebration. Leo moved in temporarily with me. Even though I wanted nothing more than to get back together, I wanted to start it from a different place. I was not sure if it was the right moment, but we had no time to think with the big event in Kiran's—or, rather, in Leo's—life approaching.

Somehow we could not bring ourselves to admit that we were not ready yet to get back together.

The first signs of it were being revealed to me by the alienation that I felt as Kiran was preparing for his coming-of-age ceremony. I felt lost and excluded for not belonging to the clan. At least the children sort of half belonged; I was nobody. I looked at everyone—even my nonbelieving sisters-in-law felt totally at ease. Of course, one is born as a Jew, it cannot be fully acquired later in life. Even after the painstaking conversion process, many of my friends said that they still felt rejected by the tribe. From that point of view, Islam and Christianity were more welcoming, more accepting. Even your half-Jewish children could not help you to belong to the club.

I couldn't help but feel that I was being magnanimous by agreeing to Kiran's bar mitzvah and taking an active part in organizing it, albeit hesitantly, as I justifiably questioned my role in it. Leo noticed my hidden dilemma, which must have sometimes slipped out. He could sense that my heart was not 100 percent there, that it was fraught, we knew each other well enough for him to detect that. What Leo saw was that I did not *wholeheartedly* take part in it. I could not have done that, facing a religion that thrived, especially in Israel, on its exclusivity. On top of that, I was a nonbeliever. I thought I did my best, but he said one day when I was sitting glum-faced at the synagogue, "Why don't you sometimes just try to make me happy?"

"I am trying, can you not see?" I whispered in frustration and tearfulness.

It was not a good place to start from, after we had fallen apart so badly. We had not gone through the proper rehab course that was required for confidence building and regaining inner resolution that we would not return to the same site of wound. Part of me was content, despite my unease at the circumstantial pull that brought us back together prematurely. I was tired of our two homes, I grew tired of having Shabbat in his flat and walking back late at night on my own to my lonely house, I grew tired of letting the children go away with him every other weekend. My resolve faltered toward the end and I had been inclined to overlook the nonfulfillment of our promises, that we would strive to be different people, to start again from a safe place.

"I am doing this," Kiran said, "so that Dad can never say again that I never tried."

"I am doing this too," I said to him, "so your dad cannot ever say to me that I did not try to belong."

Strictly speaking, my own family consisted of my two sisters in Britain, whom I chose not to invite fearing they would feel totally out of place among Leo's extended family. Besides, my little sister, Leela, was going through a bizarre and painful time herself: her estranged husband had stolen their only child from a north London primary school, left Britain, and was now hiding with the boy in a Bengali village. There was an international search warrant in place and reputable lawyers were involved to locate him and return him to his mother. Leela could hardly be my confidante; she needed a lot of support from me, as I was closely involved with her case, finding lawyers and chasing the police and judiciary to make sure the boy was declared a ward of court. The only person I invited and who I thought would understand my confusion amid the celebrations was Kiran's old Czech au pair, Katka, who was with us in London while Leo lived in Morocco. Katka understood how it felt to be "goy" in a Jewish coming-of-age ceremony. But still, for her it was exotic. For me, I was the gentile mother. It was the hardest thing to swallow.

In the end it was not all alienation arising from the feeling of being a trespasser in the Jewish synagogue. My moment of pride and inner jubilation came during Kiran's speech, which he wrote by himself, based on his own interpretation of the selection from the Torah that he read as part of the service. Since the ceremony fell during the festival of Passover, Kiran was taught a section of the Bible that concerned the flight of the Israelites from the bondage and slavery in Egypt. It is called Shirat HaYam, the Song of the Sea, a beautiful, haunting piece of poetry. Kiran, my boy who now suddenly was an adult, gave his own interpretation of the poem to a packed synagogue. My heart skipped a beat, and I sat there victorious, beaming with my own private smile.

Kiran said that the song was beautiful, but he did not think that the story was all too pleasing. As he understood the story, he said, it was about praising God for drowning those Egyptians who followed Moses and the Israelites to the Red Sea. Passover was supposed to be a festival of celebration, he said, and this was hardly festive.

He then added that in some sense the Palestinians were like the modern-day Israelites, trying to break free from occupation.

Later that evening when all the festivities were over and our little family retired to the Musrara house, I asked Leo, "Did you help Kiran write his speech?" Luckily we had no guests staying with us in my house; we had settled them all in Leo's flat. We were alone, proud at having succeeded in putting together such an important event. My earlier feeling of self-pity at my gentileness was put on the back burner for the time being and there was instead elation at this little success story amid our family's history of failures. The humane message of Kiran's speech was still spread over our minds like a soothing balm.

"Not really, why should I help him? The Song of the Sea was chosen for him to read at his bar mitzvah by the rabbi, and Kiran chose to write his own speech based on the song."

"He must have discussed with you, the message of it and etc."

"Well, the only thing I suggested to him after I read what he otherwise wrote on his own was the link between the Israeli occupation and the Egyptian slavery."

"I thought so! Aren't you proud of your son?"

"I am. Aren't you?"

Words would not have expressed what we both felt, so we just smiled as we held each other. It was probably the closest moment in our lives since we fell apart. Since we could not reach a common ground for happiness, we had reconciled at some point in our turbulent life that we had the children, the sole joint project in our seemingly unrealizable marriage.

Leo lived permanently with me in Musrara now. Maya settled in comfortably in the Jerusalem lycée. She spoke and wrote perfect French after less than a year. Her Hebrew started to get rusty, to our dismay. But we accepted that, we had chosen the lycée for her sake and we should just be glad that she had adapted so well within such a short period. She also started to show certain political consciousness. Her "Israeliness" was peeling off, and there grew instead a new universal identity and maturity not fit for a child. She was now in a class full of Palestinians— almost two-thirds of her classmates. To them, the lycée continued to be a sanctuary from the grinding mill of occupation. Maya was careful not to be found out in her class that she was a Hebrew speaker. She was still asking loads of questions, but more and more they showed her new political awareness of the place she lived in. Walking around the house, brushing her teeth, or doing her home-work, she would suddenly come up with a totally unre-lated topic and insist that we elaborate it.

"There were shootings in the street outside my school today."

"I don't think so. I would have heard something. Your school is not far from the house."

"But I'm not lying! I heard bangs."

"Might have been fireworks."

"Mummy!" She looked really vexed at my comment. "It was in the middle of the day!"

Maya's big eyes that resembled chocolate Smarties—dark brown with thin circles of gray-green—were about to pop out.

"Well, maybe some naughty boys were playing with firecrackers."

"No, there were shootings. Israelis were shooting Palestinians."

"I don't think so."

"My teacher, Monsieur Daniel, told me. It was playtime and we had to all run inside."

"Monsieur Daniel told you that?"

"He told us that the bangs were gunshots. But I know who shot at who. Palestinians won't be carrying guns in the street!"

"What else did he say?" I would not have been remotely surprised if the teacher had said that the shooting was indeed between the Israelis and the Palestinians, people here shared an awful lot of terrible things with the children. For example, all the children in Maya's class knew that a Palestinian suicide bomber had blown himself up almost a decade ago on the Prophets' Street outside the school gate; his body parts including the head flew over the high wall and fell onto the playground.

"He said that there was a Jewish procession to the Kotel for the Jerusalem Day and some people tried to stop them and so the shooting started."

So, I thought, I was right—he did share an awful lot of information with his class!

"It was probably the soldiers, firing in the air to scare away the protesters who are against the march. What a fuss these fanatics make every year to celebrate undivided Jerusalem Day, just to mock the Palestinians, to show them that the Old City, the Kotel, all belong to the Jews. So childish."

I should mind my words and the rising tempo in my voice, I said to myself. They did not suit a child's ears. She already knew and heard too much.

"What is Kotel?"

"The Wailing Wall."

"You mean the wall with the writing on it?"

"What writing?"

"The wall in Bethlehem with all the writings on it?"

She had seen the part of Israel's security wall around Bethlehem where activists and clandestine revolutionaries had scribbled in spray paint antibarrier slogans. She had seen the famous lines in red from the album *The Wall*, sprayed by Roger Waters himself during his recent concert in Israel.

We don't need no thought control.

But "Kotel" stood for the western remaining wall of the Temple Mount, built in 19 BCE by Herod the Great. I turned to my daughter and said, distractedly, "No, the *wall* with the writing on it is a barrier that Israel put up to stop people from coming and going. The Kotel is the only wall left of the ancient Jewish Temple."

"Where the golden dome is?"

"Yes, where the Dome of the Rock is, which is also called the Temple Mount."

"Which the Palestinians say is theirs but the Jews say should be theirs?"

"The Dome belongs to the Palestinians, it is the highest point of the Temple Mount. But one of its walls, the Western Wall, the Jews say is theirs because that was part of their old Temple that used to be on the same spot."

Maya looked pensive for a second. Then she gave a very grown-up sigh before saying, "So many walls everywhere. But the tallest and the biggest one is in Bethlehem. My friends Layal and Rakan come to school every day from Bethlehem by school bus, through the big gate in the wall. They can't come with their parents. Grown-up Palestinians can't cross the wall. The children can, but only by school bus. Layal and Rakan said they have never seen the sea, because they are not allowed to go to Tel Aviv. They are Palestinians."

I noticed for the first time that Maya had dropped the extra "ni," she stopped saying "Palesti-ninians." When did that happen?

.24.

DESPERATE TO

BELONG

I was busy the rest of the year working on my film. I collected and filmed some forty reels of interviews and footage of the members of the community, of the girls and women who had run away from home to avoid murder. Many of them who stayed behind told me that they were always waiting for their turns—anything could trigger the customary fate of women in the neighborhood of Juarish, of being killed by their own family members. They were afraid of inviting that fate by acts as innocent as sending a Facebook message to someone unrelated to the family. They told me that there was no point in trying to even fight it. I was totally consumed by my attachment to the story, taking frequent trips to Ramle and making Hamoudi work almost for no money, as I had run out of funds. A small relief after each stressful and sad day of filming came with Hamoudi's quirky humor. I was also beginning to get used to his obsessive smoking of the Lebanese hashish that was available in abundance since the second Lebanon War. The soldiers, Hamoudi claimed, had come back with a bountiful supply of the freshest harvest. I felt more relaxed now even when we were passing the Route 443 checkpoint. We made a point not to mention the killing clan of Ramle during our comic interludes.

"How come you have no qualms about smoking with me?" Hamoudi asked me one day as we were driving back to Jerusalem. "I worked with many foreigners. While some of them were very tempted, they still wouldn't accept it, at least not in bright daylight. They would very happily do it, though, in their living rooms or in their secluded gardens in their nightly parties. But never in public. What's wrong with you?"

"Well, I grew up with my grandmother, who used to smoke stuff."

"What did she smoke?"

"She smoked a hookah, a smaller nargila, if you like, filled with ganja or even opium." I added the latter substance to keep the story going. Although my grandmother did confess to me that she had occasionally smoked opium for medical reasons.

"What? Opium? Was she a drug addict or something?"

"No, it was normal in those days. My grandmother used to say that one could buy both ganja and opium at the village grocery store. Ganja to relax and the opium as an alternative to painkiller. She said that many women in her time gave birth easing the labor pain with opium."

"What a civilized society you come from," Hamoudi said with a marijuana-relaxed sigh.

"Well, it's no longer possible, of course."

"When did it stop?"

"I think in the 1970s, after paracetamol and other Western patented painkillers flooded the market and the poor grocer risked imprisonment for selling specific unauthorized substances. Apparently there was a lot of pressure on the government from some foreign agencies to stop the village grocers from selling the traditional healing drug and to promote instead paracetamol cure."

"They even own the copyright of our maladies—and what remedies we must choose," Hamoudi said, taking another deep puff and releasing clouds of smoke slowly, pensively, contentedly.

Finally, in December 2008, I finished the rough cut for the long version of my film, *Deadly Honour*. At the viewing with close friends and the crew, there was a tremendous sense of satisfaction—we had managed to put together a powerful visual story with next to no funding at all. I considered it my best work, counting all the BBC years. For the first time I genuinely felt that I had no regrets leaving that organization. In the past I would say it to justify my action but had hidden doubts, as I had nothing to show, nothing to offer as an alternative achievement. The film had now established that I had not become the typical wife of the ambitious man who convinced herself that it made her happy to give up her career for the family, that she did it out of her own choice. My biggest surprise came when Israel's first channel

bought screening rights for three years followed by its pre-
miere in the country's most prestigious documentary film
festival, Docaviv, in Tel Aviv. It was the most absurd turn
of events that I was living a more "Israeli" existence than
my Jewish husband; his first port of call was still the international community, even after he had stopped working for
the Washington-based think tank. He had given up being a
Middle East analyst and joined journalism once again, the
profession he had a natural knack for, with his tireless pursuit of stories from the greater Arab world. But still he reported to London, while I was bizarrely pegged to this place.

Leo seemed amused by my new exposure. He teased me
when the Israeli Foreign Ministry paid for my plane tickets
to film festivals, saying that I had sold my soul to the Zionist
state. But I felt smugly pleased that I was mentioned on the
database of Israeli filmmakers. What would have appeared
to any observer as being pathetic was a clear-cut realization
for me that I had a childish yearning to belong. Anywhere
that was available. Any spot on Earth that would embrace
me and offer security. I concluded that it was what happened to floating souls, after much wandering, bragging of
independence, and detachment from the world of religion,
nationality, and kinship.

With the unexpected attention I received from the
Israeli audience following the release of my film, I became
more confident. So whenever people in the street or in my
everyday life unwittingly questioned my ethnic status in
this country, I was able to demonstrate a certain brazenness
and humor that I did not possess before.

When I was speaking to a packed audience after my film was screened in Warsaw, then in Marseilles and Brussels, and was asked which country I was representing, I shockingly heard myself say, "Israel."

I could explain this only as my way of turning the table around. I was overcoming my insecurity. I did not spend much time pondering what anyone thought of my new laughable "allegiance" to the Israeli state. It was just very comforting.

For now I was content.

One evening when I came back home after celebrating the official release of the film with my crew at Askadinya in East Jerusalem, I could hardly believe what I was experiencing: the long-forgotten, familiar nausea. In the early hours of the morning, unable to sleep, I drove to an all-night chemist and bought a pregnancy test. The pack came with two test sticks. Both proved to be clearly positive.

In the stillness of the dawn with only our heartbeats to hear, I looked at Leo in amazement. How did that happen? We neither wanted nor tried for a third baby after what we had gone through in recent years, but it still happened, and the only way I could explain this was that it was just part of the good-luck package: getting back together, Maya settling in school, Kiran's successful bar mitzvah, the recognition of my film in Israel, and a new *Israeli* baby on its way into our family. I felt protective toward the atom of life inside me and the half creator of that life sleeping next to me. There weren't very many moments in our lives together when I felt such affinity with Leo, such conjoinedness of our hearts and bodies.

PART
FOUR

.25.

HOPE, CAUTION

The hope and possibility for a solid continuity of our family that looked so plausible at this juncture would turn out to be a house of cards, the first alarm bell ringing at the three-month ultrasound scan of our third baby-to-be, which showed white spots in her heart.

Things moved fast after that, they had to.

It started in Jerusalem, the first part of losing the baby. I boarded a plane to London, where my two other children had been born and where I wanted to leave the baby that was not going to be mine. We were not meant to have a third child. It was not planned, but that did not help soothe my grief when I was actually losing her. Once she had been embedded in my body, she became part of me, we grew together for one hundred days. The security at the airport asked the usual questions. But this time I was traveling on my own, and a single woman is considered to be the highest threat in Israel's security profiling. I realized as I arrived at my turn with the security personnel that only a handful of times had I traveled out of Tel Aviv without one or both the children with me. I felt exposed and extremely uncomfortable. The last thing I wanted was to answer blankly to routine questions such as where I was going and why I was going there.

"Are you traveling on your own?"

"Yes."

"Why were you in Israel?"

"I live here with my family."

"Is your husband Israeli?"

"No."

"What does he do?"

"A journalist."

"For which paper?"

"He freelances." I was too tired to give out more information.

"And you, do you work?"

"I am a housewife."

I maintained the standard reply, which always saved me from answering more questions about my work. Luckily the security here did not carry computers with Google. If they had, they would have learned about my work activities, and that would have complicated matters more since I was here on a tourist visa. For now, my housewife status seemed to have satisfied them.

"You know that you are not allowed to work here," said a stone-faced junior officer, through her Ethiopian curls that fell over her stern eyes.

Thank goodness I had not mentioned anything about my filmmaking! Why do they always have to be Ethiopians, I thought. I often found them to be the most hostile of the interrogators. The most deprived group of the aliya makers in Israel was struggling to prove itself to the Ashkenazi elite. But I couldn't be concerned about the sorry state of the Ethiopian Jews when my baby was trickling away from me.

"Yes, I know." On a visitor's visa I was not technically allowed to work in Israel. But everyone did, including foreign NGO workers, in order to avoid a lengthy bureaucratic application procedure for a work visa. "Of course I know I can't work, I am on tourist visa. I leave the country every three months in order to come back in again," I said.

"But you can't go on doing that for too long. You must have a long-term B2 spouse visa stamped on your passport through your husband's work."

They put my hand luggage through the X-ray machine, then I walked through the X-ray gate. This time I was like all the others. This time I was not the privileged wife of a Jew and the mother of two half-Jewish children. I was being treated like any other single, high-security-risk passenger. They asked me to step aside and gave me a number for the bag check counter. I walked sluggishly toward the counter. I had no intention of fighting. I thought of our relatives: Yakov, Michal, Amos—the names that would get me out of trouble in an instant, but I could not articulate my thoughts.

They asked me to open my case. I opened it and then unzipped my wash bag. I took the camera out of the pouch, which one of the security guys seized from me, turned on the LCD screen, and went through all the pictures. I regretted that the pictures that Leo took of me crouching down to pee in the roadside bushes on a recent trip to the Dead Sea were not there.

"Where did you buy these sweets from?" asked the man behind the counter with a strong Russian accent after he had finished playing with the camera and picked up the box of baklavas out of my case.

Damn! I should not have had these in my luggage. The true answer was on the tip of my tongue, which I slid back.

"From the Old City."

The sweets were from Gaza, Leo brought them back from his last trip. I was carrying them to give to his father, who loved the sweet Arab delicacies. Dropping the word "Gaza" here would have been more hazardous than throwing a hand grenade. I was now hoping that the Russian did not read Arabic.

Bloody Russians, I could not help thinking, they were too good at languages to be fooled.

"But here it says 'Aza'"—Hebrew for Gaza—he said and stared at me unblinkingly.

"Perhaps they were baked in Gaza and then marketed in Jerusalem"—which would be impossible with the current blockade on Gaza—"or maybe a Jerusalem franchise is making the Gaza specialties. Like the sheep's cheese *kanafe* from Nablus that you can also buy in the Old City of Jerusalem. I don't read Arabic, you see."

I lied again. I knew enough Arabic to read "Made in Gaza." It was hard to know whether the Russian and his juniors who were hovering around him now believed my story. Perhaps I should have kept it short and precise and not have brought up the kanafe story. I did it because at this point of the interrogation, I was beginning to feel nervous. Did they suspect that I was covering up for something? I did not want them to think of me as one of the pro-Palestinian activists who lie down before Israeli tanks during army incursions. I had no connection to Gaza except having a husband who had a fixation on the Mediterranean strip.

"But you see, we currently have a siege"—ah, there we go, I had not fooled him!—"there's no way these sweets might have come from Gaza to be marketed in Jerusalem, unless a journalist or diplomat or a UN worker personally brought them from there." The Russian did not give me a chance to respond to his final assessment of my attempt at falsifying the origins of the baklava.

I was put through more searches; they squeezed toothpaste out of the tube and put it through a machine. They took swabs from inside my handbag and put them through the machine to check possible traces of gunpowder. More questions followed.

"Why are you traveling to London without your family?"

Yes, really, why should a "housewife" travel on her own?

"I have a medical emergency," I said, my eyes downcast, I did not want any more probing. But my reluctance to make eye contact gave the interrogating officer more reasons to think that I, the carrier of sweets from Gaza, must be hiding something. He handed me over to a female officer, who led me to a cubicle for body search. I struggled not to let the suppressed tears roll down my cheeks.

From her accent, I could tell the female officer was a real sabra, Israeli born. In the security hierarchy, the immigrant Israelis probably carried out the first steps of interrogation before passing over the passenger for final checks to the native Israelis. The female officer had an expressionless face. She asked me to stand with my legs apart and arms stretched.

"Do you have a weapon?"

"No"

"Do you have any sharp objects on you?"

"No."

"Penknife?"

"No."

She ran her hands over the side of my left thigh, right thigh, my left arm, right arm, the length of my backbone, my abdomen, the under wires of my bra cups; she pulled the elasticated middle bit, pressed the hooks on the back. Then she turned her attention to the inside of my legs and suddenly, she stopped. I waited a second before letting out a sign of relief. I thanked myself for staying calm. I looked at her face. There was still no decipherable expression, but there was a single crease on her forehead as she said, "We have not finished. Would you please take off your pants?"

"What? I can't take off my pants!" I thought she meant my underwear. She looked at me now with *two* creases on her forehead, a spark of sudden fire in her eyes—first visible sign of irritability.

"You won't cooperate?"

Why was she suddenly being so pugnacious? I thought, just because I did not want to take my knickers off?

Then I understood her American expression—by *pants* she meant my trousers.

I stepped out of my jeans and stood there cold and vulnerable in my "pants." She swiveled the long electronic wand around my back and my belly. Nothing beeped.

My baby would not beep, I told her. My baby was dying. Warm tears finally burst out and I did not make an attempt to wipe them.

She waited for me outside the cubicle while I got dressed. She collected my case from the baggage check counter, packed my things, and zipped it closed. She asked me to follow her, which I did silently. She took me to passport control and waved a special card along with my passport, I was not required to queue again to go through passport checks. I walked behind her to the waiting lounge before boarding the plane. She sat me down on a chair and asked me if I wanted water. I shook my head. The creases had now vanished from her face. But I did not care. I did not care for anything she offered or what she tried to convey, her empathy, now that she had unsettled me. I was beyond consolation. I looked blankly into the space between the flight boarding desk and the row of seats where I was sitting. Buzz off, now, I mumbled to the unwanted body of terror. I did not care about you or your country. I did not want to belong to your security state.

.26.

THE BREAKDOWN

I never thought the aftermath of losing a baby—I still refused to call it just a fetus—would be so heart-wrenching, so painfully unbearable. I woke up every morning with the recurring memory of lying on an operating table with a rubber mask dangling above me before it fell on my face, smothering me, sending me into a dark abyss, the abyss that would continue to engulf me after I returned to Jerusalem to my family. It was strange, but I lost interest in my living family and mourned the loss of the baby that I could not have. I took my healthy children to school, to their music classes, to birthday parties; I got along with life for a while in a mechanical pace. It did not make any sense what my English doctor had said to me before I left the hospital, that I would find peace by submerging myself into my family, my children. I would learn to appreciate what I had rather than what I could not have. It did not provide any solace. Day and night I thought only of what I did not have.

There was a dinner party organized by Leo days after he brought me back from London, for which I shopped, cooked, set the table, and received the guests. I even smiled and convincingly made an attempt to engage while the dinner guests talked passionately about Operation Cast Lead, the latest Israeli assault on Gaza, to which I half listened in my overall intellectual lethargy.

As I had expected, Leo did not want to address the grief that was poisoning me, numbing my desire to continue with life. He said that I was "wallowing in sorrows." I wished he were more expressive of his pain, because I was sure he felt the loss too, even if not the trauma of it. Because before the final scan that brought the terrible news, Leo was in Dubai for a conference. There he visited a Mothercare store and brought back a yellow bib saying LITTLE MISCHIEF and a cooling leg gel for me. He must have grown attached to the new reality in our lives too, a new baby that we both silently believed would bind us together. It was part of the good tidings that we felt were flowing through our lives: the new film, Leo's leaving the American think tank and getting back to journalism, the children feeling safe after we had decided to live together again.

The party soon started to sink under the weight of alcohol. But even the watermelon-and-vodka punch could not take away the inevitable discussion of Middle Eastern politics at the table. We were experiencing the second Israeli war on Gaza since we had been here. The slurry-voiced and the sober ones alike were engrossed in exchanging agreements and disagreements about their positions on whether the victorious Islamist party Hamas should be punished by the international community. Over the cheese platter and the poppy seed cake, more and more guests acquiesced in favor of boycotting Hamas. Leo, known in the city as the "Hamas man," voiced his familiar position that the internationals must give the Islamist group a chance to stay in power and run the country. "You cannot talk about democracy and deny a democratically elected government the right to govern." Have we not heard this at least a thousand times by now since Hamas's victory in the Palestinian legislative elections two years ago? I yawned in fatigue and frustration. I wanted the party to clear out and leave me to my solitude where I could go back to my lost baby.

A red-haired man with sharp eyes behind round spectacles said in a Scandinavian accent that under no circumstances should Hamas receive any foreign aid. They must first change their political manifesto to recognize Israel.

"They must be given a chance," Leo said, reiterating his earlier point. For the first time Hamas was in the government, he said. It was no longer an opposition resistance movement. The policy statement was just a popular strategy that they used to contain the hatred of the millions of Palestinians who were made refugees or exiled, stripped of their right to return to their homeland by Israel's intricate apartheid system. The Hamas manifesto was just a political ploy, they were very much interested in a dialogue with the rest of the world.

There were so many voices. A lot of ideas were being boiled, churned. Apart from Hamas talk, there were, among the dinner guests, words of adulation for some and apologies for others for various job-related ups and downs. So this was networking again. How transient everything was.

"Why do they only talk about the rotten politics of this place?" I said to Leo after the last person finally left, which was around two in the morning. "Is there no literature in this part of the world, no art, music? Can you imagine going to a dinner party in London and talking only about what Tony Blair or Angela Merkel were up to?"

"There's art, there are books, and many of these people are avid readers. But I need to see these people to be on top of things about the latest on the Israeli-Palestinian political mood, from the international angle. This is my job! I need to know what the two sides have been telling the foreign mediators. Don't be always so cynical."

"I too need food for thought, if not solace for my sorrows," I said to him. "I got nothing either way tonight. Why should I subject myself to this, especially now when I need my space so badly?"

I was sure Leo knew what I was going through, but he avoided any conversation about it. He avoided me. He was afraid of what he called my obsessive grief for something that happened to one in four women worldwide. Statistics again. I was sick of hearing it, sick of being told how I should be grieving, how much sadness was allocated for this particular loss. Life is not about statistics. "Life comes to you too intensely. I feel powerless before so much emotion,"

Leo wrote to me in a short e-mail, unable to deal with it face-to-face. He suggested that I talk to a grief counselor, but I was not interested in getting anyone else but Leo to hold my hand. The only person who could offer me comfort was him, his words of empathy were the only thing I wanted to hear. And the more he avoided the issue, the more desperate I became. Again, there was this pattern that I could identify from my earlier years, of hankering after impossible expectations.

Amid these confusing times, we moved house again. We went to live in Nachlaot, not far from Leo's old flat. The house was tall, airy, and light. It occupied the top two floors of a narrow red-stone building with three huge terraces, one at the front and two at the back. The ground floor was part of the Mahane Yehuda market. The front terrace hung right above it. The noise down below started long before dawn. More than once it had occurred to the occupants of the house: What if there was a bomb right there, at the entrance to the market where the two security guards were sitting eating falafel or just dozing off at the end of a long day? The market had previously been the target of several terrorist attacks during the intifada years. They imagined the streets and the houses and their balcony splattered with blood and body parts.

Kiran and Maya were growing up fast. Kiran was almost fifteen and had his own world and friends. Moreover, he had his music, concerts, and drum lessons. Maya was suffering. Kiran pushed her away from his new teenage world where little sisters were nothing but a nuisance. Leo was busy with Operation Cast Lead and I was lost in my white clouds of grief. Maya would sit for long hours by herself by the window watching the market, and when it became too boring, she would go and annoy Kiran, only to be pushed out of his room. Around this time she was forced to learn how to have a quiet time. She used to be unable to remain quiet. These days she stayed in her room drawing by herself, and when she spoke, she spoke pensively, with occasional clear statements in between her thoughts, rather than blabbering away as she had done until recently, asking questions almost about everything that happened around her. One day I left her at home to go down to the market to get a few things. She waved at me from the window. When I finished, I still saw her standing at the window waving at me. I crossed the narrow Agrippas Street that separated our house from the market and climbed the stairs to the living room.

She came out with a frown on her face, saying, "I was worried about you."

"Why?"

"The market is crowded. I was looking for the bomber."

"What?"

"I sit at the window a lot and try to spot the bomber."

"What do you mean?" My heart momentarily jumped out of the soup of lethargy.

"Well, the bomb, if it happens, would happen in a crowded place, won't it? Daddy said it was not so safe now to take the bus because of the new war in Gaza. I thought it was not safe for you to be in the market either. I know that's

Our house in Nachlaot

why you left me at home, you didn't take me with you. But I don't want to lose my mummy."

I decided to ignore her, I had to contain her morbid obsession with suicide bombers in crowded places.

"We are lucky that we don't need to take the bus to school," she said and went back to the window.

Yes, we were indeed lucky. The children's schools were less than a ten-minute walk from our house. As I watched Maya going back to her room, I wanted to tell her that I did not want her to stand by the window. If there was a bomb, the explosion would almost certainly reach her and shatter the glass, her room being at the front of the house overlooking the market. I did not know how to explain it to her without raising her curiosity and hence inviting more questions. It would be hard, but I would have to try. It was easier to explain to Kiran, as he was older and more reserved in his manners. But then I was not so sure how much of what I said to Kiran he actually followed. I asked him while the war was going on not to go to coffee shops with his friends or hang out among the teenage crowds in the pedestrianized Ben Yehuda Street in the city center. He always nodded when I said anything to him, but it probably all fell on deaf ears. After an uninhibited childhood, Kiran turned into a very secretive boy who hardly ever opened his heart to either me or Leo. I often felt inadequate for not being able to connect to him, but I did not have the energy right now to try to find a way to reach out to him. He grew up far too quickly. I could not keep up with him.

.27.

THE CURIOUS CASE

OF FIDA AND

TAMAR

It was around this time that Fida and Tamar, my closest friends in Jerusalem, would slip away from my life,
as they were unable to reconcile their own differences.
What I at first had thought of as a trivial matter, the reason behind their falling-out, unleashed a whole saga of
unresolved issues.

I found a message on my answering machine from
Tamar. She was crying. It was a long message and she
sounded distraught, devoid of her lawyer's composure.

"I really want to talk to you. I can't get across to Fida.
She won't speak to me, won't answer my texts or e-mails. I
can't make her understand anything. Call me."

I listened to the message again. She wanted to talk to
me? How could I help? How could I stand between Israel and Palestine, which was what their relationship had

finally succumbed to? Maybe she wanted to talk to me because she knew that I would not take sides? I vaguely remembered Fida telling me the last time I was with her in Bethlehem that when the breakup happened, most of their friends had to choose whose side—Tamar's or Fida's—they were on. So I had said to Fida, "You are both so important in my life that it would be impossible for me to take your or her side. Both of you helped me once to fall in love with this city. I learnt a lot from you, you showed me how friendship across the insidious political barrier was possible. I am so sorry. I wish I could do something to stop this breakup."

"I'm not asking you to be on my side, but if you still go on seeing her, don't tell me about it," Fida had pleaded. "And please don't tell her that I am thinking of moving to the West Bank permanently. I've had enough of Israel."

I had promised her that I would not tell Tamar.

From the whispers of their breakup I began to understand that beneath the friendship and goodwill there always lurked dark patches of conflict. In terms of their personalities, Tamar and Fida were on opposite poles. Tamar was loud, expressive, determined, academic minded. Fida was quiet, did not express her emotions too openly, and was not interested in discussing the Israeli-Palestinian conflict. In fact, she would, if she could, not even open the daily newspaper. She did not pay any attention to external recommendations for solving the conflict. She was younger than

Tamar, tall and beautiful in a universal way, whom the men worshipped regardless of race or religion. Fida was sick of the conflict politics, she wanted to have a good time. Tamar was living the conflict, every day, with each of her cases that she represented in the Israeli court.

Tamar, when she was not being a lawyer, studied. The issue of the Israeli occupation ruled her life and her vision for the future because she saw herself as an instrument for change, a slap on the face of the "Israeli colonialism."

The dark patches surfaced even when they were having a good time. The discord had been threatening to bring them down for a long time.

"Our breakup has nothing to do with the conflict," Fida had insisted when I went to see her. "It's much more straightforward. I couldn't stand her life like an open page anymore. She is unbearably loud. Sometimes I would wake up hearing her scream down the telephone line at her mother. She walks around seminaked in front of her friends. Her friends enter straight into my room unannounced. I might be in bed, might be getting dressed, they just come in to dump their bags, or just to explore the house, and they don't even say sorry. A bunch of hippies, they have all been to India and have come back with this air of weightlessness as if they are all walking on water, like Jesus Christ. They are not plugged in to this world. I am sorry, but I am fighting to live, to get *papers* to stay in *my* country. While these dossers just come back from their foreign trips paid for by the government's "normalization" fund, and act so blasé as if it didn't matter to invade my privacy. It wasn't enough that they had already invaded my country! Besides, I could never put away the thought—how many Palestinians each one of them must have tortured or killed before they went to normalize!"

"Have you ever said this to Tamar?" I asked. But Fida ignored my question and went on, "Every time I heard her scream at her mother or sister, I told her that I didn't want to know about her family not having money, or her father going bankrupt, or her mother falling out with her sister." Fida was beyond the realm of reconciliation.

"This is very un-Eastern, your attitude," I said to Fida, "not to have anything to do with personal problems of your loved ones. I must say, I would be very interested to know how Tamar's Communist father went bankrupt, he used to work for the *Jerusalem Post*, did he not, before the paper was taken over by its current right-wing owner?"

"You are avoiding the issue. I was sick and tired of her friends barging into my room when I was not dressed properly, or when I was in bed. I was sick and tired of hearing her making love to Itay—my old boyfriend, for God's sake—while I stayed awake next door. I loathed her walking around seminaked as if we were in a harem."

"It couldn't have been a harem! There were always more men than women who used to visit your house!" I said to Fida, trying to lighten up the mood. "Two women against a gaggle of hippieish men, fancy that! Has it never been in your fantasy?"

But she did not appear to be remotely amused by what I said. Her face, so graceful and Jesus-like, was tortured. It was clear that she did not want any arbitration, she did not want any mediator between her and Tamar. She no longer believed in coexistence with Tamar, her lawyer, her best friend for some time. But the most absurd thing was that she still needed her. Tamar was the one who took her case to court and was fighting to get her papers from the Israeli authorities. Tamar was representing not just Fida, but her entire family—her mother and two brothers. Was this then the sticking point in their relationship? Was it this absurd debt of "papers" that Fida could no longer live with, the Israeli blue ID that every Palestinian coveted regardless of his or her reservations about the Jewish state? Because the blue ID got you through passport security without too much trouble. With it, Fida would be able to travel through Ben Gurion airport, it would save her from crossing the Jordan River to Amman every time she went abroad.

"Then there was Betinjan, the dog I picked up from a checkpoint. She could not stand the dog," Fida said. She was unable to stop talking about Tamar. "She saw the dog as a threat. Can you believe she was jealous of a dog, a Palestinian stray dog? She was so possessive, she thought that the dog had come between us, me and her, a dog!"

"I don't like your dog either. I am frightened of that bloody wild thing clambering all over me! But I don't think it's fair to accuse Tamar of not liking your dog. I saw her kiss Betinjan, believe me, I saw it many times," I said.

"She did it to hide from you her uglier side, which you don't know."

"Fida, don't you think it's a bit silly to blame her dislike of the dog for your breakup? It's deeper than that. I am sure this has everything to do with your respective political realities. You don't want to be indebted to her."

"NO. It's simple. I don't want to know anyone who slept with my former lover. Not only did she sleep with Itay, she did it so openly, loudly, she did it with screams of ecstasy that even the dog barked at them when they were at it. She did it all through the night. I was sickened by her vulgarity, the shamelessness of it all. Before Itay, she used to bring home some of her Palestinian clients. They, too, would stay up all night having sex."

I felt deeply saddened by Fida's outbursts. She had Tamar under her skin. Tamar reminded her more than anything else that she was a stranger in her own country, whereas the "stranger from Europe" possessed permanent citizenship.

But Tamar literally held the passport to her salvation, her freedom of movement. The blue ID.

It was not an easy situation.

Their falling-out was of course related to their being Israeli and Palestinian.

So when Fida said she did not believe that their breakup had anything to do with the conflict, she was simply covering up her shame for being indebted to Tamar.

Of course she wanted to believe that it was possible to have a normal relationship, a normal friendship between an Israeli and a Palestinian. That it was possible to be normally jealous of someone's lover, job, and good fortune. But for Fida, a Palestinian without papers, it would never be possible to taste what we took for granted. Even her objections to Tamar making love to Itay had political twists. It was not that Tamar stole her former boyfriend and that led to their breakup; Itay was not even a boyfriend. Theirs was a short-term affair laden with political meanings: Itay wanted to fulfill his fantasy of making love to a beautiful Palestinian woman, and Fida wanted to see how it felt to be in bed with a Jew. And it had long ago ended in failure, the Israeli-Palestinian love story. The story of Fida and Itay, from what I had heard, was not the story of a beautiful woman and a beautiful man feeling attracted to each other, falling in love. It was anything but being in love. Love was not something that was possible across the checkpoint. Under Israeli law, which was religious, based on the law books of the Talmud, a Jew and a Palestinian were not allowed to marry within Israel. Even when such marriages took place abroad, a West Bank Palestinian or the descendant of a Palestinian refugee was not allowed to come to live in Israel proper, or to apply for an Israeli passport. There was no future for Itay and Fida's relationship. The desperate need for a blue ID for Fida and Itay's American and Israeli passports came between them and killed the spontaneity of romantic love. Itay could not be rid of his birthright to the Jewish state (and to the United States due to his American Jewish parents), and Fida could not come to terms with the confiscation of her birthright by Itay's Jewish state.

But Itay and Tamar could be lovers without these obstacles and preconditions. Tamar and Itay could sit on the sunny terrace of their Ein Karem house, share bread, soft cheese, and olives for breakfast, and talk about some obscure ashrams in India where they both had spent time. They could kiss whenever they wanted. Fida was not able to kiss Itay in public. She would risk being called a traitor by her Palestinian friends and family, and opportunistic by some Israelis.

Fida was not free to make love to anyone she liked in Israel.

So seeing Itay with Tamar—I arrived at this hypothesis —she felt terribly betrayed. Fida was deeply hurt. Tamar was insensitive to her by displaying "shamelessly" her privileged status. Fida was outshone by Tamar's show of brazenness, in the face of which her despairing insecurity became more acute. And yet Fida still could not completely sever her ties with Tamar.

———

"*Why can't she be happy for me?*" Tamar said to me tearfully when I dragged myself out of the house and came to see her a few days after her phone message. "Why can't she just be pleased that I didn't have a steady boyfriend for a long time and now I have one? I wanted her to be happy for me, I loved her."

"You know it's hard. She feels betrayed and hurt."

"But she and Itay had a fling about three years ago. Itay and I are really happy together, why can't she just leave us alone? I've spent so much time and energy to look after her, to sort out her problems. So many nights after bars and parties when she would be drunk, I would drive her home and tuck her in bed. We used to be friends, we used to be sisters, we used to laugh a lot. Why can't she be happy for me?"

"It may sound strange, but you need her more than she needs you, Tamar," I said. "You had placed too much weight on your friendship and Fida had to carry that burden. Through Fida you justified actions that you wouldn't have taken, such as living in an abandoned Arab house. She wanted to be rid of the burden. I may be wrong, but Itay is just an excuse. She had been trying to break free her image of the 'liberal face of Palestine' for some time. She brought a mad stray dog to the house to test your patience. You haven't treated Fida as an equal, you were always apologetic, always trying not to hurt her feelings because she was Palestinian. For example, you didn't tell her that you didn't really want Betinjan in the house."

"But she didn't give me a chance! She just brought that wild thing one day and said she had found it at a checkpoint. That was it. I had to live with it," Tamar said. She was crying loudly. I had never seen her break down in tears like that before.

"Why didn't you just make it clear that there was no space for the dog in your small flat?"

"Because I didn't want to make her unhappy."

"But you would have said it to any other person."

"Yes, but for the reasons that you've just mentioned, I couldn't hurt Fida's feelings. She was the indigenous person on this land, and I, the Israeli, the settler's child, was fighting for her right to reside in her homeland. You know, the biggest blow came when Fida accused me of the most terrible thing."

"What was it?"

"That *I* had expelled her from Ein Karem. It is true that I did ask Fida to leave during arguments because I was hurt by her not accepting my relationship with Itay. I would have said it to an Israeli flatmate if she had been rude to my boyfriend. But this time when I treated her as an equal, looked at her as a friend and not as her mentor, Fida didn't like it."

"Tamar, you said to me many times before that your relationship personified the political dynamic of Israel and Palestine; you are both hypersensitive to this phenomenon, and you are hurting each other in a political power game. This has nothing to do with your affair with Itay."

But Tamar could not take Fida's unilateral withdrawal from her life. She would call her and Fida would not answer. She would e-mail her, Fida would not reply. She was teasing Tamar with, "Are you still going to represent me in court? Are you still going to take up cases from other disenfranchised Palestinians who come knocking on your door for help? Are you still going to be my lawyer?"

As I had expected, Fida made it clear when I went to see her that she would reject all forms of arbitration between her and Tamar. For her, the chapter of living with Tamar in Ein Karem had ended and she had moved on. She still worked in Bethlehem but went back to live in the modern, thriving Palestinian city of Ramallah with Mahmud—*a man with a strong personality*, with a strong political history. It was their history, Palestinian history. She was born to it and she did not need to accommodate any guilt from any party. She was freer being under siege (the Israeli army hunting for supposed terrorists carried out routine incursions into Bethlehem and Ramallah, and their inhabitants would be stuck inside the walled cities until the siege was lifted) than she was in "free" Ein Karem, where every Arab house occupied by a Jew reminded her of the Naqba.

After all, it was in Ein Karem, on an adjacent plot of land, where perhaps the only recorded history of a massacre by the Jewish militia had taken place during the Arab-Israeli War of 1948. The Deir Yassin massacre blighted the valley, and Fida said that she could never rid herself of the weight of history.

In Bethlehem, she did not have to face the daily reminders of the past, the loss of Palestine. And Ramallah was young, full of hope. Bethlehem too was emerging increasingly younger after years of inertia while Israel completed the eight-meter-high security wall around it. Somehow the wall defined clear territories on both sides. The Palestinians behind the wall of Bethlehem learnt to get on with life, and a powerful resolve abounded among the youth that they wouldn't be defeated, that there was life beyond the occupation. As if they defied the wall by being normal, as it would seem to the casual eye. But what also contributed to the well-being of the people and the beautifully restored neighborhoods and churches, was the generous donation by the world's Christian organizations. Trendily dressed men and women spilled out of cafés and bars, the markets were full, men drove fast cars. By relocating herself to a Palestinian city, Fida wanted to live with the freedom that she could have *now*.

Meanwhile, in the last days before her departure for Princeton, the dog managed to get on Tamar's very raw nerves. Now that there was no Fida around, no Palestinian arbiter to soothe her Jewish guilt, the very sight of the dog annoyed her. Betinjan chewed almost every chewable item in the house and, in the absence of regular outdoor dog walks, she went crazy and started biting visitors. Tamar sent Fida an ultimatum that the dog had to be removed.

One day the dog was gone. Fida phoned the kennels and dispatched the mongrel.

On that night, Tamar said that she had thrown away the chewed-up sofa covers and mattresses. The smell of Fida was no longer there in their Ein Karem house. With Betinjan departing, the last bond between Fida and Tamar was severed. But there was one more thing: Tamar still had to win Fida's test. Tamar would still have to fight for her family's right to the blue ID. It was her last battle with the Israeli judiciary before her imminent departure for Princeton University.

———

A few weeks later Fida was summoned for a court hearing—the much-longed-for event for her and her family.

Tamar fought hard. She held back tears as she presented Fida's case in the Israeli court. She called them racist, accused the authority of carrying out an apartheid policy against its own citizens. Tamar's argument was hard-hitting, infused with rage and compassion. The whole family stood in the courtroom silently crying, Tamar crying with them, as the verdict was read out.

Fida and her family were given the blue ID, albeit temporarily, for a year, after which the case would have to be back in court for a review. Tamar had won Fida's test. She seized this remarkable victory not just for Fida, but symbolically for all her Palestinian clients, for each one of them whom she represented before the Israeli judiciary over the years.

I was not surprised that it still failed to change Fida's mind. She was not ready for reconciliation. She had left the chapter with Tamar for good. Meanwhile, Tamar transferred Fida's case to another lawyer. She was counting the days before leaving for her studies in the United States. She wanted to breathe freely away from the conflict's rage, she wanted to feel normal. Tamar no longer wanted to be hounded by her clients around the clock. She had never known life beyond the sphere of Israeli-Palestinian politics.

Tamar was ecstatic when she heard that the U.S. university was so impressed by her proposal on Israel's administrative colonialism that it offered a full doctoral grant to complete her thesis over the next four years.

So Tamar and Fida both ceased to be part of my life in Jerusalem. All the indicators pointed to the pressing reality that perhaps my time was up too, perhaps I should sever my ties with the "black widow." Distance myself from its history of misadventure. Fida and Tamar were indispensable for my sense of belonging to the city. Through them, I could make sense of Jerusalem, I could find my way out of the maze of the city's muddled history, of the claims and the counterclaims. It was possible for me to find my own attachment to this place for the first time *not* through Leo but by seeing the things that they saw, loving the cityscape the way they taught me to love it. When they left, my independent connection to Jerusalem started to fray, and I found myself turning to Leo again—for roots, for a steadfast reconnection.

In the region, meanwhile, a number of significant political changes somewhat accentuated our—the international community's—collective sense of detachment. In the elections of 2009, the right-wing camp won a majority of seats, and Benjamin Netanyahu was called on to form the government. We would enter what would become known as the Netanyahu era with an isolationist agenda, which would spearhead renewed settlement-building activities and bring the peace process to a complete halt. Israeli politics became increasingly domesticated. The Middle East talk was sidelined in the world media by more provincial Israeli daily news with one former president's indictment for sexual misdemeanors and another former prime minister's prosecution for multiple counts of corruption. On the whole it appeared to us as if the world had momentarily stopped caring about the Israeli-Palestinian conflict. The inward-looking new Israeli government shunned the international mediators.

Amid this wider political and regional hopelessness, I found myself still struggling to come to terms with the vagaries of my own personal grief. I failed to pull the reins to stop my life from going increasingly awry. There were too many loose ends that needed to be tidied. I needed help, some outside interference in what seemed like an unremitting state of detachment. The black widow had begun the process to squeeze me out. Israel's disengagement with the peace process reflected onto my inner disconnection with Jerusalem. My cry for help went unattended. The only place that was left for me and where I had turned to with feeble expectations seemed out of range. I could not reach Leo anymore. He too was disoriented by Israel's swivel toward insular domestic politics. My personal bereavement lost momentum, it now embarrassed me. But I still couldn't shake it off. Leo and I were living together and not arguing, but we were more separated than ever.

At least when we argued, we still had the raw and visceral attachment to each other. Now we were treading parallel directions and our paths hardly crossed. I was struck down by lethargy, inner and outer, as my once beloved city looked on.

.28.

THE CITY OF DOOM

It was glaringly white. I squinted my eyes and saw his face,
a blurred face with a question mark. I had not seen this tormented face on Leo in a long time. My mind was numb, but
I knew that something was terribly wrong. I could not work
out why I was here, in hospital again. There were no doctors near me, but I saw them in their green gowns everywhere, scurrying around the room that I was in, zigzagging
between metal beds, emerging in and out of the green curtains that separated the beds. I jogged my brain for clues.
I was adrift in an emerald sea. There was a muffled noise
around me as if of distant waves; I was disoriented by the
voices of the people who were not talking to me. I was in a
huge room with many beds. I was wearing a green hospital
gown under a blanket of the same color.

But I had already left the hospital, I had returned home.
I had left the hospital in London, gone to the airport, and

arrived back to my family in Jerusalem. We moved house, we lived together with all our things in one place on the top two floors of a quaint house above the Mahane Yehuda market.

I opened my eyes again and saw Leo on the other side of the room, talking to a woman. "She's up," I heard him say to the woman in a doctor's gown. She came to my bedside and I could smell antibacterial hand gel. She bent over me and asked if I could hear her. If my head hurt. She told me that when I felt up to it, she would send the officers to take my statement. Which officers? I thought of asking, but I was not sure why I should be asking such a question, why I should be talking to any "officers." I tried to stretch my arms out of the hospital blanket and realized that I had a drip attached to my left arm.

There was a terrible stench around me. With my free right hand I touched my hair; I felt wiry, sticky streaks and realized that the smell came from my hair. It was the smell of vomit. The doctor saw my puzzled eyes. "You have been through some nasty experience. You need a wash, but before that, the officers need to know what you can remember. Are you okay to speak to them in Hebrew?" The doctor's voice was kind and compassionate. I was not in my old hospital in London. I am here, in Jerusalem, she wanted to know if I could speak Hebrew. The "officers" did not speak English.

She went around to the other side of the bed and checked the bag of fluid that had now been emptied into my veins. "It is going to hurt a bit," she said and gently pulled out the long needle. She pressed a small cotton ball where the needle had been in the inside of my left elbow. I stretched my arm to get rid of the numbness and saw that the cotton had blotted up a small drop of blood. Leo was hovering near the doctor, watching everything intently. He had sleepless, bewildered eyes. Why should I be in hospital? I did not have an accident. Why was my hair matted in vomit? I did not remember throwing up. But I did remember walking out of a restaurant, the new nonkosher seafood restaurant in Mahane Yehuda where we had gone after months of emotional detachment. It was our first proper outing since I returned from England, our first night out in glowing contentment.

I remembered ordering a hotpot of langoustines, mussels, and crab. It had a tantalizing aroma when the waiter put it on a burner in the middle of the table with the crab legs poking out of a lemony, parsley-infused broth. I was happy. I felt for the first time in months that I was finally coming out of mourning. We could not stop kissing each other. We could not stop appreciating the tenderness that we both still felt toward each other after fifteen years of marriage and many upheavals. Other people around our table in the galleried dining space were amused by our overtly physical manifestation of endearment; we must have looked like new lovers who were showing off. They must have thought it was strange, if they had noticed my wedding ring. From the gallery, in between our display of mutual infatuation, we watched the kitchen below, the wok on fire as the chef threw flaming food in the air before catching it on the awaiting diner's plate.

I wanted my eyes to stay open, but they refused to. The covers were pulled up to my chin. I felt too warm, the blanket felt heavy and I wanted to remove it. But I could not. I did not have the energy. Eyes closed, I tried to move my toes, to get them out of the blanket's folds.

It must have been an emergency ward, there was a lot of noise around me and too many feet scuttling about the room. I felt exposed under the fluorescent lights and Leo's glare. Why was he not holding my hand? Why was he standing so far away from me, staring at me unblinkingly? I wanted to be hugged. But I could not say that to Leo, I could not utter a word. The doctor asked again if I would be able to speak to the officers in Hebrew, and I nodded. I waited for the moving, rushing feet in the room to stop, for the lights to be turned off. I wanted Leo to come and sit next to me. But he did not. It was strange. If I had been in an accident, if something terrible had happened, surely he should give me comfort, I would be in his arms. He was standing as far away as possible. Did he bring me here? I wondered. I put my arms across me as if to protect myself from the glare. I felt sticky and dirty. I desperately wanted a wash.

I tried to put together a jumbled-up jigsaw puzzle. I knew it had something to do with my walking out of the restaurant, walking in the streets of the market and then into a bar.

"You were in a bad way when we found you last night. How much do you remember?" said a voice. I opened my eyes and turned to the two silhouetted men in police uniform. The kind doctor was with them, giving me a reassuring smile. "I'll translate if you need me—would you like me to stay here?" I nodded. I needed her to be here for my comfort and security. I was in a bad, irreparably bad place, the officers did not need to tell me that. "What do you remember?" they asked again. I stared at them blankly, racking my brain, trying to translate my English into Hebrew that would make sense.

"Your husband told us you'd recently had a miscarriage, quite a late miscarriage. We are sorry. You are understandably distressed, but we would really like you to tell us whatever you remember. How did you get to the place where we found you?"

"Which place, where did you find me?"

"When we came, you were unconscious, in a stranger's house in Nachlaot. Did you, do you know him?"

How could it be possible? What stranger's house were these men talking about?

"Do you and your husband go to bars often?"

"No."

"Do you often speak to strangers?"

"No! I don't know why you keep referring to *strangers*."

"Did you speak to anyone in the bar where you were last night?"

"I remember being introduced to someone by a friend who was at the bar. I remember the man said that he was a filmmaker. I remember Leo walking into the bar and we all talked. He wanted me to come home. But home didn't seem like a safe place."

"Why is that so?"

"I don't know. I was upset."

"And were you drunk? How much did you drink?"

"More than I could take."

"Do you drink every day?"

"No. Until recently I was pregnant. I was almost four months pregnant."

"So it did not take very much, then, to knock you out. Your body was not used to alcohol."

Was it a question? Was I supposed to answer it? Yes, he was right, my body was unaccustomed to alcohol. It was probably the first time I drank in five months.

The officers asked, "What do you remember? What happened at the bar?" They said, "Take your time." I was told that I had been in and out of consciousness for over ten hours.

Slowly, bits of what happened started coming back to me.

I remembered walking out of the elegant seafood restaurant when Leo, after we had had our fantastically happy, engaging time, brought out from under the table his laptop bag. I had not realized that he had brought the bag to the restaurant. Looking at the clock on the wall, he said, "Oh, it's the end of office hours in New York." I did not at first understand what he meant and kept a smile on. He went on, saying, "I'll have to proofread this quickly and send it off to my editor in New York, it's on my recent trip to . . ." I had already stopped listening; his flustered smile had turned to a disconcerted smirk. I paused to think, only for a moment, because there was nothing to think. It didn't take me long to jump to a quick conclusion that my night, which only a minute ago seemed so endless, had come to an end.

"I beg you," I said, "don't let's fall into the familiar pattern tonight. Let's just enjoy what we have here, now."

"I am sorry," he said and went back to a stack of papers on the table between us where there had been earlier in the evening two aperitif cocktails, our conjoined hands and elbows, a bottle of sauvignon blanc, our laughter, my crustaceans, his sea bream, and on-the-house vodka shots. "I have to read this before America goes to bed," he said without looking up from his papers.

"BUT I am here, we are here now, and it's not often that we feel like this. Please do not spoil the night. Please stay here, with us." I hated my voice as I pleaded with him. As a journalist of course I knew about the importance of deadlines, but this time I reacted strongly to his all-too-familiar escape from intimacy, because of my personal circumstances.

"It won't get published if I don't send them the final copy in half an hour," he said and hesitantly but surely went back to his proofs.

The officers stood there looking puzzled.

I continued piecing together the rest of the conversation in my head. I was tired. My throat felt dry.

"I'll only spend half an hour," he said. I pleaded whether it could wait until we went back home. He said NO, it could not wait.

"Why did you come out tonight, then?" I asked.

"Because it seemed so important to you," he said meekly.

"Respect it, then," I implored.

"But I do need to send this." His voice was assertive. I was left feeling that I was making a fuss out of nothing. But I also felt strongly that I did want to make a point, that it was not right. He would not have done that if he had gone out with a friend, or one of those internationals. It was not acceptable that he had taken me out and then chosen to cut the evening short, without a warning.

I looked at the faces of the officers. They were neither kind, nor were they unkind. They were just doing their professional duty. Which was fine with me. Because any word of kindness would have melted the thin wall of mock security that I had created around myself to stay composed.

"We wish you a better future," they said and asked me to read and sign my statement that they had written down. It was all in cryptic Hebrew, but I did not care. The kind doctor asked me if I wanted it to be double-checked by her, but I declined. I did not care. What difference would that make now that I foresaw my future? Now that I already saw that once again I would be saddled with the burden of separation because my despair had brought upon us this latest calamity and which, a great part of Leo believed, I had orchestrated to avenge his single-minded involvement with the Middle East and his emotional detachment from my grief? Otherwise why would he be hovering over there at the foot of the bed with dispassionate stares and not standing by me? Why did he shake his head when I said to the officers that I could not remember how I got to the "stranger's house"?

"Please do not put me on trial. Do not put me on trial," I implored silently. My head hurt, my vision was blurry, and I felt guilty for being in such a void. I wished I could take away his pain. I wanted to tell him that I wished I could remember everything. I was deeply troubled because I didn't know what had happened.

I opened my eyes and saw him still standing afar, inspecting me with quizzical eyes. His mind had been made up by what he had seen and what my amnesia had obliterated. He did not believe that I did not remember.

A few days later, I would visit our friend Yoni, who was in the bar on that fateful night, and ask what he knew. He would tell me that both he and Leo had left me there after I said that I didn't want to go home. Yoni said that he had introduced me to his friend, an Israeli filmmaker who was sitting at the bar.

According to the account that Yoni heard from his filmmaker friend, I had continued to drink and the filmmaker had asked me at one point where my house was. I had apparently looked at him with expressionless eyes. He had offered to take me home, and I had vomited on the way, then in his house, all over my clothes. He had poured buckets of cold water over me, to clean up and to bring me back from my befuddled state. He had removed my dirty, wet clothes and put me to bed.

Leo would later tell me that he had gone back to the bar when he woke up at home and I was not in bed. The bar woman was cleaning up and closing the premises, but she had told him that I was last seen with the filmmaker. She had also given him directions to his house.

When Leo arrived at the filmmaker's house, he had knocked on the door for a long time, but no one responded from inside. He became worried and called the police, who arrived at the scene very quickly. They tried to wake me, but having failed that, called an ambulance.

Yoni would tell me that the police had arrested the film-maker and taken him to custody where, according to Yoni, he had undeservingly spent several nights as a suspected sex offender.

He would be later released for lack of evidence, after the medical examination was negative.

Seeing Leo at the foot of my bed looking at me, I felt so sad that I had burdened him with this. I wished I could rewind the night.

"You are still probably feeling light-headed. But the drip has thankfully replenished the lost fluid, and you are no longer dehydrated. I'll leave you to rest awhile. Once you've rested, a nurse will do a general physical examination, if that's okay with you. Go and have a shower after that. I'll bring you a towel and some clothes," the kind doctor said after she checked my eyes with a little torch.

"Light-headed." It was more like being in a trance. I could feel everything that was going on around me, while I was hovering in midair. I did not see the police officers leave.

I told the doctor that I didn't need to rest, that I desperately wanted a shower. A matronly nurse and her assistant promptly arrived at my bedside and escorted me to a room to check me for any physical signs of violence, forced or consensual sexual conduct the previous night. There were none. I was relieved.

The same doctor arrived with a dress—black with white polka dots   and a towel. "Most of the hospital clothes are large sizes, this is the smallest that I could find." I wanted to laugh at the absurdity of it all, I had no idea that the hospital had a clothes bank for the patients' use. I urgently needed to get out of the hospital. I wanted to wash the dried-up vomit off my hair. The doctor walked with me to the shower room. Leo was standing in the corridor.

I struggled to come to terms with the purgatory of the unexplained hours of the previous night. Even though a physical rape had not taken place, I felt violated all the same. I was ashamed of my recklessness, my propensity for doom. It also left me disconcerted that I was more worried thinking how Leo was feeling than how I would deal with what I was going through myself, what I had just been through. How I was going to leave this hospital and start a "normal" life again.

When I came out of the shower, I realized that I had no shoes. The hospital clothes bank had no subbranch for shoes. I walked like a zombie after Leo, barefoot, my hair dripping water, smelling the antiseptic liquid soap that I had used to wash myself with from the wall-mounted dispenser in the shower cubicle. I followed Leo to the hospital office where he had to sign various bits of paper.

I was surprised to see the same doctor trailing behind us. She had huge, expressive eyes. She gave me a hug and said, "My name is Keren. Call me tomorrow and I'll put you in touch with a grief counselor. You need help. Don't let anyone tell you that you have done anything wrong."

She then looked at Leo and said just one sentence: "Take good care of her."

In the coming weeks, the kind doctor would call me many times to find out how I was coping with life. Her solicitude was a great example of Israel's superb medical care.

Leo did not say anything either to the doctor or to me. His face was a mirror of his inner conflict, the trauma of the recurring vision of what he had seen. Their collective impact was tearing him apart. I could read it all.

The rest was predictable. The rest was just a repeat of the act of separation from two years ago, only this time it came to me with a dose of stoicism.

In the taxi that brought us home, Leo did not sit next to me. I did not fight him, I left him alone. I did not have the courage to try to change the inevitable course that the next phase of our life in Jerusalem was about to take. The next phase that had already been determined.

I knew he walked up to our flat—our joint home in Nachlaot after our most recent reunion—only to pick up his clothes and his laptop. As he ejected himself out of the house onto the alleyway, he might have been crying. But he was not to be comforted by my empathy, not even by my apology to him for inadvertently bringing upon us this unexpected tragedy. Nothing upset me more than Leo's tears. The last time I saw tears in his eyes was after Kiran was born following a complicated cesarean section and I had fainted in his arms. He thought he was losing me. So were these tears for the same reason too, that he was losing me?

If he felt that, it was not because I pushed him away but because he chose to stay with his own conception of honor, at least that was what I believed. I had told him in the taxi that I understood his pain, I was sorry. I deeply regretted my loss of control. But he was inconsolable. His pain was greater than mine, his wounds were deeper than my agonizing remorse. I was left to deal with my own private ignominy.

My one act of recklessness exonerated him from his responsibility in this dark hour. All that mattered now was Leo's pain, his doubts, his mistrust of my innocence, his fury.

Perversely, I thought, as I saw him from the balcony running out the front door into the pedestrianized alleys of Nachlaot, that perhaps deep inside I wanted to see him break. I secretly wanted him to have a taste of my despair. So I succeeded in breaking him, albeit at a huge price. I paid for it with the loss of a large chunk of my self-regard. Why was it so unbearable for me then to see him in pain?

.29.

THE BLACK WIDOW

STRIKES

A month after our calamitous descent behind irreconcilable frontlines, we were facing our fifteenth wedding anniversary. This year the date came with cautious expectations, because it was on this day, four weeks after I saw his tormented face disappear in the alleys of Nachlaot, that we agreed to meet in the presence of a mediator, Deborah.

We saw Deborah separately first for three weeks, then together. The sessions together often ended with both Leo and I feeling more traumatized than before we went to see her, but soon we were to realize that it was a normal process. That we were supposed to let it all out, tear each other apart, reach the lowest point of hope, in order to feel remorse and be ashamed of ourselves. We waited several weeks before the blessings of the joint sessions started to make a difference.

The alleys of Nachlaot

Exactly a month after our fifteenth anniversary, Leo came home. I heard the key turn in the front door and the familiar footsteps on the stairs, as though he were coming home after work. We all had dinner together, after which he read Maya a story and then we sat on our terrace overlooking the market with mugs of tea. "To us," we said, and vowed, as we had been instructed by Deborah, not to utter another word about ourselves; that was fine with me, but Leo found it difficult. He felt that he had compromised more, that his requirements for reunification had not been satisfied, his doubts remained unattended to.

This sad episode in our life came to a sudden halt in early December 2009, when my agent, Ruth Diskin, called to tell me that I had been invited to attend a film festival in India where, among others, one of my favorite filmmakers, Jane Campion, would be present.

This news somehow totally sidelined my woes. It was not the film festival. I could hardly contain my joy at the possibility of staying next door to Campion in the same hotel, bumping into her in the lobby and sharing meals with her at the hotel restaurant. She was more than just a celebrity, I loved the way her films, such as *The Piano* and *In the Cut*, dealt with the dark side of the human psyche, giving both sexes the quirkiness that their characters demanded, irrespective of their gender, without sending an overtly feminist interpretation that her era often promulgated.

Ruth pulled her strings and the Israeli Foreign Ministry paid for my round-trip to Delhi. I was surprised to discover how unimportant the devastating events of the past weeks appeared to be. I arrived in Delhi a day after Campion, who was staying in the same hotel with her daughter, as I had expected. And we did meet as I had dreamed, when I came down to the lobby to ask about the opening ceremony. But I did not expect the bad news that she came to deliver. Barely four hours after my arrival, I was informed by Campion that the festival was a sham. No one was present at the airport to receive her, which was the case with me too, but I had thought that it was just a matter of miscommunication. Despite being at the hotel for more than twenty-four hours, no festival organizers yet contacted Campion or any other filmmakers, and now the hotel management was being difficult, as it did not know who was going to pick up the guests' bills!

I still kept thinking that there was a serious "third-world-style" communication problem, it could not possibly be happening that one of the world's best-known directors was staying in a lower-midrange hotel and no one had been there to welcome her! But the more I looked around, everything confirmed what Campion had just said, that there was no festival. None of us—there were around fifteen guests staying in the hotel—were picked up from the airport. I had arrived at four in the morning and had spent two hours at the airport arrival lounge pacing up and down looking for a placard with my name on it. I had then asked every single waiting hotel crew whether they might have misplaced my name! I waited until it was light outside and decided that there must have been a mistake and took a taxi to the hotel, which was a small, naphthalene-smelling, holes-in-the-sheets establishment in the outskirt of Delhi. There was no reception area as such, just a table and a chair by the door where the guard sat, and a bench in the hall for the waiting visitors—up to four people could sit on it.

It was humiliating at first to accept that the festival was a scam, an attempt by a bunch of crooks to amass money from various Indian ministries and, as it soon became clear, they had pocketed the money and gone into hiding. It was the most elaborate scam that I had ever experienced in my life. The opening ceremony was supposed to have taken place on the day I arrived, and most of the local newspapers published full-page color supplements on the festival with the announcement of Jane Campion's participation. In the evening there was no ceremony, just us, a group of mostly women filmmakers drinking room service tea in Campion's room, feeling very unsettled and concerned about our safety.

A group of Turkish filmmakers stayed in their rooms, locked their doors, and lived on room service meals for three days. When they saw me, they thought they had found an Indian whom they could trust, and I hesitantly took charge of their daily schedule for sightseeing until their flight back to Istanbul. I was embarrassed by their experience at the hands of the festival "organizers"—who happened to be fellow Bengalis—and took personal responsibility to make sure that they were at least having a good time during the rest of their stay in Delhi.

Still reeling from the shock and disappointment at the "Indian experience," but nevertheless enriched by my friendship with Jane Campion, I returned to Israel.

What awaited me here unnerved me beyond my wit's end.

On arrival, I found myself facing the most bizarre encounter at Ben Gurion airport. After I showed my passport, the woman in the cubicle called some security personnel, who escorted me to the Interior Ministry office without an explanation. It happened very fast, as if they had been expecting my arrival, and their subsequent actions followed a clear plan, details of which had been entered into all the computers and they were acting in unison. Tired after the long flight and confused by the new, unprovoked, totally unexpected twist in our Middle Eastern tale, I sat on a bench at the Israeli Interior Ministry's airport branch and waited. After about an hour, a female security officer entered the waiting area and called out my name. She asked me to follow her to a different waiting room, where a third uniformed female security officer was waiting to receive me. I saw from the name card that she wore around her neck that she was called Ronit.

Ronit started her interrogation by saying that my husband was an illegal element in Israel and as his wife I was illegal too and they were going to deport me back to where I came from. I was too shocked to speak at first. When I managed to open my mouth, I asked them why my husband was illegal. She said that his work permit had not been renewed. The Interior Ministry refused to extend his work visa, as after five years in Israel, his time was up and he must leave the country. He had, according to their report, already overstayed and they had the order to deport the whole family. I said, meekly, that he was Jewish, and that Israel, under its own Law of Return, had to give sanctuary to all the Jews of the world. "Why did he not make aliya, then? If he wants to come back in, he can apply for aliya from his home country. Until that, neither he nor you will be allowed to enter Israel," said the officer.

I said that it was my husband's decision whether or not to make aliya, but I was a British citizen and was not entering the country illegally, I never overstayed my visas. "You cannot deny me entry without a reason!"

They said they did not need a reason. I was, along with my husband, planning to "settle" in Israel, and they could not let that happen. Since my husband was not willing to settle here as a Jew, we were seen as illegal intruders.

"Whose side are you on, may I ask?" was the question that had been thrown at Leo recently at the Allenby Bridge when he was crossing from Amman. This was how he had replied: "Who's *us* and who are you considering as *them*? How can I be on your side if you are thinking this way of almost half the population of this land?"

Well, it looked like his reply did not go down very well. It probably exacerbated his already murky "Arab sympathizer" profile on the Interior Ministry's dossier. Otherwise why would I be here? I had not knowingly committed any act that could be considered as politically leaning toward any specific group. Even my film, many of my Arab friends jokingly said, bucked up Israel's witch hunt against the Palestinian people. They said that the majority in Israel would love my film, as it might serve their Islamophobic agenda. I was aware of it and had been very cautious while filming the survivors of honor crimes. I was very upset when Leo echoed the same view, that I might not like it but I had played a minor part in strengthening Israel's Islam-bashing policy as well as a similar trait that was very much on the rise in the West.

The Interior Ministry official had meanwhile clarified with her bosses and come to tell me that I was indeed being deported. It was not just a threat. Until then I had been relaxed, and it did not once cross my mind that the fuss they were making over my husband's status and overstay would actually see me deported from the country where I had lived for five years. After the final order came from some unseen superior, I was pushed from one room to another under police escort, and none of the Interior Ministry representatives would speak to me, hear my story that I had actually been sent to India by the Israeli Foreign Ministry and that I was a filmmaker and a state guest in Delhi, representing Israel! I even dined with the Israeli ambassador to India, Mark Sofer, and his wife, Sara, at their private residence.

They were not interested. At one point I managed to convey the message, with a lot of noise and tears, risking arrest and possible overnight incarceration, to one of the big fish at Ben Gurion working for the Interior Ministry. He came out and said that he did not care whether or not the Foreign Ministry had paid for my ticket to India—because he was going to ask the same ministry to now pay for my deportation.

I think the only reason they did not put me in custody for the night was that whoever was deciding this at the top had a real personal vendetta against Leo and did not want the court to intervene in the meantime to overrule the deportation order. Overnight custody would gain more time in my favor. When I was screaming at the officials who were putting me through such an absurdly dark, bureaucratic trauma, saying that I had already called my lawyer and that they would not get away with such acts of savagery, I heard the officer in charge telling his subordinates in Hebrew—assuming I would not understand—that he would see who got there first—the court's injunction to stop the deportation or their effort to kick me out.

Suddenly I felt nauseous, faint. I blamed it on my incessant crying and shouting at the ruthless Interior Ministry officials. I was astonished that no one was interested in explaining to me why they were going ahead with such a drastic decision to throw a British citizen out of the country. Even the janitor who came at night treated me as if I were a foreign worker caught being in Israel illegally. In my frustration, I said to no one in particular that I could have become Israeli anytime over the past years had I wanted to, my whole family could have, but we refused to, and now I could see that Leo had all along been right, that he could not be part of this xenophobic apparatus.

Amid hunger, thirst, and extreme fatigue, I could not face boarding a plane again. I had been traveling, with a stopover in Turkey, for almost twelve hours already. Some part of me still refused to believe that this was happening to me. It felt really strange that I was ravenous despite the nightmare unfolding around me. When I asked for food, I was told to use the vending machine—all it dispensed was *bamba*, peanut butter puffs. I thought of the children, of Maya, she loved bamba. I wanted a sandwich. I was told no, no sandwiches at this time of the night. I remembered what Leo always said: "If you ever want anything from Israel, don't try quiet diplomacy. Just shout and make a huge fuss, only then would they listen." So I made a fuss, I insisted on having a sandwich for myself as well as for everyone else in the room waiting to be deported: there were activists from the Popular Front for the Liberation of Palestine and housewives married to men whom the state considered "seditious elements"—the appropriate term would probably be "self-hating Jews." ("Any Jew would become self-deprecating if they came to Israel," Leo started saying lately.) Oh, and there were some Filipino foreign workers who had probably overstayed, as many do, one with a very young child who was fast asleep on her mother's lap.

The sandwiches came in the end, for everyone. So Leo was right, you make a noise and things happen in Israel. This reinstated my self-confidence and I resolved that I was not going to be deported.

I called Leo as soon as they allowed me to use a phone. My own mobile's battery had died earlier when I was talking to a lawyer friend, asking for his advice. I borrowed a phone from one of the activists. I realized that, as I had feared, Leo had been going through exactly the same treatment around the same time at the Allenby Bridge. He had flown to India so that during the last of my two weeks there we could spend some time together, just the two of us without the children, who were in the UK with their grandparents. We had Christmas dinner with some friends in Delhi and flew back separately two days later— I on Turkish Airlines to Tel Aviv via Istanbul and he on Royal Jordanian to Amman and then taxi to the Allenby Bridge. I had an inkling when they stopped me and put me through the deportation process so quickly upon arrival that Leo had already been nailed by the Israeli security at the Amman-Jerusalem border crossing. The Interior Ministry predators probably could not believe their luck that I had shown up almost simultaneously at Ben Gurion airport. Leo told me not to worry, that the lawyers were working very hard to get an injunction against the deportation order.

I even tried to use the children at one point, saying that I must get through to see my two children in Jerusalem. They knew of course that I was lying. It was not a very convincing lie, knowing how hawkish the security was in personal record keeping. They kept a tag on every Palestinian in the country, and I was just fooling around saying the children were in Jerusalem when a simple computer search would have revealed that they were not.

Luckily, I thought, Kiran and Maya were on Christmas holiday in England. I had packed them off before leaving for Delhi.

The ordeal lasted six hours, during which I was treated like a convicted criminal—I was photographed, fingerprinted and, due to a computer glitch, they had to repeat the whole process. I was stripped and searched by a girl wearing white rubber gloves. Finally I was sent to a room with a security guard, without any explanation regarding what they were doing to me. It had been by then fifteen hours since I left Delhi. It was very, very Kafkaesque. My phone had no battery and the activist whose mobile I was using was no longer in the room. Our lawyers could not contact me with an update on the situation.

At one point I was escorted to the baggage claim to identify my suitcase, which they opened, took out every item, and X-rayed them one by one. After having done that, to my disbelief, they repacked my things and checked in the case onto the next Turkish Airlines flight to India! I saw the baggage tag hanging from the handle: Tel Aviv—Istanbul—Delhi. I still did not understand why no one was talking to me. They were using single-word commands: Go! Sit! Come! Open! Apart from that there was no communication. As they wheeled my suitcase away to put it on the plane to Delhi, I tried to tell them that I needed a visa to enter India and I had only a single-entry visa that I had already used.

"If you want me to leave, I'll have to fly to England, and I would be happy to buy my own ticket!" I cried. My earlier determination was waning.

"You are going back to where you've flown from, that's the rule."

I was waiting to board a Turkish Airlines plane to India, when our lawyers made a breakthrough, they won the race against time; the Interior Ministry was virtually minutes away from putting me back on the plane to Delhi and Leo in a taxi to Amman.

To make the long, humiliating story short, the lawyers managed to get a court injunction after securing two letters from the rabbi who had conducted Kiran's bar mitzvah service. The first letter said that my husband was Jewish and that they could not deport a Jew from the land of Israel unless he was involved in seditious activities. The content of the second letter would be revealed in its context shortly, but for now, Leo and I were allowed to enter Israel on one-month entry visas. We were given a month to sort out our suddenly precarious status in the country.

When we finally met back in our house in Jerusalem, Leo seemed unfazed. He was not making hundreds of calls as I had expected, to hold the authorities to account. All he said was that he was not surprised; somehow his unwavering reluctance to integrate into the Israeli state for all these years was finally vindicated. He was victorious with the silent but clear message: "I told you so! You wanted me to make aliya, now you know why I didn't!"

I was shaken by the experience. For the Israeli airport security, our family with its Jewish connection never used to pose a risk, and we used to pass through lightly when we traveled together. Before I started going to film festivals, I hardly ever traveled through Ben Gurion on my own without the children. Occasionally when I did as a single traveler—like that unfortunate time when I was on my way to London as I was losing the baby—I would be stopped and interrogated as part of their "terror indicator" profiling. Nevertheless, I had kept my spirit high, and these security procedures did not seriously prejudice my views about living in Jerusalem.

This time though, after I came out of the airport following the lawyers' intervention, in the taxi home I seriously considered going back to England. I did not want to live here feeling powerless against such abominable treatment in the hands of a bunch of power-crazy, xenophobic security personnel.

Of course the Palestinians face such trauma every day, far worse than what Leo and I had to go through. But I was not Palestinian and this was not my conflict. I could live with civil liberties elsewhere in the world.

When the woman from the Interior Ministry handed over my passport with a one-month visa after crossing out the initial ENTRY DENIED stamp, she threatened to deport the children when they were due back in a week's time. We did not want to take any chances and so we faxed over the second letter from the rabbi to Kiran to keep with him in case he was turned back. Our son was horrified when he read the letter:

I am familiar with Kiran (UK ppt no: ***) and Maya (UK ppt: ***), who were born to Leo, who is Jewish and a member of our synagogue and our community. Kiran has attended *****

synagogue regularly. I taught him for his Bar-Mitzvah and carried out his Bar-Mitzvah service in the synagogue two years ago. To the best of my knowledge, he is circumcised. I am the Rabbi of ***** synagogue in Jerusalem, and can be reached on telephone number: *****.

.30.

THE "GOOD" BABY

The New Year of 2010 arrived, marking a different note to the cycle of unfortunate events and our struggle to keep afloat. We were still aghast at the attempted deportation that we had overturned, but amid the confusion and loss of faith in this country, I had been experiencing extreme fatigue. After a New Year's Eve jazz jamming session at a neighbor's house, as we were about to toast the arrival of 2010, I felt sick. I ran out of the room, unable to bear the smell of champagne. I walked back home without telling anyone, rummaged through the medicine cabinet and found an old pregnancy test. With much excitement that I did not know whether was of joy or fright, I carried out the test.

I sat on the toilet seat with my head in my hands—this could not be possible, this could not be happening to me. And then the fright set in. I was convinced that it would end in disaster again. It would tear us apart, it would tear me apart. This was the final mockery of the gods, in whose hands we had been unwitting marionettes.

When Leo came home, I found it hard not to tell him. But I wanted to first undergo some initial tests at my doctor's, to be 100 percent certain, before I broke the news to him.

That night, as I lay in bed awake, the night's tranquillity set in, and my thoughts transmitted a qualified welcome to the special cluster of cells in mitosis, deep inside me, an exciting new prospect.

———

We put the new baby in his car seat and carried him gently from the maternity ward to the car park. He looked serene and oblivious of the fact that he had been around a mere twenty-four hours. This was his first outing into the world, bathed in a merciless August sun.

Only a year ago I had left another hospital in a different city with the same soreness, but without this bundle of hope. What was then a depressed calm before an all-tearing storm was now heavenly serenity before a still possible future.

From the utmost acts of self-humiliation on my part, I had been beatified with mother goddessness. I was protective of the baby and stood sheltering him against the sun while Leo went to bring the car to take us home. The inner strength that I felt seemed strong enough to shield us all from our family's susceptibility to doom.

He was a strange thing in our house, an object of curiosity. Leo cleared a shelf in our wardrobe to make room for his tiny clothes. It seemed bizarre that we had a new, fifth member in our family. I would often just open the door of our walk-in wardrobe and look incredulously at his single shelf of Babygros and vests. Does this creature really belong to us? "Where do you come from, little thing?" I would whisper to him, and he would stare back cross-eyed at the strange woman hovering over him, his face tickled by the ends of her long hair.

For a while our family life seemed as ordinarily perfect as possible. The baby had his brit on the tenth day after his birth, not on the eighth as required by Judaism since he had infant jaundice and was kept in hospital for observation a few days. I was brave and prepared this time to remain in the same room with him when he was circumcised by Jerusalem's most celebrated mohel. There was a moment of awkwardness, as the mohel did not conduct the religious service that usually accompanied such a ceremony, since he sussed out within seconds after he entered our house that I was not Jewish. Leo was furious and upset, and he wanted to confront him. But I said that it was not necessary, as by now I was acclimatized to Jewish exclusivism. I told Leo that it did not matter that he did not pray for our baby. It was important that he was healthy, and he survived the ordeal. Leo said that this time round he was not sure whether the brit was as important to him as it had been after Kiran was born. It was a bit too late, I thought, but did not say so. He wanted both his boys to have the

Abrahamic slits and he should be happy that his little baby hardly even bled. It was a clean cut.

But a scar all the same. Even in the sane and collected state of mind that I was in, I could not help feeling that we had no right to subject our perfect baby to this ritual physical meddling. But I wanted to avoid conflict and I thought of a hundred reasons why the brit was worth it for the greater good. I did not want a repeat of what happened when it was done to Kiran. I had run out of the house in protest but did not succeed in stopping it; my protest only generated more conflict in the already conflict-prone relationship. This time I was wiser and had learnt to take into account other matters that were important to the people closest to me. My mother-in-law flew from Wiltshire, Leo's extended Israeli family came to attend the ceremony, and it was an occasion that brought us closer. Or that was how I liked to think, in the serene state that I was in.

For a while life for us seemed normal.

It was time to move house again. Our sixth in as many years. Each time we moved, we did so subconsciously to turn a page, hoping it would be a happy page.

We moved to Jerusalem's second and the last "politically correct" neighborhood of Yemin Moshe. Every house in this city has a story. Each spot of habitation has a history that one must know and tell to make sense of one's life here.

Our new house in the shadow of Montefiore's windmill— a Jerusalem landmark—overlooked the Jaffa Gate of the Old City and the city wall. From our terrace in the evening, the city skyline looked like a Gothic birthday cake. Layers

Our house in Yemin Moshe

of mostly gory history around Sultan Suleiman's wall were just a stone's throw away. It was strange while having a shower to be looking at the city wall. The absurdity of the incredible panorama was particularly mind-blowing in the evening when the walls were lit up. When the illuminated turrets, the ancient citadel named the Tower of David with its sixteenth-century Ottoman minaret, the clock tower of the Dormition Abbey, and the deep valley beneath looked out of a fairy-tale painting.

We were happy in the new setting with a new baby. The "birthday cake" vista around us celebrated the newness.

The baby had arrived looking serene, with Leo's features, closer to my complexion, and as he grew older, he

The "birthday cake" vista from the terrace of our Yemin Moshe house

started to show a headful of Leo's curls. He was surreal. I had been pregnant for so long that sometimes when I had to provide his doctor with the details of his conception and birth, I did not know which pregnancy I was counting from. In a way, it felt good, the lost baby merged into the new "good" baby that found us. His arrival was a minor miracle.

There were no major miracles in terms of how we handled our lives together. With the Arab Spring breaking out, Leo would soon start traveling. The region called him, and the roving reporter in him responded. Kiran and Maya were delighted with their new doll of a brother and they played funny games with him: Kiran would place him at his drum set with one of his drumsticks to hold and suck on and Maya would make him dance to "Yellow Submarine" in his outsized dungarees. My life with a new baby, with two older children one of whom was a teenager with frequent grumpiness, appeared to be something I still had to come to terms with. Life at this stage caught me unawares, the sudden seemingly pulled-together phase less than a year after our worst ordeal to date had, despite the joy it brought, certain setbacks. There was a great deal of sorting out to do, and a great deal of growing up, to carry on with our marriage and the huge responsibility to bring up the three children, each at a totally different stage of growth and need. It was overwhelming, and for a while I had no time to look back on the old personal conflict between Leo and me.

The Arab Spring shook not only the Arab world from Libya to Morocco, it also somewhat toppled the relative calm that we achieved for a short while in our new abode, politically correct, scenically beautiful.

But one could not be so complacent and ignore the fire that was burning the old regimes throughout the region. Leo left first for Libya, then Libya again, followed by Egypt, Tunisia, Morocco. And the cycle kept repeating in different order from then on. I found myself often at the Allenby Bridge, dropping him off or bringing him back as he traveled back and forth carrying with him the spirit of the Arab revolution. He, as many others around me, felt optimistic about the infinite possibility of the power of the people for the first time in this region.

I understood his urge to respond to this call. It was an absurd situation. I was expected to understand the region's greater need of him. Our lesser need seemed trivial, and I was expected to rise above it. But we had just begun life in a new home with a new baby after much turmoil, and we had told ourselves that we would try to treasure what we had just achieved in our private space, as a family. But that space had overnight been invaded by a greater achievement by the heroes of Arab democracy. I came to accept that duties to one's family receded in importance in this context. I felt embarrassed to ask more of Leo. I watched him leave at short notice, often none at all. I would wake at three in the morning and struggle to remain calm as he would announce that it was the call again, the taxi was waiting for him outside to take him to the Allenby Bridge and from there on to Amman, Cairo, Benghazi, Tripoli, and so on. The regional upheaval pushed aside our petty, personal turbulence. One could not afford the complacency of home comfort when the region was reeling from a recent revolution.

But it also became clear to me that there was no shame in wanting to have what a "home" usually provided: security and reassurance. It was no lesser need. What mattered at this stage in our life was how we strove to achieve these to safeguard our marriage, how we found a balance between the personal and the global.

POSTSCRIPT

Leo and I did not have that space that separated warring couples with a breather, what one could define as no-man's-land. So in our lives, war perpetuated and spilled over the frontline. We were too intertwined with similar drives, ambition, and passion: mine perhaps were emotionally too extravagant, his were intense with a grave sincerity.

It may sound strange, but we found peace.

He found his, as he went on roaming around the post-revolution Arab world, having been able to stretch his heart for the first time in his years in the Middle East. He was liberated from the claustrophobia of the Israeli-Palestinian conflict. From the futile perpetuity of peacemaking.

And I found mine by writing this book.

Peace also derived from what for the first time clicked, something I had heard many times before but never paid attention to because I never thought that it could be relevant in my life: that you cannot change another person, so you must change yourself. Not necessarily to surrender, but to adapt and to move forward. After all, that is part of peacemaking.

———

Fida is living in Toronto with her husband (she did not marry Mahmud; Mahmud did not have the passport to her freedom from the shackles of statelessness). She now has two children with a Canadian Palestinian and is waiting for a Canadian passport for herself, so that she can return to her birthplace in northern Israel to visit her mother and brothers, on a tourist visa.

Tamar is finishing her final year in Princeton. She also married and had a daughter with a U.S. resident Israeli businessman, who enjoys self-imposed disconnection from the "conflict" in their country. Tamar wanted her home to be a quiet zone, after years of inviting radical politics into her private sphere. Whether she has it, I do not know.

Hamoudi married a Frenchwoman and had two children very quickly. Why should he be deprived of the passport to freedom in whichever way that can be achieved? As he started spending long stretches of time in Bordeaux with his wife and children, the Israeli authority caught up with him and warned him that he risked losing his Jerusalem ID, which meant he would lose his residency in his country under Israel's absentee property law. He did not want to take any chances and moved back to his house on Via

Dolorosa in the Old City with his French wife and the children in 2013.

I never spoke to Orli again.

Amos, Leo's cousin and our babysitter, the good soldier Švejk, a year after finishing the army turned emphatically a-religious. He threw away the kippah and started appearing in the liberal late-night bar Dewan on Friday nights.

ACKNOWLEDGMENTS

I am indebted to the following people for providing support and inspiration during the writing of this book.

Rebecca Carter, who descended as a savior and said, "I am really excited about your book," when I found myself disoriented in the dense jungle of would-be writers. Rebecca restored my confidence, and when she became a literary agent after many years working as a distinguished editor at Random House UK, I was privileged to be one of the first authors whom she wanted to represent. Without her expert editing skills and unwavering optimism, this book would still be sitting in the "My Documents" folder, as do a million words of two unpublished novels.

Judith Gurewich, the publisher of Other Press, who sent me an e-mail from the plane after our first meeting and three intensely resourceful days in London, in April 2013, saying, "The process is always more gratifying, what matters is to enjoy every step of the way." Working with Judith on the final draft was the most stimulating experience. Every step of it was suspenseful, action-packed: disputations over transcontinental phone calls on the law of eugenics; reading aloud together more than three hundred pages, around the clock over a week in her house in Cambridge, Massachusetts. "You have to kill your darlings," Judith would say, repeating the infamous literary quotation. (However, she did let me keep some of my darlings!)

Libby Riefler from Other Press, whose crucial editorial comments helped me address some important omissions. Yvonne E. Cárdenas, Paul Kozlowski, Marjorie DeWitt, and others who saw the book through to production.

I am immensely grateful to my three children. They were my familiar comfort zone, my fall-back-on gods, who kept me aloft with their laughter and cries and the snippets of life from outside during the lonely months while I wrote this book.

My oldest friend, Miti, whose unorthodox, exuberant use of language I have envied since I was eighteen.

Fuchsia Dunlop, who always stood by me, despite being dragged all too often into my stormy voyage through life.

Hami Verbin, for the most constructive criticism of the book and for going over the Hebrew translation.

Christopher Gunness, Ari Porat, Ruth Diskin, Natasha Dudinski, Mohammed Jaridi, Nitzan Israeli, Charo Lucas, Yasmin Barghuti, Hugh Fraser, Shlomo Lecker, Harriet Sherwood, Victor Gurewich, Anna-Christina Winterstein,

Emmanuelle Fouquet-Lapar, Sara Benjamin—they were pillars of wisdom with unlimited enthusiasm for my writing.

Very special thanks to Gillon Aitken, Ayesha Karim, and Andrew Kidd.

Finally, my husband, the unwitting companion on this journey. By challenging everything around me, he provided the vital stimulus for my creative inspiration. Life with him has never been repetitive. There's always excitement, trouble, travel, and unpredictability. Our children rightly say, "We'll grow older before you!"